STORE

A Story by

Kathleen Y. Robinson

Copyright

Copyright 2014. All rights reserved.

ISBN-13: 978-1494930196

ISBN-10: 1494930196

Cover design and interior design and preparation for publication by Mark.Fletcher@jabop.com

Cover Artwork: Original Oil Painting of Rob's Foods by the Author - Kathleen Y. Robinson

Names of customers and situations are "fictitious" and no inference was intended to be of anyone living or dead.

Thus saith the Lord,

Let not the wise man glory in his wisdom, neither let the mighty man glory in his might; let not the rich man glory in his riches:

But let him that glorieth glory in this, that he understandeth and knoweth Me, that I am the Lord which exercise lovingkindness, judgment, and righteousness, in the earth: for in these things I delight, saith the Lord.

Jeremiah 9:23, 24

Acknowledgements

Thanks are due to so many:

I felt the Lord directing me to write, my story, years ago. All honor goes to, Jesus Christ, for leading my thoughts and giving me "key" people that wanted to assist me.

First, I would like to thank my supportive family. All my children.

Three daughters, Cozette, and her husband Darron Pettigrew, Annette, Paulette, and my son Warren Robinson III and his wife LaDonna. They gave me the wonderful blessing of motherhood. Now, I am a Big mama to, Mia Pettigrew, Logan and Liam Robinson, my three beautiful grandchildren. Then LaDonte and LeKari, are LaDonna's two older sons, whom I love as much.

Then there are other " Special Children" in my life.

Dwight Robinson, my late sister-in-law Charlotte's son. My Shaggy, the son Rob and I met in Nigeria. Vernita Royal, Brando Murphy and Charrelle, also, Christopher Wathen, all of California. I'm blessed with their love too and all that call me Big Mama.

After years of writing and self-editing, I came in association with Cathy Cleary. She read my manuscript and assured me I wasn't a writer, but worked closely with me for marked improvement. Colossal thanks goes to you.

I attended the Sun City Library's Writers Group in California. Its leader Carol Kaliher, encouraged me to share my writings each week. Thanks for each listener and valued participant. You know who you are.

Elated and fueled with the possibility of a future publishing my story, I made several 'attempts' to do my homework.

I did a quilt of Rob's store; it even won The Judges Choice award in a local quilt show. I voraciously read many books on writing techniques.

The book that spurred me the most was "If I can write you can write" by Charlie Shedd. Thanks Charlie.

My friend Jeanne Dukes, of California helped me paint with oil for the first time. With her direction and persistence, the artwork of The Store on the cover of this book was completed along with a portrait of Rob from a photograph I had taken. Thanks Jeanne, I love you dearly.

Several friends read my manuscript. Kelly's mom, Emma Redmond gave me feedback. Thanks Emma.

Eddie Morier made several red marks in to give his support. Thanks Eddie.

Janet Wells my treasured friend encouraged me. She lived in The Pocket, worked 4 years in, Mrs. Fain's, store while attending, Hyde Park High School. Also her father, Thurman, married my Aunt Eleanor. Thanks Janet.

Mark Fletcher did my first prototype of the book front cover and rear along with the web site, www.thestorestory.com, then finally publishing my manuscript on Amazon. This wouldn't have happened so soon if it wasn't spurred by him. Thanks Mark.

My friend, Ann Leavell, God said use her. Thanks for everything Ann.

Listening to a sermon by T. D. Jakes, titled "Don't Settle" I said "Why Not Me" publish the book on my 50th Wedding Anniversary, June 12, 2014 or else! That date in '64 was so special for us. Rob would have celebrated big style, if he were here. That's why I did it, for him. Thanks Rob.

There are so many others to thank. My 90 year old cousin in Denver, Val Tanaka. She made movies of, The Store, ages ago and mailed them to me. She was so excited to help set up my web site, so everyone can share the history of our lives living over The Store. Thanks Val.

Vendors, wholesalers, Dearborn and State Street Wholesale, that assisted us to stay in business. Thank you.

To all Rob's customers, how could I ever have done, The Store story, with out you? You supported our little corner store, sent our children to college and all for coming in to buy something; May it had been only one time, or each day.

My friends that support me, and love the Lord Jesus Christ like I do.

The Grace that He gives is priceless! These are Gwen Digby, Shirley Scanlan, Georgia Williamson, and Gloria Jean Moody, all in Chicago. Thank you.

Madeline Morgan you are in there too, so much support. There isn't anything you wouldn't do for me. Thank you, thank you, and thank you.

Technical support and friend, Dennis Weatherspoon, thank you.

To the block clubs, the Comer Foundation, and all who support the Woodlawn neighborhood. Each worker and committeemen. Thank you.

My California friends. The WOGGIE ones, Women Of God Giving Infinite Exaltation, are Loretta McKinney, Marie Walker, Cathy Cleary and Odessa McGiffert. So much fun to be with and I thank each one of you.

Charles and Sharon Martin, Pat Smith, Teri Whitman, and Lajuana Malone are friends indeed. Thank you.

My neighbors Tom Hughes and Mr. and Mrs. Chuck Miller you were sent into my life to watch my house and for that I am grateful. Thank you

And finally may I thank my churches, Apostolic Church of God, in gracious memory of Bishop Arthur M. Brazier, where I attended his services since 1987.

My current blessing, New Life Covenant Church, in Chicago Illinois, where all my children attend. I have an anointed minister of the Gospel there, that's a "Lion in the World." Pastor John F. Hannah. Thank you, and to your beautiful wife Anna.

Thank you both churches for seeking God's heart, begging for souls and therefore leading thousands to the saving knowledge of Jesus Christ each week.

My book is dedicated to you Pastor Hannah. You help so many women get their lives back on track and if I had you when I was growing up ... oh, well.

In loving memory of my best friend, and mother, Paula Johnson, (1918-2005) and the reason I am eternally grateful to God for allowing her to reveal to me her wonderful Saviour, Jesus Christ to me.

Mrs. Fannie Mae Fain (1921-1984) In blessed memory and a treasure, indeed.

**This book is prayerfully dedicated to
Pastor John F. Hannah
New Life Covenant Church
Chicago, Illinois
and to all God's children everywhere.**

Thank you.

Foreword

For more than 35 years, I lived over a little corner grocery store my husband owned and operated, on the south side of Chicago. I began to question his loyalty, as time passed, and his Dream took over our lives. I left many times; physically, mentally and emotionally, as my thoughts dictated.

This is my story: my beginnings, along with each hurdle; through courtship and the bliss, that contrasted with the turbulent reveal, of what my 'marriage' was.

No matter how often I was told, that my life was God's blessing; in my mind, I thought otherwise.

The Store was a thief. She held our family hostage. But first, I had to get my husband released from her spell.

This became my quest.

***

She's got it all wrong. My shelves supplied everything she needed: toilet paper to talcum powder, Orange Crush to fresh-cut pork chops. I was only seconds away, right downstairs from her cozy apartment.

Her husband did give me much needed attention, 'cause, I couldn't operate without him. Yes, he spent long hours nurturing me, but I was giving him status in the neighborhood, and respect among the customers.

He was extremely popular, all because of me.

***

Everything about operating The Store excited me. Sure, it was hard to explain the special attention I gave her daily.

To relax, I would leave to spend casual time with my customers, listening to their problems and it endeared me to them. They told me their secrets.

My wife, whom I love with every bit of my soul, will write The Store's story: from her perspective.

I've divinely left the scene. Hopefully I've left a legacy and highly thought of, by my loving wife, the kids, my friends, and customers for greatness and never my weak moments.

The Store

"Hey, today must be your birthday!"

"No, it's not my birthday, but I've heard about you. You're Rob."

I notice a feeling in this place, looking around at the crowded shelves, and the man behind the counter smiling at me. It's not just a little grocery, packed with goodies, it has uncommon charm.

"You married? Kids?"

"Yep, they're here. We live upstairs."

I stay and talk awhile, to this responsive guy, that has the neighborhood buzzing. He's young, maybe too young to own all this. The first thing I want to know is: if he's genuine, because I like him.

"Hey, you're sure new around here! I haven't seen you before. Do you have a name to match that face?" Rob says smiling, as I complete my tour and put a couple of can goods on his counter.

"I'm your future friendly competitor; been thinking of buying a business, over on 71st Street in a month or two. Thought I'd mosey on over and find out, who I'll be neighbors with."

"Thanks! That's what happens to a lot of us." Rob continues. "I've been caught up in this area's magical web, since back in sixty-nine. You will too. Back then, few

The Store

people, like us, owned real money making businesses. I'll help you, if I can."

Rob's front door, in need of fresh paint, had a metal bell that swung back and forth, as another customer walks in.

"Boy, I can see you're a busy man. I'll be back, and we'll see what you can do. Here's my card."

I finish making my purchase and Rob places everything in a brown paper bag, throwing in a mint.

"Thanks for stopping in. Did you find everything? This was your first try!"

The history of this place is stimulating; "Nothing" but "Something." Why is it, that everybody likes this grocery store? I've heard it's made a name for its self for years. I remembered all the stories; that he's like; -kind, -friendly and down right -helpful. I will never forget his way of making ME feel like an 'instant' partner. His little store has it all!

As I leave, this little kid is straining to open the front door, holding her money tightly in her fists. Her tiny nose will be flattened against the glass in seconds, where her favorite candy is kept. I laugh at Rob, trying to find the very piece her fat finger points to. The very one, her tummy craves.

"Yes! I sure got what I came in for. Very nice meeting you, Rob, see yah."

I found out that this, brown skinned owner, is a serious business man and he's exciting! I felt his energy. He's interested in his community and really settled quickly.

Okay, he's got a wife and four kids. In fact I like the sound of professionalism with kick-back friendliness in this community that I'll soon be a part of.

Chapter 2
It could happen to you

I have a name.

For now, they might refer to me only as, "The Store".

For years my name has changed, from this name to that awful one, I want to forget and not mention; since I've been here on this corner, even before the turn of the century...flatter me, I know I don't look my age.

I'm stately and proud. My eye-windows face east when I open them at day. They're big and clear and when they're washed, I'm glowing.

There are trees, sidewalks, pavements, and lots of people traffic at times, to look at, and houses over the area that just stare. We've made our agreements to share this area and it's okay with me.

My boss has chosen to christen me, 'Rob's Spotlight Foods' several years ago, and I'm still thrilled with his choice. Everybody knows me now. Not like before, when I was taken for granted. I feel safe, with a younger owner in all sorts of ways; mostly with his watchful eye, promoting and parading me to everyone he knows. And, I've never been robbed.

He has to feed me electrical currents for my rich energy to flow. I mean paying my bills on time. Legal issues are fine, but there are my taxes, fines and dues. My upkeep is expensive. It cost 'big' to keep me happy.

I need cooling in summer and plenty of raw heat on those blistery winters this Chi-town is known for. Let's not forget to mention my water, gas, and other maintenance: manicures, facials, bathing and such. Please understand. He's going to speak for me when I am shy or can't scream

The Store

loud enough. But, I can shut down in a minute and he knows that too well.

Today, Man, I'm jolly excited about his cool idea. I'm getting a blue awning over my big eyes, he says to protect them. I've promised to cooperate up to a point; if there is too much attention at night, I'll lose some rest. We'll see.

He has to be faithful. No other store must he go ah courtin.' We talk for hours on end about what the two of us can accomplish. I'll do this, if he'll do that, back and then over again. I always win. I'm cute that way.

He knows I give my blessings nightly. It's proven when he counts his receipts, because our partnership is sealed, promised and sacred, for several generations to come.

***

It was October 4, 1969, on a cool crisp evening, when our family moved above The Store. My husband was the new owner and he spent the majority his time working. At first, I thought nothing more of it.

While walking the streets around The Store, I'd see some two flats, but mostly single-family homes made of brownish red brick. These houses stood a whisper's distance from each other on narrow lots, so it wasn't unusual to know everyone. I adore kids and children of all ages peppered the vicinity. Often people would be sweeping their sidewalks, picking up trash thrown down by those kids. Neighbors hung out fresh washed laundry to dry in the breezy sunshine. Most were the friendliest I'd ever seen. I'd offer them a "Good morning, how are you doing?" or made a brief reference to the weather, "Sure is pleasant today," with a nod of my head, then the gesture was echoed.

The Store

There were beautiful trees everywhere. Roses of varied colors, morning glories and honey suckle ran up the sides of various homes. Some places rivaled Better Homes and Gardens' center pages. It was hard to resist opening their gates and climbing up to rock my girls on their porch swings. The area had made a swift change from one ethnic group to another.

On this particular afternoon the girls and I were on a stroll down Woodlawn, to observe the street where we lived. Owning the grocery store on the corner was still foreign. Cozette, my four year old, was walking three steps ahead and, Annette, five months, was saddled on my hip.

I hadn't liked moving from my adorable apartment in Hyde Park's quaint higher class community, but no one there greeted us, or wanted to know us, totally unlike this place. I hadn't realized people knew of us, although they soon would call me Ms. Rob.

An elderly gentleman leaves his porch. "Excuse me, we saw you move in." He greets me with a smile, and then extends his hand, taking off his glove. "My wife, Sadie and I, sure wanted some good people, like you, to re-open that store." Then he paused a long time, to look over towards it. "There was a strange mystery about her." He stammers. "Darn it, how come, I mean that young Mr. Toliver, its previous owner, so nice, was murdered?"

I didn't know what to say to the nice man. "Yes, we will find the person who did it." I shared.

"Miss, your kids are cute." He says, tips his cap turns away. I thought about it for a second. *Maybe one day, we'll all find out.*

I hollered out to Cozette "Wait for me, honey you're too far!"

The Store

Heading back home, I see the most adorable nappy-headed children playing after school. They are jumping rope, others are riding their bikes or playing baseball in the middle of the street. A few are running to our store, to buy candy.

So, these are the kids my girls will be playing with, I thought. Cozette lingers a bit watching them too. We stood there for the longest, smiling at them.

The Store has everything. Along with basic necessities she had a certain mystery. Some inquisitive neighbors might be bent on finding further clues. But, in time, I would soon learn to hate her.

We had nothing to do with the murder of my husband's uncle, Mr. Toliver. I sure wasn't interested in it, at the time. I had my girls, my newly acquired apartment and my husband's preoccupation with his new business, to occupy my mind.

***

All day, various people run inside for cigarettes and other vital supplies. Once inside it was like a trap. You come out with a grin on your face and an unconscious resolve to come back. You'd met my husband, someone who truly wants your business.

His hand was always ready: to shake yours, lift a package too heavy, give a pat on your back, or lay it on your shoulder in his friendly neighborly way. In other words he was there if you needed him. His big brown eyes looked straight into yours and you'd come away feeling like; now that guy could be my next of 'kin.'

Older people found our little store a haven at the crack of dawn. I'm up with my coffee and cigarette sitting in the kitchen, before my girls were up. If The Store wasn't awake

The Store

and Rob was still asleep, you'd bang on the side door leading up to where we lived and holler. "Get a going, young man!" A half hour later the aroma of coffee percolating on a hot plate, encouraged grins and laughter, from you and some other bearded old men, ready to start the day.

The smell of chewing tobacco, and smoke from stinky cigars and rolled cigarettes filtered the air. Rob sleepily listened to your heated discussions of newspaper headlines or countless stories of, The Good Old Days. Seldom did you buy much, you just wanted to, 'shoot-the-fat,' in The Store, that had become your, 'second home'.

The stories were wild every morning. Rolling hoots and hollers wouldn't stop for hours and by 8:45, Rob's energy shifted to the straggling kids, trying to get to school on time. Then later, you'd wander out the door, hanging with the guys and go on home, until the next time.

It always amazed me, how many women planned their dinners, from Rob's posted sales scotch- taped around The Store. Meat specials, poor-boy deals, and items marked for a quick sale made the list.

I had never seriously shopped in a small grocery store. If Rob had depended on people like you and me, he would have gone out of business the second week.

As you'll find out, the same customers coming in with their grocery lists also brought a variety of stories: about mishaps, miscarriages, abortionist and abortions, misgivings and marital woes, which spawned unexpected excitement! People shared their lives: misunderstandings in their homes, marriages, dating life, weddings, births and even their nasty dirty habits, that should have been left unsaid. Mysteries were solved right in The Store, and created there too.

***

The Store

Mrs. Loretta Townsend, confessed about her husband's unfaithfulness, each time she entered, The Store. "Your friend stayed out again, and it's been going on for months now." Her voice stumbled through tears, buying a loaf of bread, a lemon, two tomatoes and a gallon of milk. Rob could do nothing, but stand behind his counter and listen, with all the compassion of a big brother. Then, he softly said, "I'll mention something to him next time he comes in." He assured her, with a token of comfort. As he bagged her things, throwing in a couple of candy mints to make her smile.

***

Mrs. Lucy Larson, has several situations that would tickle Rob, each time she came in, with her funny self.

She couldn't stop laughing, while trying to tell yesterday's horrible story.

Her prized bird, Mickey Mouse, flew out the back door as she changed the newspaper in its cage.

"I saw an article that I wanted to clip, and darn, if it wasn't the worst timing. My kids opened the back door." She paused to catch her breath. "That's the second bird I've lost that way!" Banging her hand on the counter, "You'd think I'd learn my lesson, and keep 'dem kids locked out!" Her eyes bucked wide, "That's two hundred bucks, each bird, Rob!" They both would laugh and she'd make him swear not to tell a soul.

***

Rob has several customers that come to see him regularly. Is it The Store that draws them, hanging around, or

The Store

Rob? What The Store and Rob do on a daily basis synchronizes them; it's hard to separate them two. Rob's personality was designed to show off in front of each customer. The Store was his platform; with a royal performance each day; so genuine and sincere every time you see him, it couldn't be fake.

***

The décor of The Store is quaint. It's filled with fresh produce that punch the air and it has a home-style, comfortable atmosphere. It all derives from Rob's simple upbringing. Nothing fancy: coolers, cases and display racks, to get his food stuff off the shelves and into your cabinets. He has this knack of making you relax, laugh a lot and spend your money, because you feel just that welcomed, it's kinda like, it's your private store.

Reaching for a candy bar you see something twice as nice beside it. It's a secret that you can't explain. You end up getting both, or a bag full of groceries with your "Why-not-get-it-now" attitude. The price is right and you'll need it anyway.

Being the neighborhood hub, you like the 'excitement' of going to The Store even when it's crowded. Hit songs are playing on the radio. Musical after effects of your favorite jam, and its vibrations are alive; it even puts a 'bounce' in your step.

"Excuse me, hey, hey, boop te boo bop!"

"Excuse me."

You pivot your way to the back around the shelves, then slip while softly humming, through this man and that woman. Hey, hey, they are going in the opposite direction, while you are singing, on your way to the rear of The Store.

The Store

You are just happy to retrieve your item, which drew you inside in the first place. You have to pass other people. "Excuse me. Hey, like that watch you've wearing." You had noticed it when you passed the pretty girl before.

You wait in line too. It's your turn soon; there are only a couple of people in front of you, smiling, rocking their heads humming their offbeat tunes. You often run into your friends and neighbors. You exchange pleasantries: words "Hey!" a hug or hump, hand shake, or a grin with a tip off your head, knowing, "We, are at The Store, hey! hey!" No one seems to mind, standing in back of the line either, you and everyone wants to be here!

You finally, get to the register, to put your arm load of groceries on the counter: pork chops, loaf of bread, gallon of milk, pound of butter, tomato sauce and a couple of bags of chips; Whatever!

"Yo! You waited for me didn't you?" Rob says as he gets eye contact, and with another remark; "In a big hurry today?" Then He grins, as he reaches over and touches each item to tally, on that old green register, you know so well.

"You know I'll take care of you." Rob says softly with concreteness, only found in The Store. Then you get one of Rob's famous quips, which trump all the others.

"I **know** it's your birthday! Your bill is only $9.57, and 'The Smile,' is on me!" There's plenty of laughter between you. Your stuff is safe inside his brown paper bag as you walk out the door, humming. "Boop te boo bop…"

***

Finding a store that had so many varieties of grocery items was wonderful. You didn't have to go to the big

The Store

supermarkets and the prices were cheap compared to other places.

Pork chops were the right thickness, when Joe the butcher, ordered the entire loin and cut each chop by hand. Then he had them, one by one overlapping all neatly on trays.

Rob had, jumbo ham hocks, pig feet, boiling bacon, all to season your cabbages, collard greens, or string beans. He provided onions, potatoes, yams, and hot peppers, corn bread, stuffing mixes, cake and pie fixings and rolls, all for his choice customers' enjoyment. His store was a big mama's shopping delight.

There were countless accounts; of all their money lost gambling, petty jealousies between their families and, running games on people, were just some of the stories Rob patiently listened to. He never gave a mumbling word about what was told to him to anyone. If someone confessed as to who was then, selling drugs, where to get them, who was caught in adultery, their own vices, and even who they wanted dead.

Rob's trusted customers became friends: they brought in their kids and grandchildren in –for a 'tiny taste' of what being at the little crowded store, was like.

***

Over the next couple of months, Chicago's pleasant weather changed. It was frigid outside. I relinquished walking Cozette around the vicinity for good. She pressed her little nose against the window pane and drew pictures in the ice crystals that her breath made, wishing she could play outside. She watched television while playing goo-goo with Annette.

The Store

I beamed with pride seeing my husband enjoy his new establishment, during those first weeks. I was there as each new customer's loyalty was courted. I didn't work in The Store by design.

Slowly, I withdrew from the entire neighborhood that adored my husband and The Store. I got busy perfecting my household decorating crafts, and cooking skills, while sewing adorable clothes for me and my daughters.

Now, I've learned to observe the customers going in and out from looking down at the surrounding area, entirely from my second floor windows. Perceiving the excitement and camaraderie, the daily miracles and can't participate.

I'm not invited.

On a February morning before Rob opened The Store I said that another baby was due.

"The doctor said November."

***

I had a lot of babies for my husband. I still tried to keep my figure, but each time it was a battle having so many children. I didn't want to look-like I lived over a grocery store. Staying thin and beautiful became difficult. Having two daughters made me wish… if only. My thoughts were that I would bring home a son. I'd feel important to my husband, like before – when I was the sole object of his desires.

***

I hadn't realized the importance of The Store; her significance to the area, her customers, and the many friends that depended on her, even for their vital social outlet. The Store was beautiful and shapely, self-assured and popular – she had more bricks than she could count – and with her bricks and plaster coving her cracks and seams, I saw her cunning ways.

The Store was a place that got all of Rob's devotion. I hated her and despised the foundation she stood on. Her low-priced signs, adornments, her cheap painted walls and deodorant sprays to keep her smelling sweet, when she wasn't –that all got to me.

The iron clad grip The Store had over Rob had to end.

Act I

Chapter 3
My story had a glass slipper that didn't fit

Since I am neither famous nor a celebrity, a personal explanation of how I got to survive my life, living over The Store and the twenty five, exhilarating years, leading up to it, may be in order.

When I think of my humble beginnings, I smile. Who cared that I was a Negro, born November 25, 1942, in Chicago, Illinois, at The Cook County Hospital. You couldn't be more of a Chicago native than that.

My mother, Pauline, delivered me healthy and full of life. Mom's firstborn daughter, Lillian Rose, died at only three weeks of age. When Mom saw my blue eyes, she knew she'd been given another chance. I was treated very special by both of my parents, my grandparents and all my relatives.

No one told me how poor I was; never deprived, my mom took pride in her two daughters, me, Kathleen Yvonne and 15 months later, my only sibling, Claudette Anita, was born.

I was a secure kid; until drifting into my twelfth year and then one day, it all fell apart... For all my life, I'm known as an energetic, free spirited, pale faced, skinny girl, trying to have enjoyable innocent adventures –minding my own business; despite a crazy upbringing of being displaced – dozens of times.

Chapter 4
I want it just right
... isn't it supposed to be

In late September, 1960, I meet through a girl named, Phyllis, an average looking deep brown skinned guy. He really becomes 'close' to me out of boredom. There is nothing about, Warren Robinson that is appealing. I'm in-between casual friends and Warren has his own car! That's rare within my circle of friends. He is non-threatening, not all over me sexually, and he's what I call 'safe' to be with. He never gives me the slightest inkling of what he's really thinking about, when he looks at me. I flirt innocently with the entire situation.

I agree to go on an outing one Saturday night. He picks me up in his 1957 black Chevy, in front of my Aunt Eleanor's place on 70th and Harper. I am hoping he's dropping off, two friendly guys somewhere else, but they stay in the back seat. Their conversations throughout the evening are upbeat and funny. I enjoy myself sitting all night listening to their wild accounts of what they do: lingering at Hyde Park High School's park grounds, messing with the seniors; competing with each other, racing their cars on the Lake Front or playing black jack or poker. All the guys have jobs and they consume plenty cans of beer and I enjoy their bar-b-que.

I find out Warren, who seems shy, never dated anyone seriously. The guys repeatedly tease him about me. We end up at, The Point, overlooking Lake Michigan and I am surprised when the sun shows up. The hours passed so quickly. How funny, now everyone can see each other.

Warren hurries to his mother's store on 70th and Dorchester by 7:00. It's his morning shift. I'm stunned this store's location is quite close to my place up the street. He

The Store

and his friends pick up the Sunday Sun Times newspapers, tied in bundles.

Warren opens the grocery store housed in a large frame three flat building. I stay in the car. My hair is a mess and I finger my hands through it. The rear view mirror isn't my friend, as I dab on some lipstick. The neighborhood is quiet. The area is full of really nice single family homes. I can hear birds chirping. The morning air is clean and fresh, not a cloud in the sky. Everyone must be still asleep as I glance over it momentarily.

The store looks ordinary, as I sit for a moment and observe it. Not much to brag about. The entrance has one door covered with iron bars. The windows on both sides are blocked by aged-wood boards that need painting. There is a neon sign and the name of the place above it.

Still in a jovial mood, out of curiosity of what's inside that store, I get out of my seat, pull my skirt down and close the car. I flick my last cigarette butt over on the dirt. I brace my body against the heavily decorated door, advertising various things, and step inside.

Warren and the guys are still flipping switches, as I creep around sheepishly, with a grin on my face.

I've never seen such a tiny store. It's sparsely filled with stuff on the shelves: two cans here and three cans there. The potato chip rack is filled. As I walk toward the back area, there is a meat counter lined inside with pork chops, chicken legs and ground beef. I'm thinking his store looks dingy, as I complete my trek. The overhead lighting is awful. The boarded up window at the front, has forgotten to let God's light in. Warren turns some other switches, but the atmosphere doesn't improve. It seems as if one 40 watt bulb is burning, and that's all the light the little store gets for the day. I was out with the gang for an evening of innocent fun,

The Store

that has spilled over to a bright morning. I think nothing more of it.

I feel the floor creak at one point going around the outer aisle. Looking up, graying paint is missing from the molding under a chipped plastered ceiling. The walls don't look much better. It's unimpressive. Shoppers start to come in, the radio is turned on, and the atmosphere improves. Warren, from his grin, seems to adore the place.

From two buddies, the one that lives near, PeeWee, gives Warren a weird handshake that I failed to understand. Both of them leave when I wavered a bit 'bout staying.

"Hey, Jr. you take care." said Vaughn as he busted out the front door, laughing hilariously with his friend mimicking him.

My eyes get accustomed to this dim interior, that's about as big as a one room school house. I make myself busy picking up cans and reading the labels but shocked at the prices of some.

I straddle the stool behind the counter, as soon as Warren offers it. I can't keep it still twirling it back and forth. I'm not nervous, just ridiculously tired and my back slumps a bit. I must look a wreck, with my eye make-up in panda bear style, and there are no mirrors. I'm near an old fashioned register that makes noise when a sale is made.

Warren has this fresh newness about him or is it shyness? I don't know what it is about him that keeps me here. I live so close. I could easily leave too and walk up the street.

My arms lean over on the slick slick surface in front of me. It's sorta like my daddy's lunch counter that I like to wipe clean with a soapy cloth to act as if I were busy.

Warren hides another grin as he rings up the few customers that are standing in line. He piddles: rumples

The Store

papers, puts penny candy in jars, and counts quarters. Then he rings up an order of chips and a can of juice for me.

"Thank you." I say, smiling. "How could you know I want Mango juice?"

"I didn't – but you must be thirsty, and, and I want to take you to breakfast later," he stammered.

Warren, in rare form wants to talk now, for he hadn't said two words all night but kept his eyes glued on me. He moves closer and wants to touch my hand, leg or brush accidently against my body in some way.

Some rare customers, since he's trying to have a cozy conversation; get their stuff and leave, while most can't keep their eyes off me, as if I am the "it" girl.

Warren asks several questions, "What do I need? Where have I been? What do I like?" I share all he wants to know, since he's polite. But I don't ask him personal questions, because I really don't care.

The little store has a lull every now and then, but there are times when traffic never stops. Everyone likes this place it seems, and they treat it, lingering like they do, as if it's special to them. The radio starts to play some sacred selections and a few customers, use their musical talents, by singing a stanza or two. I turn up the volume on a few that I know but don't dare sing. I can't.

The sun sneaks inside the store as the door opens frequently. This store is more popular than I originally thought. Warren wants to share about the very store I'm sitting in. I could care less what he says, but he continues anyway.

He prides himself with helping his mother. "There isn't anything I won't do… mop floors or sweep the entire neighborhood if necessary."

The Store

"I haven't ever met anyone like you. You're not afraid of hard work are you?"

"Never, my mother is worthy of all my devotion. I'd do anything for her." He's awkward and acts bashful. When a customer that he knows comes in, and he knows them all, he's Mr. Congenial –overboard with compliments and downright personable. Which one is he? Funny he switches back and forth from a hilarious jokester with the customers, then to a mere mouse next to me. We talk while he works; sometimes he's running all over the place.

I find out a lot regarding the grocery business. He's that talkative, however, most of the "finding out" is about his mom that he calls, Mrs. Fain. From his description, I thought of her as likened to The Statue of Liberty, with a personality to match; only, she's dipped in chocolate. She is a pillar of this south side neighborhood, located in an area called "The Pocket." He explained later why the enclosed area was called that.

Warren, at my cue, continues talking. I feel he needs to talk about his mom because, she is colorful, exciting and important and he isn't. I perk up and give him another smile and ask a loaded question. "So you think she holds out a flaming torch to her kids, her family, friends, neighborhood and anyone willing to follow her?" I am copying what he's said just moments ago. "Yes, I do" as he shares about the mother he loves.

"My mom, Fannie Mae, we all call her Mrs. Fain, is almost 6 feet tall without heels ... with her tenacity and wit, started this grocery store business in May of 1957. Some say she's successful because she listens to her customers, wears expensive clothes that are hard to find, and drives the latest automobile, that I take care of. But everyone wants what she's got. She loves: anybody's kid, cooking favorite recipes, going to church, outdoor activities, fishing, and family gatherings or parties, maybe not in that order.

With her good work ethic and an unwavering determination to own something (if given a chance) she leaves Mississippi and migrates here to Chicago to help bring her family out of poverty. She was tired of working in 'dem cotton fields.

Because of a horrible accident, soh eerie, I shiver thinking 'bout it, her little fortune came. While working over at the R H Donnelly Company, her left arm gets wedged in a big loading machine. Horrific screams from her gut could be heard all over the entire plant, she said, as her three fingers got cut off. Then, she gained a handsome settlement. She purchased our two flat building up the street on Dorchester and opened this store in The Pocket."

Warren stops and reaches over to wait on another customer. He greets the man by name then tries to continue his mother's story after Mr. Barns leaves. With an upside down smile he sees some awful drips I'd made on my white jacket. He leaves to find a clean rag. The stain won't budge; yes a ruined garment, and we both laugh as it matches the rest of me. "Your mom seems interesting." I say while wiping myself. "I'd like to meet your mom, ahh, Mrs. Fain."

He says confidently. "Yep, I know you will –in fact I promise."

The Store

We have several interruptions. Even the phone calls were interesting. People are asking all sorts of questions, wanting everything from fresh bananas to corn bread mix. The number one request is if he has their cigarettes. I'm smoking his, several Winston's all morning.

Warren yearns to give, 'The-Whole-Story' one more try but I tell him I'm tired and I look that way. "Please arrange to take me home." I spin around again on the squeaky stool though it's not going any faster than before.

He never mentions Mrs. Fain in detail again. His step father, Mr. Fain, comes to relieve him. He is: caramel colored, a stout elderly gentleman with a round belly and kind eyes. He has a questionable look on his face as his head tilts to the side. His raised eyebrows convey, who I might be behind his counter? "Just a friend," Warren tells him.

Secretly, that makes sense to me because I am not coming back any time soon. It will be a relief to snatch that elusive sunshine that has tried to peep in all morning. I put out my cigarette, gather my belongings and leave my secluded post. I wobble behind Warren leaning on his shoulder, assuring him he doesn't have to carry me.

My eyes squint in the sun. The Chevy has residue of our party that he brushes aside for me to slip in and throws most of the stuff in the back seat. I smooth my skirt to my knees and finger what is left of my curls.

"We sure need sunglasses today." I say taking a welcomed breath. "You'll be home in a second. Sorry 'bout your jacket."

The short zip to Aunt Eleanor's was silent. I leaned back and thought of nothing but getting upstairs and jumping in the tub.

The Store

I say "good-by" twice. He lingers a little too long. Turning the ignition, he sits for a moment longer. He strolls around to open my door. He's grinning.

I'm not interested in Warren. (I'm afraid he likes me too much) He's a nice guy but there are a lot of nice guys in the world. "See you later, Warren. Nice talking with you." Holding the door wide; he's standing right there. I awkwardly pivot around, making sure to keep my skirt down – just trying my best to stay ladylike.

"When can I come over 'n see you again?" He reaches for my hand. "I wanted to take you to breakfast m-maybe a movie tonight?" His brown eyes turn blue as he repeats what he'd said earlier. I want to say "Never!" so badly but can't. Darn it. I'm too tired to make a quick response seem natural. I look up lazily towards the sky, count to five to prove I'm thinking hard. "O I'll see … but it was nice, thank you, seeing you."

I leave him at the curb and I don't look back, half skipping up the sidewalk to burst through my vestibule doors. My energy returns as I fly up the stairs, two at a time, to my aunt's third floor apartment. Reaching each landing, I'm hollering. I'm not seeing that guy again! I am never seeing that guy again! And I meant every word.

***

Warren is 'history.' I have other things to think about and finding a job might be one of them.

One week, two days, three hours and 43 minutes later Warren is parked outside my apartment building!

"Oh, I remember you!" I say, after I roll my eyes then back at him. I'm headed to the cleaners on Stony Island.

The Store

Three and a half steps and Warren lures me to his car with a quick question.

"If I tell you the back seat is full of flowers, just for you, will you take them?

Chapter 5
It only happens in real life

I smile and let my guard down when Warren tells me he has literally counted the days, hours and minutes since I was with him. I see so many flowers. "Are these all for me?" I'm grinning wide now. "No, you can only have one," he teases.

I am proud of the flowers in my arms when I come through Aunt Eleanor's doorway to her kitchen and show them.

"These are yours!" I tell her. She lifts her hands up to her mouth in amazement telling me to hurry, "Quick, let's put them in water!" She knows where the vases are. I take them down from the cabinet over the refrigerator. "Did he hold up a funeral car?" she screams.

Warren eventually gets invited upstairs. He congers up a legitimate excuse to be in my living room again and then more than again.

One clever way Warren uses to see me often is, he brings my aunt a quart of her favorite hand-packed vanilla ice cream. How did he know that she even liked the stuff is beyond me. I must have told him that Sunday while watching so many pints leave his store.

Aunt Eleanor, although average, attracts men like flies. She's on the floor sitting with her back to me while I pin curl her short hair. It takes me twenty minutes to finish as I twist the hair around my finger and slip on a bobby pin. I secure that curl and start another. She's laughing at me between licking the spoon never sharing any of it. We're both watching Warren. He's seated in a chair across from us. She slowly enjoys the delightful sensation until her entire carton is empty. "Thank you Warren." She says every few minutes or so. "It's my pleasure Ma'am. Anything else I can get for you, say so."

If I need stockings, Warren brings up stockings in the size and color I ask for.

If she needs: cigarettes, straight pins, cookies, laundry detergent, cat food, milk, eggs, whatever, she will have them. Most times he brings them and sits. I shake my head.

"Cathy, its Warren on the phone!" She says every evening holding the receiver up in the air. 9 o'clock means closed for the night.

"Cathy! Warren wants to talk with you!" She screams.

"Tell him I'm not here!" I holler back from across the room. "Warren is on the phone!!" She tells me twice; her voice firm and determined. "I'm not home, Aunt Eleanor!" I know he hears us. Man, I wish he didn't have our number.

One day I melt and agree to answer his persistent call. He can take me to a party at the dance hall on 43rd Street and then drop me off in front. Another time he waits all night for me to leave a dance hall on 63rd and Cottage Grove. I can't believe this guy. Warren is leaning against the building. He asks if he can escort me home.

"You don't want to be alone on this dangerous street, do you?"

"I am fine Warren, but yes, you can take me. Thank you."

***

I end up seeing Warren more often than I want to. But he's that comfortable. I'm using him and his generosity but he knows it, and seems as if he's betting or waiting. I don't intend to get seriously involved.

The Store

During a winter storm we throw snow balls at each other; delightful romps as he ducks when I try to slosh him. The snow falling from the sky glistens through the street lights as blankets of wonderment surround us. We drive in the slush to a store around the corner just to buy cold beer and sit warming ourselves in his car turning up our favorite tunes on the radio. He comes close. I do let him kiss me for the first time; his lips are soft but his nose gets in the way.

It's refreshing being with a boy I feel really likes 'Me.' Almost, well as if he loves the ground I walk on.

How could I know: *I am dating a prince, a real tiger, a lover in disguise; but will the shoe fit?*

Chapter 6
Little girls make pretty pictures

From five years old until I was twelve, I lived in a low income housing development called Altgeld Gardens, on the outer limits of the city.

In "The Gardens," as it was affectionately called, we had green grass where kids could play, and everyone took pride in their yards. Our entire vicinity was an oasis compared to the crowded tenements near 43rd and South Park where I was born. My prideful area of The Gardens was called block one. It didn't matter; all the blocks consisted of families trying to survive.

Thinking I was privileged; coupled by the way I talked, and looked, I didn't fit in with my peers. I didn't like that "Kathleen" was pronounced "Kath-the-reeen" in my community and my nickname "Cathy" seldom was.

My resourceful parents acquired a new novelty: A 10" TV set. Kids in the neighborhood, Kenneth Carter, and his friend David, Kinkie and Billy would pile in my house to look at the phenomenon. We had a 1949 Chevy coupe that Mom drove with her white gloves perched proudly on the steering wheel. Telephone seats, called gossip benches, were pieces of furniture. Because of the 'party' line, we shared those lines with two or more different callers at a time, and because of the short cord, we needed a place to sit.

Our place looked the best inside. Mom inherited beautiful, ornate, living room furniture from her well-to-do relatives. My favorite piece was a huge floor model mahogany radio. My ears were glued to it listening to, The Cisco Kid, The Lone Ranger and Life with Father.

The Store

Mom's kitchen sported the latest appliances: a mangle to iron linens and curtains, a washing machine, and other electrical gadgets, that Mom said were so necessary.

My bedroom had brown metal bunk beds, mine on top, with fluffy pillows, chenille spreads and clean sheets. I had a dresser, mirror and a closet packed with adorable clothes.

As I grew older, The Mickey Mouse Club was never missed. Later, I loved to see older kids dance on American Bandstand. I looked weird the way I bounced out of step.

I noticed something more important as I matured. My body didn't: long lanky legs, slew footed, and I was flat chested to a fault. Worse, most boys didn't like me, especially when they saw my sister's pretty face, that matched her perfect body. It never stopped; my loss of male attention. Claudette's skin was flawless, with golden highlights over deep bronzed caramel. Her long black wavy hair reached below her shoulders. My hair was short, unruly and dishwater brown. My pale washed-out skin tones, that I'm sure glowed in the dark, covered a pencil thin frame.

My parents were celebrities to me. Mom was young and beautiful, and almost every man told her that. She sure agreed with their assessments. She had a pretty skin tone like milk 'n honey. Her hazel eyes fluttered and flirted and her legs went all the way to the floor. Men called them shapely she said. Her nose, mouth and teeth were perfect and her hair was medium length, brown and silky. She let me comb her soft curls and paint her nails with red polish. She wanted so badly to be 'domestic' by trying to sew and cook.

Mom could have gotten an award for her acting performances. It was weird the way her body would go through a metamorphic contorted flip when she heard a compliment directed towards her. Claudette and I hated the way our mom performed. We vowed to never be caught dead

The Store

acting like that by putting our thumbs and fingers together in our secret handshake.

Daddy was handsome. Mom said he reminded her of a deep tanned Clark Gable. Daddy had a smooth easy going personality with a charming smile. His average frame looked super in modern felt or straw hats. He wore a silk stocking cap to smooth his hair slick to his head at night. I enjoyed watching him maneuver his razor while he carefully edged a pencil thin mustache each morning.

Daddy loved to watch 'Shoot-em-ups.' His favorite cowboys were Billy the Kid, Gene Autry and his number one and mine, Hopalong Cassidy. He would stretch out on our sofa for hours in his pajamas and silk robe. Then I'd change the channels for him.

But I remember my daddy most around our dinner table. Before he left for work we couldn't keep still in our chairs for wonderment. The stories of his exciting life on the farm in Memphis were grand. I had my favorites and we begged him to retell them over and over again. Daddy scooted out soon after dinner. The Key Club on the north side of the Loop is where he made lots of tips opening doors all night for the rich and famous.

Daddy didn't drink hard liquor but Mom hated that he loved to gamble. He would lose all his money at the race track, oftentimes holding a pencil tight in his teeth peering through racing forms ready to circle the winning horse.

Mom said my teeth had to be straightened. I went downtown on the South Suburban Bus called Big Red alone to my orthodontist's office for my monthly appointments. Having braces wasn't popular plus it increased my feelings of looking peculiar. Only one girl I knew had them, Brenda Verner, who by the way, was my 'bestest' friend. We'd talk about movie stars like, James Dean, for hours and stuff, but I told her about some of my secret crushes. They were on two boys: one named, Cubby, the cutest ever and the other, Cody. It never did any good; these boys and others didn't know I was alive.

I didn't realize growing up that Mom wasn't in love with Daddy, who was nine years older. She married him in 1939 because, being pregnant, she had to. Her mother left their family and ran off with another man and that devastated my granddaddy. Mom was only nine years old, thus forcing her to help nurture her three younger siblings. She emulated her devoted father, so she taught Bible classes in our home on Tuesday nights, the way he had. Mom liked religion and announced to everyone that she was a Christian.

As I grew older, I heard some bickering between my parents, and didn't know which side to take. I loved them both.

Well, Daddy was a real sad case after their divorce. I don't think he ever loved another woman. Mom claimed all men adored her and I sure remembered every creep she dated.

Chapter 7
Just the facts, only the facts

In contrast to me, Warren was privileged as a teen. He had parents who cared if he went to school, ate the right foods and what time he had to come in at night. Often, even in the south living with his grandparents, he was told treasured family tales until he fell asleep on their wooden floor. They loved to spoil him. Their old-fashioned way of raising children still included: whippings behind the shed, eating after adults finished, not talking until spoken to, and they frequently reminded him that children were to be seen and not heard. Unlike me, Warren always obeyed.

Yes, I grew up with whippings while in The Gardens. Mom would have me touch the floor as I leaned over a low stool while her strap would come down hard over my rear. I jumped all around the room until she thought I'd had enough. But those whippings were seldom.

Although there was no current church attendance for either of us, we were both interested in God: Warren, from sitting on a mourner's bench every Sunday until he saw the Light. And me, I must have believed one of Billy Graham's sermons or I certainly heard about The Lord Jesus dying on the cross for my sins, during one of Mom's weekly Bible classes.

Chapter 8
The color is blue

One spring day during an early class period my 6th grade teacher asked me to come up to her desk,

"Kathleen, there is an escort to take you home. You have to leave right away."

"Why?" I asked coming near her as she opened the hallway door.

"You must leave with this young man." She was pointing to a big boy with round cheeks and dark glasses standing outside. "And take your things from your locker."

"What for?" I didn't want my classmates to hear me but I was curious so I lowered my voice but looked straight at her. "Did you hear me? Take your things, he's going to take you home."

In my mind my teacher sounded as if I was leaving school for some kind of punishment. I was thinking. What did I do now? I didn't get into that much trouble but every kid blames it on what they did or didn't do. Maybe I didn't turn in my homework on time? Or didn't do it last week? I couldn't remember.

I didn't have much in my locker: Wrappers off chewing gum, a sandwich that was molded. I left all that. I took my stinky gym shoes that I was supposed to take home to clean for gym inspection, my red sweater with holes in the sleeves and three books because she said, "Take 'ALL' your things."

I had the boy close the locker behind me. I looked back towards my teacher. She was standing in the doorway making sure I did exactly as I was told.

The Store

My teacher didn't smile at me but went back into her classroom. I heard her door. It made an echo down the empty hallway as closing the locker did. I walked looking at the tiles half way up the walls and the polished floors that seemed to go on for miles that I never noticed before. I could hear my brown oxfords keeping in step with this boy. I don't remember if I was sad. I do remember saying, "Feely-Dee."

Walking across the play lot wasn't bad for the ten minutes or so it takes to get to my house. The sunshine is exceptional. It's close to noon and the entire day is going to be great! I can tell… I'll get a Pepsi Cola and have a pork chop Mom fixed last night. Then, glancing over at this kid, I have no idea why he has to "escort" me. I know my way to 13040 S. Ellis.

I start kicking the sandy rocks as I skip along singing inside myself, just smiling sheepishly, thinking, *how lucky can I be? I am twelve years old and I've always wanted to be home alone.*

As I approach my house, I think *something looks unusual*. I dump my stuff and start running crazy like. My mouth is wide open and my mind tells me that *this can't be!*

No!…O no… no! My eyes can't get wider! I can't believe ~ It's devastating!

Everything I own, my sister owns, and my mom's furniture has been kicked outside our door –

***

I am sure: the sun fell down, the earth shook, and my world that I knew, stopped. But I wasn't aware of it. For several moments I left Me …

Yes, oh, yes I am sure it's my address. I recognize everything: My mattresses, dressers, chairs, clothes and linen

The Store

all heaped up. That boy brings over my things that I dropped and leaves me standing. I can't look at him; so ashamed.

Mom comes running minutes later. "Mom what happened? Why is our stuff out here?" She sees the trashed mess and stands stunned at what is spread out before us. I start to cry louder, "Mom, whyeeeee?" Like in a daze, she doesn't hear me. I receive no comfort or reassurance; she is overwhelmed at what is before her too. Her hands are over her mouth as she continually walks through and surveys the things she's treasured for years. Another boy brings over Claudette. She's crying and won't stop.

At first Mom must feel infuriated and then helpless like us. She can't put into words what her reasons were for deceiving Daddy. But she lost this battle. The same authorities that arranged for me and Claudette to leave school had contacted both my brainless parents, but I don't see my daddy, he never comes.

I am so ashamed, tears flood my eyes. I walk through my prized belongings crying; this looks like junk, the way it is thrown all over. My piggy bank is missing. My favorite blue dress I don't see. My coat and boots are here but my paper dolls and the box they were stored in are all over the place.

I wish: it was night time; no one could see me, the stuff, my tears, the kids from next door. Billy Hornsby and his friends, they stare.

There is nothing I can do. Can I go hide from them, pack up my stuff? I'm trapped. I can't do anything but sit on some quilts and wait. "Wait for what?" I say out loud as Mom keeps walking around. "Mom, what are we waiting for?" *I remember: running away, packing my stuff, being downtown, rambling through the floors of Marshall Fields, at the Chicago Theater watching the stage show between a movie, all that... coming back home rejected, I had few choices. I've*

The Store

always run away: the kids teasing me – jeers and cat calls. Now this…

I huddle near my sister, she won't stop crying. I wish someone; anyone would make the entire day go back to where it came from.

***

Mom may have called one of her boyfriends at the time, Johnny. Maybe he was the guy she and my daddy split up over. He's not here.

All sorts of visions race through my mind. I regret fighting my sister: *wanting to tear out her long hair from the roots, twisting it through my fists – gritting my teeth – making her beg to stop. She's so perfect – laying her clothes out for the entire week –* now she's worthless too, like me.

I sit feeling scared and empty. What did I do for this to happen? I'm lost in space and can't 'trust' my parents anymore. Just hours ago, I had musings of coming home from school to celebrate freedom.

I've been searching Mom's face for clues as to what's going to happen to us. Entangled with another man's affections, she still expected Daddy to pay rent and simple utilities. Constantly gambling, he didn't. I guess no one took care of anything.

Before dark Mom's brother, Uncle Ross unknowingly became my hero. Sadly he packs all our things in boxes and uses a borrowed truck to take us to his house in Chicago.

Chapter 9
Make that two please

That word "shame" followed me for a long time. What were relatives, classmates and friends saying about us being 'homeless?' I did hear whispers and saw some compliant looks loaded with pity. *"They got kicked out of the projects!"*

I couldn't understand whose fault it was. I had no idea that this feeling of not trusting anyone: *trusting their love for me, trusting who takes care of me will never leave, until I "run far away, to another land," up where no one can find me.*

I just want my own house again; a place of my own, even if it's a shack near the railroad tracks.

To a twelve year old brain everything's gone. How does she get her bearings when she no longer trusts the sun coming up? She has to grow up and growth is 'Pain' – a great teacher –

I never went back over the play grounds to Carver school; those classmates, my teacher, my things, The Gardens, all gone. Strange: after we left Uncle Ross', I never saw that stuff again. That sunlit day is forever etched in my brain. The pain haunts me. I relive it on occasion and not because I want to.

Whatever my parents are going through, they were putting my sister and me through Hell. They have trashed The Gardens, the only place I had any stability, along with their marriage and now me.

Transferring right away to another school was the first of many traumatic experiences. I continued to feel awkward:

The Store

new teachers, different kids, the strange curriculum, finding my way around, fights at school, always trying to catch up, assuring my sister, all was good. "We don't have to leave this school, Claudette." But we did, over and over again, someone told some officials we didn't legally live in the area and we had to go.

I am caught in a crazy cycle by shifting from place to place, school to school and I prayed hard for it all to stop.

***

What started tearing my sweet parents apart? I think it was a six stool lunch counter inside a Rexall drug store on 67th and Cottage Grove. Their combined lease of it flips back and forth between them for five years, up to, during and after their divorce.

Daddy flirts with his customers, but my mom does too when men take her flattering eyes too seriously. All their marital turmoil surrounds a certain male customer, Red, the butcher. Daddy's jealousy and circling accusations are too much for their fragile marriage. In frustration, Daddy leaves our home at her insistence.

I don't know why but he reluctantly relinquishes the thriving lunch counter to Mom and the 'butcher' next door, who's working in a grocery store. Within a year she's forced to give it back –almost in total ruins – because she's unable to properly manage it. (Years later Daddy ends up losing the business anyway because of IRS woes.)

During those five influential years my parents can't get their act together, much less help me become stable. Mother spends her time searching for a better boyfriend. Daddy can't stop gambling. My living conditions consist of going back and forth between relatives. Claudette and I go to a different school each semester, on and on.

The Store

No one wants us in state custody, which was called ADC –Aid to Dependent Children. Daddy's three older sisters squabble between themselves as to who will take care of poor Kathleen and Claudette. We were handed back and forth between them, like face cards in a poker game; the loser gets both of us to take home, and the winner is released.

But what is this doing to me? Often I'd come home from school to find my things packed. Mystery solved. Another relative would show up, peer through the door and say "Let's go."

Ugh, I'm staying with Auntie Lulu now!

Chapter 10
It's real hard landing on a glass floor

Near 80th and Michigan, is an area peppered with charming brick bungalows. Mom eventually finds a place in a building and rents a nice apartment for us. The various locations around Chicago, where I've stayed are cemented in my mind: I felt Aunt Hazel's home was too clean and neat; I couldn't stay that dirt free for long. I really enjoyed Aunt Romeo's apartment. It was my favorite; she's carefree and didn't mind me eating in front of the TV. Aunt Nancy's was too strict and my Aunt Alice too old.

Now, for the first time, back in with my mom, I'm secure and graduate from 8th grade at Hookway, but so far behind it's embarrassing.

In the fall I attend Hirsh High School. It's within walking distance. I meet some kids and melt into that environment the two semesters I stay there.

Mom dates a creep named, Paul Herndon, while working her waitress job in Lake Meadows. I don't like him, because he drastically interferes with my renewed relationship with her – but she's so happy. Then guess what? She ends up marrying him. She changes her name. It's Paula instead of Pauline. She's so in love. There's a popular record everyone's playing. The duet of Paul and Paula singing their hit "Hey, hey, Paula I want to marry you."

I struggle terribly in school by flunking Spanish and two other subjects. Mom's new husband moves us near 47th and Drexel. This move gives me a golden opportunity to transfer to the famous Hyde Park High School. But regretfully, trying to fit in and have more fun, I take my innate relaxed attitude (it was called 'Happy-go-Lucky') with me.

The Store

I'm eighteen now: smoking cigarettes, practicing inhaling, hanging out in the park, ditching classes too often and this is all because I "feel" grown up. Sounds like I should be wearing a black leather jacket plus riding a motor cycle, but I'm scared of them, and the kids that do 'anything' out of the, NORM, as they say. I just don't get mixed up with questionable shady characters. They are around or I must be divinely shielded from them.

– I do develop a serious 'earth quake' crush on a certain boy that keeps me not in the least bit interested in school. I just don't have my education paramount in my thoughts. He is.

I am also reluctant to tell people I have yet another address, now at the SouthMoor Hotel on 67th and Stony Island. – not proud, but ashamed of staying there.

Mom and Paul move to three or four more places. I stay on Mom's trail until I can't any longer. She follows Paul to Buffalo, New York, his home town. Whatever he told her; she ends up leaving us behind, to fend for ourselves, just like her mother did.

As the final semester of my second year drags by I am more ashamed of my lackluster grades, knowing it's my fault and of course, I keep my age a secret. Throughout all this: reality is weighing in on Me, I keep everything stuffed where I can't even find it. No one, including Me, knows my pain, because my 'attitude' remains pleasant and upbeat.. I hide it skipping from place to place, my head in the sand, whatever!

I'm staying with Aunt Eleanor on Harper. A week with Aunt Romeo on 75th Street, over to be with Aunt Hazel on Eberheart, and then back with Romeo, then Claudette and I end up staying a lot longer with Aunt Eleanor and her husband Thurman on 70th and Harper. Again!

Eleanor had married mom's brother Uncle Ross years ago, before I was born. Their divorce hurt me deeply. Now I

The Store

continue to bond with her. She's fun and boy does she give me a 'different-education' about other stuff. She keeps a liaison with the man downstairs on the second floor. Why does she tell me that crap? But that's her 'lifestyle.'

Okay, Mom is working as a maid in another state, maybe with Paul. She's not around, never is.

'This' and 'that' and Mr. 'Other' lead me to entertain several unwise decisions about everything going on in my, not-to-understand but always hit-me-in-the-face, stupid life.

Mostly I'm running from boys that always talk about sexual stuff; that alone scares me (they buzz around like flies now)… And I am tired of hiding, lying about my living status from place to place, my age, and no money.

– will I ever find "Where in the heck is Me?"

> I have set before you, life and death; …therefore choose life.
> Deuteronomy 30:19

***

One day early in May, I open my eyes, look up at the clock, turn over and never get up to brush my teeth, put on my clothes and walk twenty blocks to school.

I drop out.

I don't get reprimanded for my life-altering, stupid decision.

Someone could have said, "Why are you in bed? Get your lazy butt up and out of here young lady!" Oh, if anyone had said something: anything parental, intelligent, or even brutal.

'What the heck' was I thinking?

Every relative, I had been with, including my parents, lived in fear: that I'd get pregnant on their watch; I am a liability; a time bomb, and if I continued with my education or not, who cared?

Nobody did!

Chapter 11
He loves me, I love him maybe, not

When I left the Gardens I had accepted the Lord Jesus Christ into my life. I knew Him personally. I prayed to Him often, mostly for my poor performances in school.

Later, in my teens I remember that my deepest prayers centered on boys. Looking back, it was a big blessing God kept them 'all' from me. I'd beg for the affection of one or the love of another. Most times the object of my prayer could care less if I was alive.

I wasn't aware Jesus directed my steps daily not answering those prayers. Too many times I was glad He didn't in the way I wanted. But, in spite of the lack of parental guidance, countless "miracles" happened that protected me. Although I was saved, I didn't know how to choose my friends based on their spirituality, nor did I read God's Word every day for guidance, but the Lord shielded me. I stayed so happy-go-lucky. I didn't need alcohol to enhance my personality. And I didn't think smoking was bad. All adults smoked.

***

Both Warren and I enjoy reminiscing about our childhoods. He tells me his sad, exhaustive episodes and I share mine. We sit for hours in his car. He's drinking Miller beer from cans and offers one to me. "This taste awful" I make a face and he laughs at me. "It's not bad if you sip it while it's cold," he tells me. I light another cigarette then try the beer he's drinking from, gulping it down fast. "That's a waste!" He says taking the can from me.

The Store

We end up boasting about which crazy part of our childhood stories gets worse, his or mine.

Warren, so talkative, shares about growing up in Mississippi:

"'You put that cotton in my bag, boy, ya hear. I'll pay your 'n share when we get home.' Grandpa would grunt about the day's pickings in the cotton field each evening. The day was hot and I was wet with sweat. I was only eight years old but I picked just as much cotton as he did. My granddaddy was firm that I hadn't met my share of cotton in the sack. My sweet Grandma had to make me my own sack when she heard her husband going on and on about the thing.

She knew he would cheat me if he could. I picked along with him, row for row, and I'd pick more than he did -faster. I know I did."

Warren laughed hard like never before. "Don't choke" I said.

"My sweetest, Sweet Mama, was a big robust woman, but she could make kittens purr." Warren transferred his cigarette over to me, getting more comfortable by unzipping his jacket.

"Yes, she was sweet as sugar candy. She'd stand in the doorway watching me and Grandpa get off the work-wagon each night." He laughs again… seems most of his memories tickle him. "I'd run up the hill and dive into her open arms." I handed him back his cigarette as he continues without a second breath…. "Wiping her hands on her apron, I can see her face still ... Cathy, she often had food fresh from her old iron stove. She worked hard for some folks in town everyday but never forgot to bring me something sweet. The house smelt so good. Granddaddy and me forgot all our bickerin' while eating the good fixin' she'd made. Her braided hair was tied up in a rag cause she stood over the stove so long. I loved her more than anyone in the world. When she died it broke my heart."

He pats me on my thigh. "Maybe that's why I'm up here to meet you."

On and on he made her sound real, someone I could love too.

"I don't share these memories with my friends, that my grandparents raised me, not my mother, and that they were everything to me."

"That's a sad story ... about you picking cotton, I mean. Did that kind of work make you feel bad? Nobody likes picking cotton I heard." I said all that knowing what he'd say. He is proud of his background: the way he was raised, his roots, deep in the South.

"None of my memories of being in those roasting hot fields hurt me. It was what I did with my Grandpa 'til I was nine. I wanted to grow up to be like him."

"I worked too. But not in the hot sun." We laughed. Warren lights another cigarette for me. The flame illuminates my face. I hope he didn't see the tear on my cheek. I am on top of him in more ways than one; leaning on his shoulder for he's got my attention as I snuggle in the space next to him, close my eyes, ready to hear another touching story.

The Store

"After moving to Chicago, I stood for hours in the cold. I was not used to snow. I waited outside grocery stores asking fat ladies if I could help them."

Why fat ladies? I thought to myself, *wonder what their weight had to do with it.* "How much money could you make doing that? Man!" I said. "That's what you did as soon as you got up here?" I am listening intently.

"**You'd be surprised.**" Warren leans back dreaming looking through the car's front windows, as if it were a blackish movie screen. It is like it's playing in 'real-time' of his treasured recollections. He keeps telling me more. His unique mild voice lower now, almost to a whisper. My head is over on his chest; his tones are soothing and deep.

"**That's where I learned my 'Look-Sad-Give-Me-Look' and I'd be smiling, glance up and say something intelligent like. 'Yes ma'am.' Your groceries are safe with me today.' Then they'd give me all their change from their purse. One woman had me wait for over ten minutes, in the cold rain before she came back. She gave me a whole dollar bill, and then patted me on my head, just for carrying three shopping bags to the back door of her house.**"

"Is that usually what happened?" I said, not lifting my head, my ear still on his chest. I am wrapped up, refusing to budge from the nest I'd made in his arms. He talks so seldom I relish every word. He is just like my daddy; telling me childhood stories.

"**Women gave me lots of money Cathy, taking their groceries home. I tipped my cap and look** pitiful. **I made my red wagon work and it was the best looking wagon too. I polished it often and the wheels didn't squeak."** As Warren holds me close, he rubs his hand slowly up and down my side, I am sucked into his boyhood, as he draws the pictures he wants me to see.

Somehow, I am there in the cold… freezing with him. Chicago winters are brutal and my 'baby' is out there waiting for that lady's money. With each description, he makes sure I can visualize me being there.

"I remember climbing up three flights of stairs, lots of stairs sometimes, carrying loads over my back, bigger than I was."

Ok, this is getting too ridiculous; he is having more fun than I think he should. Mimicking sounds: first of him shivering with his teeth chattering, and then panting, **ahah, ahah, ahah,** like he is out of breath. The beer is apparently making him too relaxed, and I tell him so.

I hadn't been with anyone that had done hard work so effortlessly, making sport of it. Maybe he was put on this earth to carry out a predetermined agenda. I have enough sense to know he **is** rare. The guys I knew were bums. They ask their parents for money to take me out. Warren doesn't ask anyone for anything.

When he was free to do as he pleased-- he'd be hanging out with his buddies, shooting dice, or racing his car. Now he's enjoying being with me, snuggled, sharing his thoughts.

"Yes, people wanted to read the news and I delivered their papers." He continued…. **"When dollars came in the form of icicles, I shoveled their snow. I mowed lawns because grass grew… anything that I could do to help my mom."**

The Store

    His strong body hovers around me. He plants a tender kiss on my scalp through my hair. My eyes open when he paused, as his kiss is a surprise. His car is dim inside for no canopy of stars blessed us. I have fallen totally inside his dreams. If it weren't for a street lamp twenty yards from us, I would not have been able to see him or the steering wheel that was in our way. He's refreshing. He shares his life with deep conviction. I could stay all night, but he has to get some sleep.

    He coaxes me to stay. I lift my head then draw his smooth chin next to my lips. The beer cans are empty, the aroma of ribs still permeate the car and I burrow in for the last bit from his warm chest, then peel myself away to the other side of his car. His brown face is in silhouette in the dark car. I understand what makes him valuable to his mom. His strength could be transferred to me if I wanted his heart.

    He opens his door then looks over sheepishly towards me. With the cutest grin and body language, a twist of his head suggests for the umpteenth time, he has to go again. He finds a bush at the rear of the parking space to relieve the pressure.

    Our spot is secluded on a strip that he's familiar with along Lake Michigan. All night the ripples of the lake were soothing us in the background. It's so quiet outside; just a cricket competing with the water he's making as his urine flakes the dead autumn debris.

***

    I keep dating this guy and he grows on me. I had always dated boys who talked about sex and what's in it for them, and never anything else.

    Several times he drives by his mother's store. I sit in his car smoking a cigarette patiently, listening to my favorite

The Store

jams on the radio. He runs in for something he's forgotten, and then apologizes for staying too long. "Next time promise, you'll come in, so Mrs. Fain can meet you." He reminds me often.

Chapter 12
The glass slipper didn't fit

On a brilliant spring day early in the evening, I meet Warren's mother, Mrs. Fain. Warren stops by her store. I decide to leave the car as a surprise and follow just a few minutes behind him. He had gone to the back where the meat counter was and sat down before retrieving the cigarettes he came for. He is leaning backward in a tattered leather chair that has missing arms.

The little store is loaded with customers clamoring around the front register; a cashier is handling the crowd. Music is playing a blues station's rendition of Muddy Waters singing his favorite hits. There is a haze in the air; it's hard to see having left the bright sunlight moments ago.

I meander towards the rear thinking I would meet this lady that owns this place. He's there chitchatting with his mother and I go and stand near him. Warren had picked me up an hour ago from the beauty shop, where his friend's girlfriend goes.

His mother has no idea that we are together. By the look on her face she is wondering what I am doing coming near her private area reserved for invitees only. I am surprised at her overwhelming presence. I am not frightened, but she looks threatening and not the nice woman Warren portrayed her to be. It only takes moments for her to lash out at me but something holds her back when she looks over at Warren for a clue. His eyes land up on me. I look at her look at him.

I was thinking how her son was so good to me, buying me nice things, having dinner in soul food restaurants on 63rd street only to have me take full advantage of him, his money and his car. And for some other good reasons, today, while I

The Store

look my prettiest I want to thank her for raising such a nice young man.

I remain frozen and silent, trying my level best not to stare, but feel conspicuous and regret that my mouth stays open.

Is it me, because the atmosphere all over the store has changed? Warren must not know why I am spellbound. He doesn't look at his mother but keep his eyes on me, like I am a lollipop. Momentarily I don't notice anyone or anything but Mrs. Fain. I've walked in to what I thought was her normal everyday little grocery store. She looks back over at me, lays the meat cleaver hard on the butcher block that she's using to cut some ribs for a customer. Because I came in unannounced, his mother yells out before Warren catches her!

"Hey, it's private back here. What do you want?"

Now, I've become the main attraction on a tiny stage! I feel every eye in the place has been diverted towards me as a hush comes over the store. Even the radio pauses and Muddy isn't belting out his cries of pain. I wish I could have read her mind as she rounds the corner to see me full figure. Warren lunges out to grab her.

I moisten my pink lips with my tongue and bite it too. My hair is curled with bouncy lightness and the flowing dress I chose was bright turquoise with yellow daises floating through to the hemline. Spaghetti straps compliment the clinched waistline. I had on a necklace set that Warren had given me our second date. It matched the golden earrings dangling from my ears with several wrist cuffs to match. A beige sweater draped my shoulders. My shoes were medium heels and they picked up the hue of the outfit perfectly.

Her eyes darted over me up and down like lightening. I see them widen and she looks amazed when I reach out my manicured hand to her. She acts so fast Warren isn't able to shout anything except, "Mrs. Fain, this is Cathy!" As he lunges out to grab her I am not offered her hand with its missing fingers.

She begins **Act II**, by talking through a forced smile, showing all her teeth.

"So! You are Cathy!"

"Yes, that's me." I wet my lips and look behind her at Warren for support, but he's mesmerized. Thank God, he doesn't seem to notice my awkwardness.

"How are you? Would you like me to call you …" I hesitate seconds then say, "Mrs. Fain?"

She has on: dark grayish overalls, which matched the décor, a white butcher apron wrapped around her waist, which accentuated her wide figure, her sweat-laden forehead showed thru her black, curly wig, and her large facial features suggest she could have been a man.

"That's fine. Call me that." Her voice was curt.

Experiencing the full brunt of her disagreeable side we fully knew that a full separation between us was imminent.

Everyone called her "Mrs. Fain." She wanted the respect of younger people. Southern ways were different from the liberal North. Every child should address an elder with a title of respect: Mr., Mrs., Miss., Auntie, Uncle and so on. Mrs. Fain has kept her name 'formal" with me and certain customers as a barrier and today I am treated as the chief intruder.

I feel Warren has told her everything about me. She finally sees his girlfriend, Cathy, for herself.

Her high cheek bones create round mounds of thickness under searching eyes and when Fannie laughs she expects me and others to laugh with her. There was nothing to laugh about with my first introduction and I tried to force a smile

The Store

after releasing my mouth from its astonished position before greeting her.

Warren pulls a stool over that was against the wall, then tries to get my attention by snapping his fingers over at me. "Cathy …Cathy." He points to the area and gestures for me to sit. His face is sporting the biggest grin and he sees I'm a bit anxious. I fidget as he touches me, mad that I came in the store. I say, darting my eyes, then invent a smile, "No Warren, thank you, I'd better stand, can't stay long." I couldn't get comfortable sitting knowing his mother won't keep her eyes off me. My eyes are honestly searching around the store for somewhere else to stand. I keep my sweater close to my body and conceal uneasy hands. My purse, dangling from my shoulder, doesn't bother me. I am at a loss. I want to run out the door but how silly would that be?

I think I know what she's thinking: Her mind is clouded by my pale skin, or self-confident attitude or the way I am dressed or the proper way I talk or my tone of voice I use that are all different from hers. Or better still, she might have admired me too much and that would complicate her relations with her son. If she teased me about him I'd be scared-to-death! It's a good thing she's half trying to ignore me.

I feel Mrs. Fain chooses to be distant initially. Not offering to take the time to know me, or ask why I am interested in her precious son. Why I keep him filled to the brim with things I'm doing.

Maybe that was what she thought as she looks at me sideways and up and down. She made no other remark to me. I wanted to find out from her what she thinks of me but it's obvious, all the physical signs show it. Grovel at my feet, you pale, yella, wanna-be. Who do you think you are?

She's used to people going out of their way with sugar-laced words, wanting to win her approval. Something has

The Store

turned her against me from the start and it's not my job to repair it. I see Mrs. Fain as the mother of the guy I am dating. When she showed signs of going back to her duties: chopping the block –slinging her hatchet. I managed a smile, if only to myself, then walked away from both of them.

Mrs. Fain continues to wait on her customer, her cleaver pounds the table. She wraps up the meat she just butchered and continues to converse with her son.

I don't like this store. Some folks obviously do, with its one-room-school-house charm. I sure don't love her son. What's more, I wouldn't give Warren the time of day if I had someone else to take me out and wine-and-dine me. Any "Mr. Wonderful" will replace him in a heartbeat and he'd be history.

After a few minutes I holler back at him opening the door. "Warren I'll be waiting. Mrs. Fain, nice meeting you, I've got to go."

Warren doesn't say much when he reaches the car. I stay quiet most of the night. "I'm so glad …you met my mom tonight … you look wonderful." Warren blurts out awkward sentiments trying to assure me my beauty treatment, and the encounter with his mom was a good thing.

What an evening. All dressed up and going nowhere special. In my mind Warren noticed nothing. I felt awful leaving him, closing the car door behind me, knowing how badly everything seemed. I sure couldn't be my Happy-go-Lucky self.

I don't recover from meeting Mrs. Fain for days.

Chapter 13
Let's try one more time

My Aunt Eleanor's abrupt announcement that she has to move makes me think. I need to get out on my own. I'm not a kid anymore.

I have to find a job. A friend of mine pulls some strings and gets me a full time position at Jackson Park Hospital. I like waiting on patients and helping put them to bed at night. I also make sure they take their meds.

In the Sun Times Newspaper's want-ad section I search for 'Rooms for Rent.' Claudette has found her a cute mini-apartment. I want the same, but can't afford her taste. A vacancy near 74th and Stewart Street earns a red circle around it. It's well within my price range, by twenty dollars.

The room is nested in a two story Victorian-style decorated home with a charming older couple and the wife's sister. I am sitting in the living room which brings fond memories of my place in The Gardens.

I try my level best to act older and wiser than my years, answering questions, intelligently (this is my first interview, ever) from a delightful, but reserved, Mrs. Webb. We go back and forth about my work history, which is "poor" but I'm employed at the hospital and where have I stayed before … Oh, well.

Whatever I said, she liked it. She accepts me and the beautiful room is mine!

A couple of months pass.

I've lost contact with Warren, by accident, during my abrupt move. I kept telling myself the relationship wasn't going anywhere. Warren was not my type, maybe one day he'll find someone that truly is into him.

The Store

Meanwhile, I get introduced to a handsome guy named, Leon. He is a friend of my sister's boyfriend.

One person that adores Leon, his persona and the sweet love letters he gives me is Mrs. Webb's sister, Pearl. She wants to talk for hours about my 'boyfriend' and I amuse her.

Well, everyone raises an eyebrow when they see Leon. It's hard to describe a delicious looking man. Leon is: tall, has beautiful dark coloring and has a regal, Roman looking nose, curly black 'straight' hair, a tad older than I am, married before but he doesn't own a car.

I date him steadily, going everywhere, for a couple months. Each night he meets me after my, 4 to11 shift, then we board a 75th Street CTA bus.

Once on my porch we stand outside my door. We caress one another, moving our bodies in the dark, well beyond midnight. The good-byes get sweet and last longer and longer.

Mrs. Webb's neighbors complain.

***

"Cathy, bring your company up to your room, honey. Please don't stand there on the porch all night saying good-bye," Mrs. Webb sweetly says while sipping her coffee one morning.

I could never thunk it ... in a million years –

Cathy Lyons, bring her boyfriend up to her room? In Mrs. Webb's house?

This older woman surprised me. I knew she liked me but bring Leon in? Up to my room? The only time he'd been through the doorway was to be in her living room on an ornate couch too pretty to sit on.

"I'm so sorry Mrs. Webb. I'll do better." From then on, I didn't kiss Leon on the porch. I told him Mrs. Webb's neighbors complained about us. He promptly left every night after giving me one lingering kiss.

***

By chance, on a brisk sunny day I learn Chicago's south side isn't as big as I was led to believe.

I'm coming out of a fast food place on 76th and Vincennes when I run into Warren. He pulls over his car to say "Hello!" He's so elated to bump into me. Within a short conversation, I tell him where I'd moved, how things were going and other stuff. I couldn't stop smiling remembering all the fun we'd had. But I feel sorry for him. He likes me too much plus I can't return the favor.

He asks a simple question. Can he stop by? Still grinning, I say "Yes, why not."

***

Several times Leon and I walk very slowly hand in hand from the carline (since he's not ever going to be invited up to my room.)

I'll see Warren's car. He's parked there in front of Mrs. Webb's house watching us. Leon leaves. I go over and lean on the open window to say something. Some nights I sit in his car and we talk about old times, laugh and I smoke one of his cigarettes.

The Store

This Friday night at my porch, still holding my hand, I lovingly thank Leon for taking me home then whisper, "I have someone waiting for me." Leon turned his head to see a man's image in the black Chevy with the motor running. Hunching his shoulders, he sadly looks into my eyes, puts a kiss on my lips and politely says, "I'll pick you up tomorrow, Ms. Cathy." I close the gate behind him and sit down on the step, lean back on my elbows and wait.

Warren doesn't hesitate to leave his car, then saunter over and rest against the railing.

He softly says, "Hello, I'll **never** stop waiting for you."

By Monday he picks me up from work.

We go on innocent dates, just have fun, and do nothing but silly things. Because of Warren's car, I don't ever invite him up to my room…

Chapter 14
The color green

The second time I get to see Mrs. Fain I had torn my stocking getting into Warren's car. He promised to replace them. "Look what your car did." I teased him when the tear became evident, if I couldn't get another pair it would ruin our date. I wasn't going to 'trust' him to find the exact color. So I came along inside his mother's store.

The dimly lit place was crowded like before as several customers hovered around the checkout counter. Warren knew them all. He grinned shyly, knowing they knew I came in with him.

My stockings had to match my prettiest new dress. I felt exceptionally special that night. The rack for panty hose was to the right of the entrance. Warren had stupid suggestions about the color and size using ridiculous examples, 2x, 3x and 3xxx, laughing at each and inviting everyone to join in.

Mrs. Fain beckoned with her eyes and a flick of her head for Warren to come over to her, as a cunning woman would. Obviously we were having too much fun, disturbing her solemn mood. Her instinctive maneuvers spoke louder than she realized.

I saw Warren's wrinkled brow; as the elation of the moment crashed like a balloon expelling air, never to rise again. He touched my arm and asked me to sit on a stool next to Janet, the cashier. He'd be right back. He's only twenty feet from me having whispered conversations with his mother and his back is facing me. I divert my attention from them while Janet helps me.

The Store

Mrs. Fain never left her meat counter. I knew not to intrude. I could see she was scolding him by her finger strategy.

She thinks she is hiding her true feelings about me. As far as she's concerned, Warren has chosen a "whore" to bring home for her approval and she abhors sluts of any kind. Her eyes were sharp and narrowed with several glances over at me. How could I have the audacity to enter her middle class family, be one of them when I have no family structure?

Mrs. Fain had become firm in her belief that I was totally responsible that her son's affections towards her and her business had changed. She was living The American Dream and she'd be darned if I'd take it from her.

How could I know, perched on my stool, waiting for him to finish, that he was pleading my case. What he knew about me was the complete opposite of her misguided view. He told her. We were going out and he didn't have to tell her everything he was doing.

Chapter 15
The rules, just play by the rules

I was tired of saying I knew all about sex. I didn't have a clue what everyone was so excited about. I didn't trust anybody I had dated; but now Warren. I am in a comfortable relationship with an easy going guy that pleases every whim. In my opinion, our relationship isn't going deeper than what it is … or get serious or marriage, none of that.

Teasing him one evening sitting in his car I promised he could come up to 'see' my room.

That one decision changed **everything**!

***

Most thought of me as sweet and innocent, caught up in situations beyond my control except Mrs. Fain. Her attitude toward me went from bad to worse when I gave her son access to my bed. Warren never gave me an inkling that she came along with the fun filled package. I don't understand that this game she started with us is going to get serious.

We are coming from a party and the conversation switches to what his goals are. "I put you before my mother, Cathy. I made a decision to separate from Mrs. Fain"

I said "Wow! Oh, no, man. Did you tell her that?" He didn't know it at the time but the ties were severed the day he saw me. He wanted to be with me for the rest of his life.

Warren knows I don't care for bars, night clubs or joints. I don't drink, swear or tell dirty jokes nor listen to them. I am totally opposite of him in every way. He is the kid glove of 'protection' and I am the movable fingers

The Store

inside. A perfect fit. We are a couple. I wanted someone that was tall, dark and handsome. I settled for warm, dark and wonderful. We go everywhere together.

Money doesn't seem important to Warren. He always has it but won't dress like it. He wears drab, colorless clothes and has on the same pair of pants every time I see him. My style of dress isn't fancy either but my things sparkle with freshness as I iron my cotton dresses, blouses and scarves. I seldom wear jeans and have never seen any on him.

I didn't notice his clothes at first. I notice how he treats me; I notice how I feel when I'm with him – Precious.

Warren loves me just the way God made me. I have light skin, his is chocolate brown. I have an outgoing personality; he is a deep thinker, quiet and reserved. I am talkative, never serious; as he listens. I am 132lbs soaking wet at 5'8" with two "fried-eggs" for breasts. For looks we both are average, but some call me pretty. I have hazel eyes that always get attention, his are deep brown, sad ones that get him in trouble. I have straight teeth that my Mom paid to fix, his are awful. His frame is muscular, making a body builder jealous at 5'10", 180lbs.

My personality is out-going to a fault, even crazy some friends call me. I'm a maverick against Warren's iron-clad conformity. He goes along with my laid back attitude most of the time. I'm not like anyone he's ever met or hoped to. Where I want to go on dates he thinks of me being fun, different and exciting, even contagious. I like him because I am totally myself with him. I **never** have to pretend.

Warren's hair cut is so short it looks bald. I wear my hair shorter than the other girls that want long tresses or pony tails. I don't use heavy grease with tight curls but let it flow after I press it with a hot comb. I get lots of justified teasing from my peers about the way I dress, with weird colors

The Store

mixed together for "that look" of pure selfless freedom. Criticism seldom bothers me.

My proper diction, when I speak makes people think I am a teacher or the daughter of one. I smile and know what they mean. Often ashamed I didn't finish high school, but I'm no drop-out, in my mind.

I like most people I meet and look them straight in the eye. I don't remember any one teaching me this. From the many places I've stayed, I've observed countless things.

Warren is solid. His conduct with the world around him is pure. He knows who he is, and he makes strides to alter his personal environment. He chooses his friends carefully: Vaughn, Harold, and his closest buddy, Gerrard. Mostly they come around him hanging for hours inside the store. He has money, resources, a circle of influence, plus his own car to explore life unconditionally. A quiet storm. He's above the crowd. He never has to announce his presence.

Warren's design to keep me around long enough to fall for him was a gamble. Changing me never entered his mind.

Chapter 16
It's purple passion all over again

Mrs. Fain and Warren had always thought of expanding her business. There was another place three blocks up the street from hers. She thought of owning it, garnering it for her son's future business. She asked him if he would search out who owned the corner store on Woodlawn and advise her of what he'd found.

Warren comes by and puts his palm on the glass to peer inside the window. The Store notices him instantly. For her, it is love-at-first-sight. For him, it was a pondering thought for three days –The Store made sure she never left his mind.

There is a sign on her with bold black letters: '**FOR SALE**'

The Store haunts Warren. He drives by several times a day looking at her. He sits for hours dreaming of possessing her and what it would feel like. He would bring her up to where she would take them out of The Pocket. Mrs. Fain and her husband, Arna, better than anyone else could have, negotiate the entire deal to their favor.

Six months past –

The Store belongs to Mrs. Fain.

***

I remember the day I went in to help clean The Store this book is about.

Warren didn't share the history of how his mom acquired the little store or how the love affair started with him and why he pets The Store so much.

The Store

I leaned on a metal guard rail and gazed out the double front window, daydreaming, looking at the houses across the street. They were well kept and we were supposed to be busy inside cleaning up the place to match its surroundings.

The area's folks seemed friendly and the anticipation of The Store opening proved exciting for them. Folks passing by would tap on the glass. Warren, looks up from what he was doing, gives a smile and waves. "When is this place opening?" some would say motioning through the pane. He would always say "Real soon" and wave back at them and we'd be back on duty.

It wasn't long after I hung my sweater on a hook that Warren handed me a bucket of warm sudsy water, a rag and a brush. I ended up putting on rubber gloves while cleaning shelves, moving boxes around the aisles, as if I knew what I was doing. Our favorite radio station was playing our songs and we'd sing and joke around having fun late into the evening that first night.

It took three days to completely clean The Store. Each shelf had to be scrubbed and the can goods placed in order, turned just right, facing the front. I choose the stamp gun that marked the prices for each can. He'd holler out the prices from an order sheet he was looking through. It was fourteen cents on a can of corn, and twenty three cents on the larger cans of string beans. Every item had the price clearly put in the center so customers knew its cost. What confused me were the twin prices. A lot of cans were marked two for a different price and if they wanted one can the price was higher.

He knew I didn't have the foggiest conception what the grocery business was all about and he repeated he didn't care. "You'll never work for me." He said later that night when he took me home. "That store will be my prized possession and I'll own her one day."

The Store

"Sure you will." I laughed at his dry jokes and his lofty ideas of owning The Store like his mom.

Never. Never, not ever, one time did I think of him, owning The Store!

I got a chance to meet more members of his family when he brought his cousin George to help us polish windows the second day.

I had promised to come back and have another day of hard work, but it wasn't easy. I put my feet up on a footstool and listened for hours as he and George talked: about their family, the grocery business, customer's complaints, entertainment and sports, girls, baseball, football, boxing, just games. Mostly sports.

They even cleaned the walls. Both men were tired but Warren wanted to go out for hamburgers. He dropped his cousin off and we drove to our favorite place, Prince and Joy's on 47th street.

We sat for hours talking about The Store and what she meant to him. He let me in on a secret, he loved The Store we'd spent so much time cleaning for his mother. I never understood then, what he meant; about being in love with her. It was just a little store.

The last day the floor was covered with empty cartons from all the stock we put up. You could smell the odor of Pine Sol and bleach over the scrubbed store. He flattens each box to take out to the dumpster. He swept the place tirelessly from front to back. He walked all over checking: the meat case, the shelves, the refrigeration units, the potato chip racks, the varieties of Dolly Madison cupcakes, a huge selection of deli meats, and cheeses. Every space was accounted for, every inch. To me it was just a tiny grocery store; slightly larger than the one in The Pocket. I thought nothing more of it. I smiled at him when he proudly said it was ready for Mrs. Fain's inspection.

Chapter 17
His momma don't tell no lies

By the third month of our intimate relationship Warren's dedication to his work and his position as manager is different. He loves his mother's business, is still dedicated but he doesn't run errands or supply stock from the wholesale markets the same way. He comes up missing when it is time to work his evening shift. He is all apologies when he comes in late or leaves early. Mrs. Fain has to find someone to take his place or she opens herself when he isn't in his room in the morning.

Operating two stores is too much if she doesn't have her son's total involvement. She fails to understand Warren has simply fallen in love. No woman on earth was designed to affect him the way I did.

Warren stays over night with me every chance he gets. I am so glad Mrs. Fain doesn't hire a hit man for me to end her pain. She changed her mind about turning The Store over to her son. Warren had disappointed her several times. His new lifestyle wasn't up to her standards and me, being a hussy, I didn't fit into her business plans. She reasoned, begged and finally offered Warren anything he wanted if he would release me, and let their lives go back to NORMAL.

I had no idea that hanging around with him in The Store on Woodland bothered her.

Mrs. Fain gives up and offers The Store we'd spent so much time fixing up to her favorite brother, William Toliver. Then she helps him secure the funds to take full possession. He and his wife, Helen, are delighted.

***

The Store

I enjoy my life so much.

We're in the car; its pitch black. I can't see the mess the bar-b-q has made all over my mouth and my clothes. Warren and I pace ourselves to see who will finish first while enjoying his can of cold Miller as it sure makes this stuff more enjoyable. Our teeth rip each morsel. The soggy potato fries and double slices of white bread soak up the red sauce in the tray …its over; He wins again.

Warren is perfect to be with. We can make doing 'nothing' fun. No one gives me the attention he does.

The only thing that saddens me: I can't picture him in my future as my husband, maybe a brother, a kissing cousin or friend. My thoughts drift to an elusive guy in high school, comparing the two is pointless. Warren comes up the winner, even to gorgeous Leon.

I have plenty of time. He promises me he'll never leave me, never marry anyone else. He'll wait.

Chapter 18
My mommy don't tell lies too

Long crazy conversations with mom convince me to leave Warren and explore new horizons in New York City. Mom lives there with Paul. Stability is new for them. In Chicago their addresses vary with the seasons. Mrs. Fain has nothing to do with Mom's decision to coax me to change my place of residence. Mom thinks she can break some hold Warren has over me. I tell her he's just a wonderful guy that takes me out and she might meet him one day.

After a long costly phone call, (I must have had my head screwed on weird that night.) Sure, I tell her I am a free spirit; I make my own decisions now... Then reluctantly, regrettably I agree: it's no problem going there to stay, get a waitress job like hers; get out on my own one day and support myself.

When we get off the phone, it's set. I leave Chicago by Friday.

Early Tuesday morning my sister, father, and close friends, including my employer at Jackson Park Hospital, all know I'm leaving. I pack some things in a suitcase I bought at second hand store.

During our weekly Keno game, Mrs. Webb and her family learn the news. I ask her to excuse the room rent. She understands; her quiet dignity saddens me. I need her blessings. Mr. Webb, who had warned me not to let Warren slip through my fingers, is given a fond kiss on his bald head. It is especially cheerless for Pearl. She had become my favorite. Everyone wants the best but lament that Warren isn't going to fare well. "He'll get over it!" I laugh along with them, never meaning it, and then change the subject. After losing the game, I finish packing.

The Store

Deep down there is no explanation. I'm scared to tell Warren where I am going. I don't have a legitimate reason. It's cold in New York too.

Why mom set her sights on me? She's not after Claudette. Seems her husband should be more than she can handle, unlike Paul, Warren wasn't threatening, had never been in jail or on drugs.

I prefer my men as dark as coal. Their skin's rich color fascinates me. The secret is in our Negro community. We just don't make our race darker by having babies with dark skinned men. It isn't my fault I have fair skin. I don't feel that way but it is whispered a lot, sometimes out in the open, that some of us are prejudice too.

Maybe I am the bad person, letting Warren into my bed. Maybe in Mom's mind and in the heart of Mrs. Fain too, that one activity between Warren and me had to stop. I could get pregnant. Nah!

Several things should interfere with my decision to relocate, and stop this crazy plan. They all revolve around Warren.

First: I am leaving the best boyfriend ever!

Second: Because I have 'tasted' him I've developed a rich dependence on his faithfulness.

Third: I have grown to be very "fond" of Warren. A cute surprise to me but I don't know it yet. We entered a different level by being personal. God's design from the beginning. Warren has challenged me. I saw him believe in himself – as if God was directing his steps; and he's chasing his goals.

Gosh, he let me get in the way. I will leave and he and Mrs. Fain can go on and live the American Dream. But, maybe I should want it too.

So why leave?

The Store

There is always this stupid nagging thought that there is "something" better out there, over the rainbow, on the other side of the fence. "*Come see New York*," a faint distant echo in my brain. Just come and see.

***

Mom's husband and I had had physical confrontations in the past. I had picked up whatever was closest to throw at his head as he ducked. I was not scared of him. Maybe they had had a fight and Mom told him she'd send for me. How they found each other is a mystery I never want to know. They are living in a tiny apartment, well a cheap kitchenette, not big enough for them. Where would I squat?

Chapter 19
It's the glam and dirt that hurts

Mom's place in New York is just as she said. It consists of one tiny area that she transforms into a bedroom, kitchen and living room. An overstuffed couch is propped up against a window that looks out over their back porch. It becomes my sleeping quarters. She really doesn't have room for me. I wonder if am crazy to be here.

After arriving, the same day I go out to a Temporary Add+ Agency on 9th Street. That's where Mom gets her day work. I don't have proper shoes but they send me on a "day job" that same afternoon in a hotel lobby to wait on tables. Same thing is assigned the following day. I end up mirroring Mom's flimsy but some time lucrative occupation.

After one week and a day going back and forth using New York's intricate subway system, I get lost in an area I thought I knew. I spend over three hours trying to get back home. By week two, I am drained, mentally overworked, homesick, and my feet are killing me.

I fail to see the excitement that New York is known for. They aren't playing the same music on their radio stations. I miss my Chicago one, WJJD and my favorite DJ, Herb Kent. Talking long distance is out of the question. I can't afford it. I don't have any friends. Mom spends her precious time after work and on week-ends with her husband.

My weekly grind is the same heading into my 25th day, in a place I'm beginning to loathe. I get off after the lunch crowd slows down at 2:30 p.m. I walk from a maze of people in the Manhattan subway system. I'm watchful to catch the right number bus, go eighteen blocks north, get off to walk 3 blocks to Mom's building.

The Store

Her entrance of marble slabs and maple carved wood is dirty. The pee stained elevator stinks; holding my nose I ride up to the fourth floor, open the iron gate then walk down the dimly lit hallway, past other sorry looking doorways to Mom's number, 418. The number four hangs by a thread.

Paul thinks I should cook my own meals, if I don't, I'll starve. I am so accustomed to calling Warren, eating at his favorite soul food place or just pigging out in his car. I miss that good food. I miss his attention but don't tell Mom these things.

I look inside the icebox, there is nothing there. I could go around the corner but my money is short. My daily tips aren't enough. I have to cover the price of my own food, carfare plus fifteen dollars a week for rent; Paul says I owe him to stay in this sorrowful place.

I miss Chicago.

I miss my sister Claudette, and my daddy.

The only thing enjoyable is I can have a cigarette anytime I want.

We can hear everyone down the hall and overhead. Eighteen families live on this floor. I swear they all come out at the same time each evening, banging doors and hollering to other neighbors. It's sickening. Our doorway mat is swept clean each night but there is something littering it every morning.

The area where we cook our meals is over against the wall next to my bed. The fumes from the little gas stove permeate the entire place. The small refrigerator is underneath the cabinet that houses the few items we need daily to cook, like rice, flour and a couple of can goods. No seasonings of any kind, just black pepper and salt in two shakers.

The Store

I wish I could tell you this place looks homey with a bedspread matching the throw over the couch. Twin pink curtains are draped across the window near my sleeping quarters, but it lacks something. I can't put my finger on it. The wall paper clashes with the dated décor. It has huge flowers trailing across it that remind me of a tropical rain forest, only it's faded and dull.

One light fixture hangs along a frayed cord from the cracked ceiling. The smallest square table with its two old wooden chairs sits in the middle of the room. That's where I am sitting to rest right now. I am so tired when I get home.

My thick bushy hair is my real problem. I can't afford to do anything about it. I hate to look in the mirror. My being here has to be out of a horror movie. I want to change the channel. I lay my head across the oil cloth table and I can't cry; that ruins my mascara. I am bent over rubbing my big toe, it hurts so badly.

The same scenario plays in my head. Mom is with a loser for a husband. He's awful, he's loud, and he's uneducated and makes everyone notice him in the worst way. Although younger than Mom by nine years, his two bottom front teeth are missing. Something spits out when he talks and **is** he a talker!

I didn't like Paul from the beginning of their courtship. I was fifteen when we were finally alone on 80th and Michigan. She brought a lot of guys home but he was the sour pickle in the jar. He talked my Mom into abandoning us. It wasn't nice being left behind knowing this creep did it. Really my mom did it, letting Paul have that much say over where we lived and what she did with us. He had her selling fried homemade pies to the guys that park cars downtown. He was a hustler using her to further his grandiose ideas. Mom was hopelessly in "love" then. To her love means everything. She told me he is the second love of her life.

The Store

I tell Mom several times a day Paul isn't the man of her dreams. He took her from us. We were staying in Hyde Park off 53rd and Dorchester where Mom managed an apartment building…then. Let me stop. I could go on and on about this loser.

But now Mom has sent for me to be with her. I'm stuck. Why did I come? Why did I leave Warren? No one put a gun to my head and made me get on that Greyhound at 2:09 a.m. in downtown Chicago.

Chapter 20
It's a skinny thing going nowhere

Warren is so in love with me. I am sadder than sad when he put me on the bus.

It's locked in my brain those last hours I was with him. He hovers around the station buying me a coke and chips. He doesn't mind sitting on the hard seats for over an hour to wait. We sit holding hands. Then I prop my leg over his. His arm gets tired lifted across my shoulder. We change position. Brushing a hair from my eye, I start to tear. It's marvelous being loved. Feeling someone adores the ground under your feet. I am leaving that experience voluntarily. Most women would fight for such a man's love. I am not 'in' love. We did have tons of fun… I made no promises.

We watch everyone madly rush in to find their loading stations. I notice so many lonely people. Most don't have anyone to see them get on buses marked for Seattle, Washington, DC, Memphis, Indianapolis, or Dallas; all the places we have never been. My bus is headed to Manhattan. He is numb as we sit together silent. Rubbing his temple I imagine he is quietly thinking he'll take me all over the world on a jet plane if I change my mind. I know him. Warren sure doesn't want me to go but he seldom shares his heart's cry.

The only thing that's moving is my crossed leg going up and down. His arm is around me. Nothing is coming from my mouth but my mind is racing. I still can't explain my decision. What do I say? I don't even understand why I am leaving. He said it's going to be impossible to go on. It's my fault. I am breaking up with him. He did all the right things by giving me his heart. But I must leave. Release him to find someone that will return the love he is capable of giving.

The Store

When it's my time to gather up my things, Warren looks at me, so sadly, then reaches over and picks up my suitcase. We walk together slowly over to the loading dock as if there is nothing to do but wish things were different. If only I would call the whole thing off, keep going, meandering through the crowd and climb into his car. He carries all my stuff: my purse is over his shoulder; my make-up case is in one hand, the suitcase in the other, and my big black teddy bear, he bought me while waiting, under his arm.

We get to the doorway marked #7, this is when he drops everything on the pavement. He takes both my hands and looks into my face. My heart is pounding but not as hard as his. Drops of sweat fall from his brow. As I look in his brown eyes I feel so sorry for him. I know he won't beg. I hate myself for causing the pain he feels right now. He bites his lip. His eyes never leave mine. I look away, and then look back up at him.

"Warren, I'm sorry." My words are sincere and breathy. I am thankful he's here to send me off but that's not enough.

I lift my arms, wrap them around his shoulders, and then up to his neck, then stand on tip-toes to put a tender kiss on is cheek. My head lies cradled in his neck for a minute. His love feels overwhelming as his strong arms squeeze me. He sporadically whispers "Don't ...don't, do not say good-bye... Stay here with me... forever!" He kisses me, twenty times on every spot on my face, neck and shoulders, burying his face in my coat. I'm helpless, but pull myself away to bend over to pick up my stuff. Slowly, I board the huge bus painted with a skinny dog running along its side.

Warren follows my window image. I creep back past several passengers to an empty spot just where I can see him. I place my bags, it seems in slow motion, one by one in an over head compartment. Then I quietly sit down on the velvet-like seat next to the window, hoping to glance out

The Store

again, trying to … is he still there where I left him? Everyone has gone that stood sending off loved ones or friends. The Chicago winds stir up papers and trash lying around the dirty ground in swirls of tiny tornados. The sound of laughter fills my ears.

Gosh, he is frozen. His eyes stare straight into mine. I can see his message, as if he's beckoning me to tear myself away; beg the driver to open the darn door and fall into his outstretched arms, he's waiting...

The motor starts, the lights are dimmed, I can smell the fumes. The bus driver announces we're off. Warren is standing alone with his arms still open wide. As we round the corner; my face is pressed hard against the glass. I lift my hand to wave. Warren: the guy that really loves me fades out of sight. His sad eyes and image haunt me for hours until I fall asleep crying soft tears into his black teddy. Soon, by the next day at 4:57PM, I'll be with Mom in New York City.

Chapter 21
It could happen to you...

Warren has the car radio listening to Etta James' *At Last*, knowing it's my favorite. When it ends, he feels worse. He has for the entire evening Mrs. Fain's brand new pink Bonneville.

He thinks he's lost me. It is a clear night. The McDonalds sign he is parked under on 67th and Stony Island has the entire parking lot as bright as day. To enjoy Mrs. Fain's car, he has invited his drinking buddies; Vaughn and another good friend, Phyllis. She tags along for free beers and cigarettes. Tonight might be the night her old boyfriend, Gerrard, Warren's best friend, is with them. That's how her friendship with Warren began, chasing Gerrard.

Everyone knows I left more than three weeks ago, including Mrs. Fain. No one has heard from me. Whispers of my where-a-bouts have reached the President of the United States for sure. I am that important in the mix of things if Warren has anything to do with it.

Four guys, Warren, Vaughn, Gerrard and Harold, the best of friends, are notorious for getting drunk, gambling, staying out late and having fun racing their cars around Lake Michigan at 43rd Street. They also build up outlandish stories about all the women in their lives. Gerrard is missing. Harold is working, and won't get off until 4:00. Since I had left Warren, Vaughn is teasing him. "Get with it, man!" Reminding Warren all evening of what fun they used to have.

Phyllis and Vaughn stay with joking sarcasms, drinking more than usual, and they start talking about me: How skinny I am, my pale skin, how funny I talk, then maliciously laughing about where I ended up; miles away in

The Store

New York City. It wasn't funny. They roared with laughter, except Warren. He sat quietly. He isn't in the mood for talking crap about the woman he loves or listening to their distasteful stories. He opens the door but they ignore him and keep up their ridiculous candor.

Memories flood Warren's thoughts and one stands out. Someone at his store mentioned, just go for a visit. He lit a cigarette, then a short time later another one. Go. Stays stuck in his mind.

Warren opens his thoughts verbally. Much to his surprise both of them agree to get out of town and it wasn't beer talking.

Everyone got their things together in perfect synchronization within an hour the trip is prepared in a forward direction that never reversed.

That one decisive scheme changed the course of history, for me, Warren and everyone else that eventually influences us. In Mrs. Fain's automobile the thought of "just a visit," no short of a miracle, took place. Warren moved that brand new car eastward and never looked back.

"How far is that place from here?" Vaughn said as he got back from packing his things, and would never leave without his 35 mm camera. "Too far!" said Phyllis. Her things were tucked close to her as she assured them she was staying to the finish line.

Phyllis did feel sorry for Warren. She knew his mental state. She had introduced him to me. I was walking to Hyde Park High School, minding my own business, when he noticed me. Always seeking preferential treatment, because of Gerrard, she reminded him she knew me. "Don't worry, I'll fix it." Being the conniver she is, everything was carefully arranged. He would casually drive her over to my place on 40th and Michigan.

The Store

They drive up and he looks up at my old building with its stone façade. He takes a deep breath, and then flips his lit cigarette out the window. She rings my bell as he anxiously waits. I appear in the hallway to follow Phyllis to the car to get in. That's the story: I realized there was someone in the driver's seat, get introduced, but thought nothing more about it.

***

It's midnight in New York: there's not a single star to wish on. I've been looking out of Mom's kitchenette window for hours. Those buildings next to me with their ugly red bricks, that I've counted many times, block the sky. My cigarette smoke floats up out of sight and hours pass, dawn must be breaking but I can't catch a glimpse of heaven.

I cry a lot. Lord, You listening?

No matter how I contort my body on this lumpy couch the stupid covers slip off. With my tiny hard pillow, it's awful. My curlers come loose making my hair untamable every morning.

All I want is 'someplace' else.

I smile thinking about a #*(&^()* situation with Warren, then another sweet one crosses my mind. I miss him. I wonder what he's doing?

Chapter 22
It should happen to me…

Warren could be having second thoughts. He is miles away from Chicago. They've been driving for 9 hours, still not even close to where I am. Cigarettes are low, along with money for tolls, and gas but it's New York or bust. Sharing an idea of getting on the road with a brand new car has gotten them all in trouble.

Warren's phone call to Mrs. Fain wasn't good. He heard her cursing for the longest and then she hung up. How could she understand when he doesn't know why he's on a turnpike going east? Vaughn and Phyllis have similar accounts. No one understood.

***

I have to hurry today for another one of Mom's assignments. I have to be at 5th Street for an interview. The position promises to be a good paying one this time. My hair is a mess. I tossed back and forth all night. Paul with his blasted TV, his weird programs I have to listen to blaring through the night. I want my own place soon and this job might be my ticket.

I smell something cooking. I peek out the bathroom as I brush my teeth. Mom is cooking breakfast and it smells like bacon. Whoa! She has some coffee on. I can have at least one cup this morning if I get to it before Paul.

I have to get to the bus stop by 7:15 and it's already 6:45. Mom told me what car line to take. I gobble my breakfast kiss Mom good bye and finish the coffee in one gulp; then grab my jacket, purse, map and sun glasses. Mom yells, "Have a good-day, see ya when you get back."

The Store

I remember everything: breakfast, clothes ready, and my feet don't hurt. The sunshine meets me and I position my shades just right.

The first bus driver leaves me; I lose my change purse, trying to locate it, my homemade map blows away. Tearfully, I arrive at the appointment site, exhausted, just before they close for lunch.

The bus ride home is pleasant, I'm thankful for a mom to rush to. I go over my project, the case manager gave me. I was hired to clean six boilers and keep them running. I stumble through the door out of breath with my face all aglow.

"I am so excited, tell me everything!" She hollers back to tell Paul to turn down the TV. "Honey, Cathy got the job!" She reaches over and gives me a hug. "Sit down, Cathy." Then she turns her face and says, "Told you!"

"Mom it must have been this blouse you let me wear that sealed it."

I settle down, unbutton my skirt, kick off my shoes and share my day. "Mom you won't believe what happened …."

Chapter 23
It was a pink horse

RINGzzz . RINGzzz.

I am eating my hamburger and some fried potatoes I fixed for dinner. My Mom and I are sitting at the table talking about my bout with the missed bus.

We are both startled to hear the doorbell buzz. I looked at Mom's face to see if she is as puzzled as I am? I get up out of my seat quickly still chewing my food. Who in the world would be bothering us? It takes a few minutes for someone to reach our door.

Sure, my Mom might have thought the super is coming to fix something that she didn't know was broken.

So, I hear this sound that will alter my life completely. That bell doesn't ring ever; no one comes over nor does Mom have any visitors or friends. I have been here four weeks and this is the first I hear the buzzer.

Mom and I look at each other wide eyed. Five or more minutes go by. I hunch my shoulders and reach over to turn the knob. Crack the door and peep. Then I open it wider. The overhead light in the apartment makes my vision fuzzy. Coming down our dingy hallway, one behind the other, back into my life, are friends of Warren's. Could this be a vision? I can't believe it! I scream! I recognize all of them!

Is this real? Instantly a flash of wonderment to beat anything that has ever happened to me materializes in front of my eyes.

What in the world!

Vaughn! Phyllis! And the last person walking is Warren!

The Store

Every memory of God's faithfulness fills my mind. There is a scripture that says *"His thoughts towards me are countless- yet I feel each one...*

No, no way! Warrrrrrrrrren!

It only happens in movies: Dirty, stinky friends walking inside my place and I can't believe it! An explosion of joy and happiness as I hug Warren like he is a Christmas present I finally got.

I'm jumping and dancing pulling Warren along with me. My Mom gets up, holding her hands over her head for she's dancing too.

Who can believe this?

Paul comes from the back of the kitchenette and wonders what has caused all the commotion in our dull lives.

These three 'nuts' are the sweetest gifts any lonely ex-Chicago girl can get. A Very "Home Sick Girl." I missed Warren more the moment I saw him.

I didn't know a thing about it. Mrs. Fain didn't know, no one knew. God gives a notion to Warren. "GO... Why not GO!" obviously God has the Power... against all odds.

God hears my secret prayers at night. I tossed and turned unable to rest. My simple 'wishes' are answered when to me its an impossible dream to be rescued.

He sends Warren to me in such a way, that it explodes my heart. He worked behind the scene for me! An attitude shift. No one ever has made this concrete commitment to me before.

Warren has walked inside my heart and refuses to give up. Somehow, I need a bang! This jolt of reality.

I know how long it takes to get here from Chicago. But I am going back! I am going back with Warren anyway I can.

The Store

Warren looks tired. He isn't beautiful or anything else for that matter. He looks like the same sad eye guy who put me on the bus. He must have said;

"I'll follow you as fast as I can come, I'll run as fast as I can run. But you will be mine someday."

Warren is so sleep deprived and worn to a thread. He and Vaughn had driven all the way from Chicago, just to 'visit' me! What a man! I finally realize he is more than different.

This guy is determined to get in my heart, that's for sure.

I find out that he thinks differently too. Not only does he tell me how much he adores me, his actions prove he will cross mountains; swim oceans; defy man, woman or child, including Mrs. Fain to be next to me, and be my man!

I had to sit back down and stare at this sight: three of them searching their way around my small place.

"Put your things over against the chair. Get comfortable. You guys hungry?" Says Mom. She knows this is special. Has anyone showed her such loyalty? Such devotion all the years she's been searching for someone to adore her?

If you want something; Get it.

If you don't get it,

You must not have wanted it.

He lives by that creed. There are times I had wished my Mom had said things like that to me. I stare at his personage. I look deep into his motives. He believes in himself.

It is Warren that digested the creed:

Lives it: Breathes it: Owns it:

The Store

My Mom gave me a priceless introduction to Jesus Christ. I pray a simple prayer to Him, almost a wish, and here they are.

Warren heads for the sofa as soon as he comes from the bathroom; he sees me, winks his eye and asked, pointing to the very spot to rest.

"You can sleep anywhere." I assure him twirling my arms around as if there were many places to choose from.

"I feel delirious, I am so tired." But he shyly smiles saying it. I remove his shoes. His feet smell terrible. I don't care.

I throw my coverlet over him; kiss his salty forehead as his eyes glance up at me. Nothing wakes Warren; like a rock he goes dead to the world instantly.

Chapter 24
Did you say spell, H-a-p-p-y?

Mom has two plates on the table, a pitcher of Kool-Aid from the refrigerator. Phyllis and Vaughn gobble the food like they haven't eaten for days. Oh, it is so sweet to stare at them. They make no apologies.

"I still can't believe you're here." I whisper so many times. I scoot my chair up to the table closer, prop my elbows to listen to what they must know as my face grins from ear to ear.

"Why are you here now? Did Warren talk you guys into coming? Tell me everything. What happened next?"

"It started with me making fun of Warren." Vaughn starts his side, chewing on Mom's left-over fried chicken. "Warren is in Mrs. Fain's new car sitting in McDonald's parking lot" Phyllis shuts him up and says, "Wait, let me tell it," and shares her side, it starts that Warren "might drive to New York."

Mom and I are mesmerized for the next hour. Then Vaughn says "Cathy, Warren iz 'nutz' about you. You know LOVE can change the world!" Phyllis says. "No one knows what's ahead of us."

They ask Mom for seconds. She has to scrape the pot because all the gravy from the hamburgers is gone; they ate all of Paul's chicken.

They continue the story of getting stuck in a little town off the Interstate and Vaughn selling his camera. He says it's nothing, pictures will prove the trip was worth it.

"Mrs. Fain?" That is a big problem I tell them. But we all agree to worry about her later.

The Store

"You nuts have come all this way to New York City.

I'm taking you guys out tonight!" I say "Follow me," as the door slams behind us. I'm so excited I gave Phyllis my T-shirt '**I LOV NY**' and me? I kept on the clothes I wore to work.

The sights become electric to me now that they are sharing this fantastic city. We tour everything along the way. The subway; an experience they will never forget. They loved the Empire State building although we didn't go up to the deck, then over towards Times Square, where the real sights of neon lights explode! I see the glitz through their eyes. We yell in unison down the streets hugging each other.

"We're going back to Chicago!" I repeat the city's name so many times it clings to my throat; "It's our kind of town!" We're having so much fun singing crazy songs, laughing, screaming and hollering, it's a wonder someone didn't throw something at us.

This city has grabbed them, but I am going back, I promised myself. I can feel it in my bones. They don't notice the lack of grass and trees or the trash cans in front of buildings and I don't mention it.

Early Saturday morning, Warren checks that Western Union transferred two hundred and fifty dollars from Mrs. Fain. He missed our jaunt through the city but said he didn't mind. Both the guys shave and shower. I was going through my things with Phyllis. So much stuff I wanted to leave as I happily threw it over the room. I discard my uniform, my work shoes, a couple of blouses and some cheap cologne Mom gave me then stuff the rest in my suitcase.

"Phyllis, I never should have come to New York." I tell her as we are resting on the couch. "We know. We are tired of him blasting the radio every time your favorite songs come on."

The Store

I needed Mom's blessing. I got that. She kissed me good-bye and hugged me like she'd never see me again. "Mom, it's ok. I'm fine. I will write you every day and call you when I get back. Promise." She leans over through the back window and says a prayer for a safe trip. Phyllis kisses her on her cheek and gets in the back seat with Vaughn. "We've got to go Mom." She didn't cry but looked sad enough to. I did try to make it in New York, and she knows that. "I love you, but you know I do, Mom." I told her that in the bathroom when they arrived. "I have got to go back with them. I must go back Mom, I must. You've got to trust God."

***

On the drive out of the city limits, my thoughts were somewhere in the clouds. I wished I had been along with them all the way. The New York skyline is piercing the morning sky, towering over commuters going to work and holding promises of another day of excitement and we are ready for ours. I am leaving this city, never to return the same way again.

"How did we do it?" Vaughn said touching Warren's shoulder as we were all full of merriment and laughter.

"Hey, I am with you guys now." I said. We stop and pack the car with all kinds of goodies to go with the lunch Mom made.

My heart is pounding. I am so happy. I am sitting in the front seat of the most beautiful car. The leather seat cuddles me and I rub my hands over the dash board and punch a few buttons. I'm naive but Warren came at the best time to be my hero. I am looking at him seriously. I am falling in love with him but don't know it yet. In fact it will be a couple of years for that realization to knock me silly.

The Store

I have nowhere to live in Chicago. I have nothing but a promise in my gut that coming back is the best decision.

I'll ask Mrs. Webb.

Chapter 25
Why fight fate. Impossible

"Can I get you and Warren some tea?" Mrs. Webb politely says leaving the room. "I'll be right back, don't stop talking, I can hear you!" She didn't stay long and brought back a tray of sugar cookies with crystal cubes floating in iced tea. The welcome was complete. We were seated on the couch as the sweetest eighty-six year old woman, wobbles from the kitchen. "Thank you." We said in unison.

She sat down in her lavish living room quite comfy in her favorite side chair. We all sip the delicious beverage and give her the compliments she richly deserved.

Mrs. Webb's face is glorious and I can see she's anticipating my every word. Her sister Pearl watches us from her throne, across from her. I can tell she's content; her big toe bobs up and down.

"We have come …" I'm a bit nervous, and (this is my second interview) – knowing my need is severe. We had dropped off Vaughn and Phyllis. Mrs. Fain was relieved to have her new car back without a scratch. She gave her son a royal grin welcome, with her teeth lined up to perfection. Now she has peace.

I don't look my best. Phyllis let me freshen up a bit at her place with her mother and three sisters in the projects on 31st and State.

Now, I am waiting on Mrs. Webb's generosity. Her oversized rental room was ideal and I enjoyed staying with her. The house has all the charm that I remembered with a three bedroom floor plan that's perfect to me. Mrs. Webb knows I trust the Lord in everything. We had had many conversations relating our views. I am remembering everything about the house even the elaborate carpets that lead up the hallway to the dining room and the stairs were fully carpeted as well. Her home is spotless and Pearl, an oversized dark skinned woman, whom I adore, is against the floral wallpaper that I've always thought looked like an English garden.

Mrs. Webb listens, with enthusiasm, as she's on the edge of her seat, along with everyone in the room as I shared the entire New York adventure.

Warren's face was fixed on Mr. Webb's as he told his account of his life changing decision. "I wanted Cathy back here in Chicago and the urge to get her was the strongest I've ever felt. I took my friends with me and almost thought I'd made a stupid decision, but now, I know it was fate."

He knew both Mr. and Mrs. Webb admired him. Warren answered all the inquires directed towards him. After Mr. Webb changed his crossed leg from one side to the other, he said, "Those accounts were no different than what I had felt as a young man." Then Mr. Webb winked at Warren. "I'd do whatever it took, to bring my future bride back with me," he said laughing out loud looking towards Mrs. Webb.

"It took several hours to make the decision to go to New York and only a few seconds for me to shout my declaration. I'm going back HOME!" I told everyone.

The entire experience became: "**The New York Story.**" It grew wider as each player; Vaughn, Phyllis, Warren, Mrs. Fain and I interject our own spin on the wild wonderful adventure.

"It must be the Goodness of God for me not to leave your place." I say when Mrs. Webb, after an hour, gives me permission to have my old room. Warren helps her out of her chair. She walks over to me reaching inside her apron pocket.

The Store

"Cathy, you have been the sweetest young lady. Why wouldn't I give you your room back?" she says charmingly, handing me a small purse, with the house key inside. Her voice is cracking. She matches her husband in age but not in coloring. She's a brown cookie, fancy in a size 12 and he's creamed coffee in extra skinny overalls. She continued to amaze me with the same rental charge. I kiss her cheek. Her heavy arms hold mine as she smiles. Pearl lets out a "hoot" and hollers "You're back!" as we laugh.

Warren goes to retrieve my things. He can't get back fast enough as we climb the stairs together.

I bounce on the side of the bed then lay backwards, sinking in, rubbing my arms across the soft chenille. Warren opens the walk-in closet and places my suitcase down. That's when he comes over near me. Comfortable in bed we agree everything looks the same.

The pale yellow spread is covering us in this double bed with two fluffy pillows and a dust ruffle skirt of lace. Pictures of roses adorn satin stripe papered walls. The single window has sheer white curtains that cover the blinds. My dresser, high boy and night stands are deep mahogany, polished to perfection.

"This was our beginning in this room months ago Warren. I had excitedly given you permission to follow me. I had promised, *All the way*, so scared, but I meant it. I hid in that closet to undress. Warren you were so anxious, all ready for me."

"I teased. *Are you ready*? No answer, you were so serious and I was acting silly."

"I crept over and lifted my sheet. Like a shivering lost puppy, your pleading eyes said *rescue me*. Quite, bashful, I inched in next to you."

The Store

"How could I know when I closed my eyes that I would feel with enjoyment the heat from your skin? Your arms were like steel. Warren, you rolled over on top of me. I knew there was no turning back; you made me feel wonderful, cherished and cared for. *–never had I been so open before.* For my first time, I gave you everything…"

"Cathy, I love you."

***

I am enjoying my relationship. I never have to cook; he takes me out nightly for dinner and after treats. Bar-b-q, is still his favorite fast food and we are known as the "happy" couple, at our preferred soul food restaurant on 63rd Street.

Warren takes me on runs gathering stock and I'd patiently wait in the car practicing some knitting techniques. He makes extra money, since I don't work, selling panty hose to neighborhood variety stores. Plus Mrs. Fain's store keeps him busy. I play solitaire with a worn out deck of cards waiting at Mrs. Webb's for him to get off. He occupies all my waking moments. Eventually, nothing can part us.

I move from Mrs. Webb's perfect room to having my own place. It came with a year's lease that I couldn't get on my own. Women aren't allowed 'anything' legal without a man signing it.

Warren secures a studio: It's the most adorable sunny place on the third floor on 70th and Bennett. We have our first experience of buying new furnishings, making both of us feel as if we are married. I hemmed and hawed before bringing home some perfect pieces: a pea green sofa-bed couch, a three drawer chest, and a dark red lounge chair.

I run all over just looking out the windows, and then opening my back door, then going again from back to the

The Store

front amazed hollering... "It is mine, all mine." It spoke 'DOLL HOUSE' to me and I am sure I'll stay here "Forever!"

Months later Warren and I have our first 'serious' disagreement.

Chapter 26
They wear boots don't they

Warren is slicing carefully a pork chop I fixed him for dinner and then stirring the gravy around his plate with the morsel he blurts out matter-of-flatly a statement, and it just comes out... "I enlisted in the Army today." I laid my fork down. Look at him sideways, and then stand up, not believing it. "Why?" I screamed.

I didn't know what to say. I know a million, zillion reasons jumbled my brain and I start crying and then begin throwing our plates and pots in the kitchen sink. I don't calm down when he tells me he has signed the papers; there's nothing he can do.

I go for a walk and almost freeze to death. Mean and angry I come back and stare at him. It is fun playing house and he must have felt horrible the way I performed with the dishes but I don't want to move to different places.

I yell at him mean things: "Warren, I am …determined to stay in one place! Stop this moving! Darn it! Always moving! Warren!" My words are sobbing, out of breath.

Then he says he wants to take me all over the world.

"Cathy, Remember? Anywhere you want to go."

"I …can't do …that! I am not going to go ….with YOU! ….Anywhere! I don't care …where it is! I can't stand what's happened; **what you've done** ….to mess us up like this!"

During pillow talk, it was President Kennedy's death that sealed it. Warren had been hanging around the recruitment offices and lingered too long. Some friends of his invited him to talk to a recruiter he said. "I just joined. I wanted to serve and get it done." His life had come to a plateau (he didn't say that word) he was going to get it over

The Store

with and serve his country and then marry me. (He meant the marriage part)

I hugged my side of the bed; so disappointed; no angry, and I felt since he couldn't have his store, he was going to hurt me. Hurt Mrs. Fain. Hurt the dog. I tossed and turned for the first time since we'd been sleeping together.

What will happen to my apartment?

Where will I go? Who will take care of me? This is serious. I don't get over it for a long time.

Less than a week later, with such bad timing, Mom visits and asks if she can stay overnight. "Mom, you can't stay here! There is no room for you sleep!"

That's what I should have screamed, but I just looked at her sad face and pitted her.

She had left Paul for the second time. Maybe she's back in Chicago to break us up too. I couldn't let her know Warren was leaving. I dare not tell her; not yet.

Yep, my mom got to sleep with us. She was on the outside, all three of us squashed, me in the middle, but I couldn't deny her. I just couldn't.

Did I mention what Warren said? I'd rather not say all that right now. It wasn't good.

We had a bleak dinner and I let Mom cook. It was a couple of days after my saddest birthday ever; a real adult, me turning twenty-one. I remember that.

He leaves Tuesday afternoon from Union Station. He has on his brooks brother's checked shirt; his favorite blue sweater, that I had given him for his birthday, brown shoes, black socks and a brown felt derby. He stored some things in the closet, and had taken the rest of his clothes to his mother's.

The Store

I brushed my teeth, combed my hair, but it didn't matter. The sun was bright, so I used that excuse, to wear sunglasses; might hide a tear.

Mrs. Fain, her husband, Arna, his sister, Charlotte, all there to see me give hugs, kisses, and see him board the train. There're lots of people, smiling, taking happy pictures of future service men, that were virtually everywhere.

I had to have Warren alone so we slipped away to a secluded spot – inside a photo booth. I held him around his waist and placed my hands up his back. We teased and kissed and then Warren leans over and whispers in my ear. "I'm crazy 'bout you" The booth camera snaps the picture. He didn't know I had fed the machine, and then pushed the button. We finish taking three of four tiny pictures capturing our last hour.

I had had enough tears lately but my eyes had more to give. "See you when you get back!" Naturally, that was all I could say. He remained silent. We left the booth. There was nothing left to do. While holding the pictures in his hand, he gives the strip to me. Parting my fingers through his, we walked back to his family. They had been watching us the entire time.

We all knew there was a war going on. The entire nation was turned upside down. I'd told myself I wasn't in love. I was thinking how cruel it was leaving him almost a year ago on my way to New York City. What a crazy flip-flop, flip! I felt that this time, with words. The only weapon I had I whispered,

"I won't be here when you come back, Warren, bet-cha, I'll be history." I wanted to really hurt him. He held me close with both arms clamped around my body then he whispered deep in my left ear. "You'll be mine ... for the rest of your life, Cathy, for the rest of your life and I'll come for you, take care of you ...even in your dreams I'll never leave you ... Wait for me."

The Store

"Not me!" I kept saying to myself, burying my face deep in his clothes. My hands couldn't leave his soft sweater alone as I rubbed the nap. He made several more unconvincing promises. I wasn't hearing any. The only thing I wanted to 'remember' was that he'd come back one day and 'take care' of me.

***

I climbed each step slowly up my third floor staircase, and tearfully opened the door to the loneliest place ever. I turned the volume up on the record player, kicked off my heels then screamed as loud as I could at the walls.

The rain tapping the windows meant the sky was trying to complete with me. All night I'm battling those relentless drops wetting my pillow.

Daybreak hurt my eyes. I begged the nagging headache to leave. I searched every act of his love and thoughts of him kept me prisoner. For hours I stayed in bed, smoking cigarettes, one after the other; staring at the ceiling. "Why me?"

I hollered at the mirror in the bathroom. "I hate you Warren!"

Act II

Chapter 27
They wear white don't they

Twenty four hours later:

I wash my face, rim my eyes with Maybelline and run out the door armed with a newspaper add advertising selling encyclopedias. I'm hired on the spot making 40 dollars each sale, by selling books door to door.

It became very challenging and I met all sorts of people. The houses I scheme my way into were of different ethnic groups and economic backgrounds.

Once I get inside your door… then I present the grand possibility of educating your family just by having my books on your shelves. I give you a rehearsed sales pitch, and unfold a huge colorful brochure and you hopefully sign a contract.

I made three sales.

My independence was very short lived because I didn't get Warren out of my mind; I had tasted someone that got to me, phoned me, came home to make love to me.

Warren eventually finishes basic training. Now what?

He had sneaked home twice, coupled with some passionate calls. But, I only remembered the last one, when he said three words. "Come, marry me." –it's another twist in my life, hopefully, maybe the last one? Remember I felt "safe" before and somehow I think he makes these shaky feelings that plaque me "go away" when I'm with him.

I start to do some serious preparation to move again and my heart rules everything.

Never say "Never!"

The Store

I'm still not in love. I think I'm lazy, or just giving up, maybe I'm tired of dating losers, because I do date. Or I feel sorry for Warren. Anyway, I quit my little position selling books, I let my parents, Claudette and friends know my plans to leave Chicago. I don't tell Mrs. Fain.

I leave: My German Sheppard puppy, Count, some beautiful clothes, pots and pans, dishes, furniture, pictures on the walls, records, books and stuff. But this is the killer… I can't figure it out. I leave this cutest place in the world; my apartment. I don't have the slightest notion; I'll never … see it again.

Overnight, I'm on the bus with the skinny dog on its side. Soon I'll be with an Army man in Fort Smith, Arkansas. Inside my tattered suitcase: a white cotton scoop neckline dress, that hits just below my knees, it has a clinched waistline, with an invisible zipper down the back, and spaghetti straps.

***

Friday June 12th 1964, is the most perfect cloudless day. I am miles from the quarters Warren secured for me on the Negro side of town. I wasn't on Warren's base quarters more than three days. This morning he told me how beautiful I looked.

We pass shady tree lined streets along Fort Smith's quaint neighborhoods with its lazy humid atmosphere that invite curious, but lonely service men. Lovers sit on corner benches, holding hands, or some stroll peering into store front windows. They also swat flies while they shield themselves from the hot sun. Few were on their way to the court house like we were doing yesterday.

Yes, on this same street, Fort Smith's official office, was like a corner store with only one elderly secretary. It wasn't like Chicago's old historic building of marble floors, heavy laden doors with thick shatterproof glass from top to bottom. This place was difficult for us to recognize. But to get our marriage license, hot and exhausted, we welcomed the tiny office and cheerfully walked inside. The lady, smiled at us and was quite efficient, handling all the papers we needed to sign.

It was exciting to see the official gold emblem on the over sized document. As we finished answering all her questions, holding it in my hands, I teased Warren so soon to be my husband. "I can taste it!"

"How does, Kathleen Yvonne Robinson, sound?" He quickly quirked, "It will be, Mrs. Kathleen Yvonne Robinson, tomorrow." He raised his eyebrow and smiled. I couldn't wait, and he assured me with his lips on mine, right in front of that lady's desk. He lingered too long. "Honey I know what you're thinking but …not now." I mumbled.

***

I carefully watch my step, leaving the second floor of the rooming house. Warren holds my hand to lead me over to his borrowed automobile parked out back in a grassy lot.

We had rehearsed 'the rules' of our marriage all night, twenty-one times or more. Each promise was made to 'obey,' with his strategically planted kiss, of all my wishes. I named so many crazy things, having fun, and he just kissed me all over and agreed to them all:

We'd never part, not for a day, week or ever.

No fighting, miss understandings or pouts.

I would handle all his money, spending, saving. (smile)

The Store

Faithful to take care of me and all the babies he wants to have.

(Gosh, he wants four)

Chapter 28
I do, if you do, I do

Warren is as happy as can be as he drives over to Fort Chaffee's little white chapel that's on base. We are on time. Everything: lipstick, comb, license, are all safe inside my purse.

The place of worship with its rows of stiff pews and polished wood floors is empty except for Willie, Warren's friend from the barracks. The sunlight is painting the walls through two tiny stained glass windows. I feel so different, something is happening to me, inside, deep. The Chaplin, who had interviewed us several hours before, tells us where to stand as he opens his Bible. The sound of a beautiful hymn in the background is hardly audible and he has us read Psalms 100. Our voices are the magical notes. They bounce back off the majestic walls, and echo in our ears.

I "think" I'm falling in love when I say "I do" repeating everything the Chaplin says. "I will *honor* you and *obey* as *long as I live*" a real **promise** at last.

I confess I'm in a daze. My white cotton dress looks perfect and my special lace panties, that he bought while in town, are wet with joy. Warren looks so serious; innately a deep thinker. I think he means what he says as his lips quiver, as beautiful words pour from them.

I hear him say firmly, more than words "I, Warren Isaac Robinson, take Kathleen Yvonne Lyons, to be my lovely wedded wife, to cherish forever, till …

This entire arched atmosphere could have been filled to capacity; laced with a myriad of flowers covering the pews or draped from the rafters. Everyone throwing rice, all screaming congratulations at us, but, I wouldn't have noticed

The Store

anything or anyone. Something is happening to me... like I am diving off a cliff and I have wings.

I look only in Warren's eyes, the most beautiful eyes I've ever seen. I know in my soul, this moment; *I'll be 'married' for the rest of my life* ... to him. I remember something about "...to death do us part" and I really meant everything and more. We are totally convinced that this is the day to remember. "The Twelfth of Never" by Johnny Mathis: His love song describes our day so well.

My cheeks are stained with tears as he vows to *love me forever*. We hold hands. His hands shiver with excitement; I "think" again, Cathy, you're falling in love right now. I can feel something, fully knowledgeable about these serious things we are saying to each other. Is this what he wanted me to do? *Just fall completely into this joy?* Our lives are irreversible now with our vow to God. "Till death do us part ... so help me God." Warren ends, as if it was his 'wish.'

He takes hold of my waist with both hands and lifts me to his mouth as eternity begins. I linger as long as I can. He whispers, "I'm the luckiest man alive." Turning to go, he assures me, "You'll be mine forever."

I can't stop smiling. The glow never leaves. *I'm married.*

Down three steps, a tiny breeze puffs my dress. I'm the most blessed bride in the world; feeling a little jolly, silly like tossing my head. Warren cherishes my hand. I reach over to pick up a masquerading daisy; really a weed along the side of the chapel. My single 'flower' was tucked in the sandy soil to remember a bride needs flowers. While still twirling it, we get in the waiting hot car. I search its meaning, placing it near my nose, for it to be there waiting, only to die, bend over limp, by the time we reach town.

Chapter 29
Just a little rain here and there

Each address on the street called Lucky, looked just alike, down Arkansas' main military strip, where the colored folks lived; poles apart from Chicago's Southside area where we're from.

We were looking for the exact number, where Willie, Warren's buddy, said he lives. They had invited us to stay with them and we're running late.

"I think we're heading in the right direction," Warren softly assures me while slowly going along the white-washed dwellings with front yards void of grass. A shady tree over hung, the address he stopped in front of.

"Yep. This is it." Warren says opening the door for me.

It can't be. I said under my breath. "Warren, I can't stay here!" Looking up at the shabby doorway.

The house was sadly in need of repair: two rotten wood steps, (splinters could catch in your butt if you sat down on them) led to the porch that stretched from one end of the front to the other, which needed paint years ago – maybe nobody ever did. A patched up screen door let flies in through openings of wear and a rotary fan could be heard buzzing inside, blowing muggy air.

Warren bangs on the door post as he hollers Willie's name. I stood behind him looking at the dandelions push up through the cracks. The sun is shining on the opposite side of the street and I welcomed the shade from the trees near the curb.

Willie, a gregarious honey colored guy, with a thunderous voice, that matches his size, spreads the screen door wide.

The Store

"Wo! Rob, you got here! ...Well, this is it!" grinning ear to ear with a sliced watermelon smile.

From early afternoon, well into the night, we talked with Willie and his wife, Tracey. They had a toddler, Aaron, thirteen months old, that crawled on the dirty floor and ate from his mother's fingers the chicken they fried for us.

Tracey had been out shopping for the fixings. She hugged me as warmly as her husband did when she walked in after setting her groceries down.

"Rob spoke so much 'bout you! I feel you 'r family." She says with her warm genuine embrace. I adored her instantly. Yep, my side of the family welcomes like this: big hardy unforgettable hugs. Well, I said to myself. *I can surely stay here with her!* She has tight greasy curls framing her face and her brown eyes were big like Warren's.

Tracey was prideful of her peas and okra in her garden. She fools her 38 years, and eats only what's good for her and her tiny waistline and smooth brown skin proved it.

The guys stay out front, but leave to bring back enough beer for all of us.

I offer to help with frying more chicken, but the word was; "we are guest." We bonded in kind, conversing, in-between swatting mosquitoes, sitting on a squeaky swing on the back porch; just waiting for our men to come back from town.

Later, I told Warren to tell Willie we'll share *everything* until we find a place of our own.

***

Fort Chaffee's army base is 18 miles down the highway. The guys get in starved every evening in time for dinner.

The Store

My days consist of playing cards. This is when I learn to listen; gather tips on cooking all while smoking cigarettes and drinking beer or lemonade.

I always look forward to Warren coming in and run to take his boots off and give him a sudsy bath. It's our private time in the bathroom. We taste our wet bodies. The warm massage over our skin with our lathered hands lets me welcome his touch any place he probes. We always stay maybe a bit too long.

"You guys through?" Willie hollers through the door.

"Man, you hold up the most important room in the house besides my kitchen." Willie cries sucking a pork chop bone Tracey had fixed.

"Don't worry about it Rob." He laughed when we sheepishly appeared. "I'd do the same if Tracey pampered me that way." He swats her on her butt and she hollers. "You take Aaron off my hands and I'd do you better and you know it."

Wilma, an elderly 39ish widow next door, shows up daily. We might pick greens, learn to can different foods, play cards, and talk about intimate stuff. Then end the session sitting on the swing, while tending baby Aaron. "You women know a lot about 'life' don't you?" I tell them. They both laugh with me.

"Why do you call my husband, 'Rob?'" I asked Tracey after Wilma left one day.

"Everyone pop-lur' gets a 'special' name 'round here ... not 'Robinson,' the name that's on his uniform. Willie and me shortens it to '**Rob**.' Nobody knows him by Warren."

Tracey shows me ways to cook traditional southern meals, and I share my northern meals of what little I know. She is from Arkansas and met Willie, almost sixteen years her junior, at a social dance club one Saturday night. The

The Store

rookie service men come in from the barracks each season. That's when she felt sorry for Warren. He met Willie when he was assigned to his unit. She laughed when both men emotionally told her they missed some good cooking. "I knew I could get 'n Willie's heart by fixing him a mess of my 'goods' and sure nuf that's what happened." Tracey beams from across the kitchen table. "Now he down right loves to take care of me and my baby."

Tracey found out I don't use enough 'seasonings' in my personal life, nor the right kind in my food. She says I have to learn fast if I want to keep Rob "hungry" for me. I love chicken and noodles. Throwing in a green bell pepper, an onion with a can of chicken soup to spice it up, just as she instructed makes a big difference. She loves her some liver and onions, spaghetti, ham hocks, pinto beans and smothered steak. And among other things, she taught me all she knew.

I learned a lot the two and a half weeks I'm with Tracey and Willie. I awake before dawn, to have my cigarette on the back steps, talk to the Lord in the morning sky, then make coffee, and kiss Warren's sleepy face. He leaves by 5:45 then I straighten our area.

I know we are in their way. Each day I hate to leave. I watch her cook her meals and tend her son. I want to apply *everything* she tells me. Then practice on Warren every chance I get.

Chapter 30
Here she comes again

In the next two weeks after moving from Tracey's and settling in on a different spot, we are on our way to Chicago. We want to pick up an old station wagon Mrs. Fain let Warren have for his wedding gift. I'm kidding, but it was a nice token. We need a car.

We load up as much as we can from Mrs. Fain's garage after the longest drive, nonstop, into Chicago.

Mostly, we want our dog Count. He has us feeling like parents. The total trip took our entire weekend, with two days traveling to get back. We had no time to smell that proverbial rose along the side of the road. I only had time to gather some things Phyllis had packed for me. She'd lost my apartment that she promised to take over until I got back. Now, all our furniture and stuff was in Mrs. Fain's basement.

Once back in Fort Smith, my mom comes to see her newly married daughter. Isn't she faithful? Maybe she couldn't believe I did it. Mom sleeps in the same room with us, but not inside our bed this time. I'd told her all about leaving Tracey and what she taught me about marriage stuff and cooking.

"I'm glad for you Cathy." Mom says the first day. We are having iced coffee, as we fan ourselves from the sweltering July heat. Miss Lilly's kitchen is the perfect place, so clean and neat. This Lilly woman is middle aged, average and quiet, never says anything so I never got to "know" her. She advertised that she needed a roomer. Warren found her note in the social hall posted saying her place was "cheap" and her beautiful house was close to town.

The Store

I am resting a bit from cleaning greens, like Tracey taught me. Later I want to fix Warren's favorite; lemon meringue pie. Mom doesn't understand I enjoy exploring the new spice rack in Lilly's kitchen and fixing delicious meals. Mom sits on a side chair; her hands under her chin with her elbows resting on the table, watching in amazement for hours. I've got flour everywhere, my face is sweaty and the floor is sticky. I love it!

"Mom, when we get back, we won't be moving all around Chicago, like you did. When Warren gets out of the service we're going to find one place and stay there forever! I promise you!"

I hope I didn't hurt Mom's feelings. But she left two days later. Warren was happy to get our room back to ourselves, when I told him, I sadly put her on the bus. She's so sweet and I love her too much. She seems to want to cling to me. I tell her the truth about her boyfriends too. I always did.

***

Six weeks later, we get orders to Fort Sill, Oklahoma. His unit will be deployed to Korea -I just don't know it yet- We get the few belongings we have accumulated and put Count in the back seat. I hate leaving Fort Smith, and Miss. Lilly's place but visiting afternoons with Tracey most of all. This is what Warren promises me every night; he'll get out of the army as soon as his tour is up – so I'll stop crying.

While Warren waits for active duty overseas we secure a small one room shack in Lawton, Oklahoma. It resembles a two room broken down trailer. The owner could have forgotten about it because it's in the back area of an enormous whitewashed frame house. Our place stood out against the green weeds and lofty trees around it. I have a stump outside to sit on for sunshine and fresh air. The one window overlooks nothing but shrubs and brush. The tiny place is heated with a blazing space stove-like-heater that is situated next to the double sized bed. Count wants to stay close to me but his back gets so warm next to the heater he develops a rash. Warren and I play with him throwing a stick to teach him to fetch and that's the extent of my recreation.

Nothing changes about our intimate enjoyment. Warren is attentive, but regrets he is constantly at the base. I have a record player and listen to Christian music during the evenings. As the weeks drag by the TV stays on with the soaps during my dull afternoons. I know every show; who's having an adulterous affair with who, and what's going on with, who-done-it and why. I know instantly which couple has the best chance of being happy, and I also know, without a doubt, my marriage will be the best ever. Warren and I will never 'fight,' or 'cheat' on each other or God forbid, will 'separate.' AND, I don't even know how to pronounce the word, '**D i v o r c e**,' less think of it happening to us.

Chapter 31
It's only a bump, baby I mean

One night real late Warren peeks through the door. He steps up on the ledge as I run over to him. He grabs me, twirls me all around and lifts me up in the air almost hitting my head on the low ceiling.

"Hey, Big mama!" He says with the biggest grin. (I'll never forget this entire encounter)

He keeps his mouth zipped, just his unique grin. "What you thinking 'bout?" I say, because I can't figure him out this time. *Maybe we can be released to go home and the USA's involvement isn't serious, and it's World Peace finally; nothing to be in the service over.*

Then he busts out with this announcement:

"The report came: Warren I. Robinson is going to be a papa!!"

"What!"...

"Wow, you're kidding me aren't you?" I scream. "Me a Mom?"

I sit on the side of our bed for the longest, shaking my head, rubbing my hands together making them hot and thinking. *I had gone to the medical building complaining about back pain. In this strange bed, I couldn't get comfortable. Warren didn't have one problem adjusting to the lumpy mattress. I thought it was springs popping through, the discomfort was so great.* "All this time, I'm pregnant and didn't know it!"

"Warren, this is scary." I get up to walk in the bathroom. Look at myself in the mirror. Me pregnant?

This bothers me for days.

The Store

I can't wait to get another opinion. We find out in the examination room that the baby is due sometime in June. "That's not good doctor. My husband will be overseas! " I cry and can't stop crying. "I'll have my baby without him doctor, …I can't do that! boo hoo hoo."

***

Our first Thanksgiving married, we want to celebrate. He will be gone by the first. We go shopping at the PX, but can't buy a turkey; neither one of us knows how to fix one of those big things. We only have a hot plate, with two burners, in our make-shift cooking area. So we boil some ham hocks in a pot, with lots of water.

Cold air seeps through the cracks. I can't even take my clothes off to shower. I am freezing all the time. We both keep our coats on during our special Thanksgiving Dinner over a metal table – alone. While sitting on wooden chairs facing one another I place a ham hock on his plate and one on mine. I wanted to have a candle or something beautiful set before us. It's plain, nothing on it but our plates.

Warren kisses me after saying our grace along with a special prayer of thanksgiving. I'll remember this coziness, cuddled. … The best ever thankful meal, as we ate every bite. "This is so sweet." I tell him smiling and yesterday was my twenty second birthday. I end up crying the entire weekend. I'm reduced to counting days for this bliss to be over.

***

It takes Warren two days to pack our station wagon. Orders came. He is off to Korea by December 29th. He has to have me settled in less than 30 days. I'm crying again. I am

The Store

tired of moving. Going back to Chicago scares me. I don't know where I'll stay. I don't tell him my fears.

We don't have a spare tire that is any better than the four we are riding on. It was a wing and a prayer that got the car from Chicago over to Arkansas three months ago. Our trip driving back home is doubtful. We are so over loaded: My clothes, Warren's army issue, shoes, record player, three suitcases, seven boxes, dog food, pots and pans, Warren the driver and me sitting beside him with room for Count and food for the trip in an ice chest, all in one car. Our car resembles The Beverly Hillbilly's truck, minus the tin cans rattling.

Warren at the last minute decides to follow Mickey, a guy on base, who has the same orders and lives near Chicago. He had the better car and we all agree to leave at three the morning.

Yes, it happened. Two hours outside of Fort Sill, and we're stranded, I think it's a blowout, not from a bump in the road. Mickey sees us; goes in reverse for half a mile on the deserted highway. Poor Mickey, the dedication he shows is wonderful. We'd be stranded without him. Warren fixes the problem with a Band-Aid and prayer. I prayed. He and Mickey reload the stuff from the side of the road and we're happily on our way again, chucking along.

The trip is lonely. I want so desperately to keep my husband with me. We are totally in love with each other and appreciate all our moments.

The closer we got to Chicago, the more I thought about our future. The baby stays on my mind. Where can I live without Warren? My parents weren't in a position. I have no one to take over and care.

"Warren, I don't want to stay with your mom." There, I said it.

The Store

I had talked about it off and on while in Arkansas. Phyllis lost our studio. Now, I'm pregnant. The thought of not having a place is overwhelming.

Fear grips my stomach, like a lump. It's devastating. I know it isn't the baby. My world is crumbling to pieces and I am stuck...

Mom wasn't a choice; she has gone back to New York chasing Paul. My Daddy is still entertaining different women and I am forced to stay with –

An "Unthinkable" choice!

Chapter 32
It's only a test, just a test

Warren was leaving for Korea in two weeks, leaving me alone for thirteen months. There we were, parked outside Mrs. Fain's. He has to leave. I have to stay.

Mrs. Fain is the only stable person we know.

Warren must have felt my pain, he had it too; by not being in control, no amount of money can help him solve this: Did he pray? I didn't.

Warren adjusts his hips on the seat, shuts off the motor and stares. Snowflakes are accumulating on the ground, but melting on the hood of the car. It's beginning to get magical looking outside, something I'd send my friends in Arkansas; a winter post card: Christmas, South Side Chicago Style. Tracey would love to hear from me.

It's been twenty minutes since we drove up. The street doesn't look the same. It's almost dark. The cars are slowing down so they won't slide in the heavy slush. No one is out walking; now the frigid air is creeping inside my bones. I don't want the dilemma in front of me any better than Warren does.

He is scaring me. Does he know something I don't?

"Warren? Warren? Are we going up?" *I'm thankful this grueling trip is over, now who's going to help us unpack? Count is eager to get out and relieve himself. Warren is silent.*

"Honey, are we alright?"

The snow covered the windshield. We left the car and didn't unload it.

The Store

I had to stay with Mrs. Fain. We didn't have hundreds of choices. He had to leave me with his mom. I wasn't showing but my mountainous belly was coming.

Everyone, Mrs. Fain, her husband, Arna and Charolette, are all glad to see us walk in. They act as if we'd come from the corner store. Their reception of me is flat. Sure, smiles and merriment but it isn't like my family would have done. Is this my new life? His family doesn't hug much, in fact not at all.

I wondered if I am the problem. I didn't contact Mrs. Fain before leaving, didn't phone, didn't do anything to announce that I was going to meet him and get married. Now I'm the elephant in the room.

I lay in Warren's arms on top of him, face to face, in his old room that had been untouched. The coziness felt wonderful against his pending departure. Glad we missed the storm. The snow had changed to sleet and the pricks hit the glass with sharp pangs. "I have to like your mother; I have no choice, and Charolette, and this place." Then, I paused seconds. *Gosh, would that have weighed in on my decision June 12th? I forgot this is my new family when I married.* "Our family, I forget that sometimes. I married them too." I smiled then searched them, how beautiful they were. His eyes. I thought: *This is the man I am to spend the rest of my life with and his family. I am in love with loving him.*

"It seems eon's ago that evening. You sitting there in your car, I never thought in a million years." I said tearfully. "I'll write every day, I'll send you my heart on each page."

"Why are we here? I said. Why does it have to end this way?" I had not been this serious since we said, "I do." *I know looking at Warren's eyes that moment I was totally helplessly in love with Warren Robinson. I will love him forever, I know it. I surrender all to this father of my child. I*

The Store

cried so hard. How can I go on? Live without him? Not now, Lord, I need him. Boo hoo. Hoo boo.

"Mrs. Fain will take care of you." His voice is serious, low and sad like.

"Wan-nah bet?" He didn't deserve that remark. I should have stayed with my mouth zipped but I hadn't learnt that yet. "Come here" He said, pulling me over to his lips as he kissed my nose. How his arms got tighter is beyond me. I am safe, right now, Lord, I am safe.

***

He left.

It's a blur to me.

He must have kissed me, held me right in front of Mrs. Fain, and I cried. He waved getting on the plane. I know he did. We saw each other until the last eye contact. I know that is what happened but I can't remember any of it. I know I was at the house with Mrs. Fain. I know I slept in his room and got up the next day looking after our dog that was in her basement.

I had Count to look after. I remember that.

Chapter 33
Yep, I fail the test

It isn't Mrs. Fain's fault. I am the one in a rain storm without an umbrella. I just don't want to stay here. Never for a long term... until Warren gets back, no way can I envision getting that close. We'd get to 'really' know each other, cooking in the kitchen, would she let me use it? She has no idea what I've been through. She looks at me pitiful like.

I have to grow up fast. I must start thinking my next move, instead of having my head screwed on backwards and stuck in the sand... Warren has spoiled me. These next twelve months will be Hell. I thought my lot in New York was bad, with, Paul, ordering me around. And my baby due, Man, this is serious.

I haven't even thought about getting away from Mrs. Fain! Let's see, how can I do that?

***

Warren calls when he gets to San Francisco. He'll be there a couple of days and thinks it is a beautiful city. I am glad for him. The call last a couple of minutes with endearments, kisses and sighs. I purposely stall and say sweet things and tell him about the weather and he tells me about his. "It's still cold here. Honey, I am bundled up every day, trying not to catch cold."

The next two days, faithfully he calls.

I don't want to tell him anything about me... my new arrangement. I've made plans to leave Mrs. Fain. I'm moving in with a girlfriend. But being in 'adult mode' says *this isn't a good time to share*. Not yet, I'll wait until he gets to Korea and write a long letter; by then I can breathe again.

He is asking about my feelings, my stomach, if I feel anything? I want him happy for me just a little bit longer. Let him get on the boat. Maybe if he doesn't ask anything personal about Mrs. Fain, I'll be able to get off the phone without hurting him.

"What's the matter? Cathy?" His voice rose. He caught on to something. As if the receiver has a picture screen and he can see my face. My eyes wide. I'm wondering what in the world can he see? I grasp for something clever to say. Stupid me… it's useless. Then the awful pause …

Pop! Goes the question. He slowly says "What -are - you -up -to, are you alright with Mrs. Fain?"

"Honey, I let, Count go, with a man, I met at a gas station. Remember? You were scared, he'd jump up, and hurt the baby?" I kept rambling, thinking quick things as I said all this, but still not saying what he wants to hear.

"Are you Okay with Mrs. Fain?"

"I'm still here, with her, but you'll be mad at me."

"Promise, I can't be angry, I love you. I adore you. Tell me pleeeesze!"

"Well, I don't do too well, with your mom, at first maybe, but now, -I think -she misunderstood me."

"WHAT!"

"I mean, she thinks, -I don't want to stay there … and I didn't, really but I thought she didn't care. So, I called my girlfriend, Minerva. She and I are, … going to stay together, in an apartment house, that her father manages, and we are going to be fine."

There, I say all that, as quickly as possible and wait.

The Store

The silence was awful.

He didn't say anything for the longest time.

I listened HARD, I only heard him breathing into the mouthpiece. Now, I envisioned I had a picture phone. I saw the sweat beading on his face, and his head lowered, still holding the receiver to his ear, sitting in a lonely booth, at the barracks and wishing… he was with me, to make everything alright.

"Warren? … Are you there?"

"Yes, honey. I'm here."

Whew! What a relief he heard me. Oh darn, I see her. (Mrs. Fain is behind me, she walked inside the room,) "Ugh."

"Warren, you are there, you can't understand me, my feelings. I need you with me, my emotions are wild!" I whispered all that, breathing inside the handset.

"Honey, you're fine. Whatever makes you happy. That's all I care about." He whispers back. Not knowing why my voice volume had changed. Mrs. Fain had been back in her kitchen while I was going through my awkward rationalizations.

Before I hand, Mrs. Fain the receiver …"Honey! Sweetheart! Your mom wants to talk."

He chats with his mother. She nods her head up and down, as minutes pass; then she looks over at me, says nothing, shakes her head and then quietly gets off the phone.

***

Early in the morning, I gather up some nerve and softly tap twice on Mrs. Fain's bedroom door. I hold my ear close,

The Store

and then ask to come in. I held the knob hoping it wouldn't turn, so I could run. When she gave permission to "Come in" I stood there. She is still in bed but invites me over near her. Her room is dark. She hadn't let the shade up and I can hardly see her face, to see if she's nice or not.

I squat on the rear tip of her bed, not facing her and tell everything. My story... well, most of it. She tells me to be "safe." No hugs or kisses, none of that. I knew we respected each other, and 'love' would come later.

"Here, this will be my new number: 555-5555." Then I quietly close her door.

Now, she knows my "puzzle" from my point of view. It is good Mrs. Fain understands I have somewhere to go, and that my resources out in the cruel world aren't dismal. I have Goo-Gobs of friends and a loving family, and an interlocking network of places to go. I told her I'll come by later and gather my things from her basement. Count is gone for good and everything couldn't be better.

Staying with Mrs. Fain, in Warren's room didn't last two days. Going by her store, I thought I left on a cordial note when I reached up and kissed her.

Chapter 34
C O Z E T T E

Our basement apartment on Jeffery Boulevard, near 75th Street has white walls throughout. Half-windows leak tiny bits of sunshine in but I hate the patches of weeds outside they block my view. Otherwise, it's an okay place to *park* until Warren comes back to me.

All my furnishings from Mrs. Fain's basement look nice in the living room area. From a second hand store, I added a single bed, speckled linen with matching curtains, along with an oval rug. A table lamp brightens my entire bedroom. The TV is always on.

Minerva's room, which she keeps locked respectfully, is off from the kitchen in the rear of our dull dark place. We share the rent and it works out fine.

It's February 15th, 1965

The radio is playing all of Nat King Cole's old songs. He died of lung cancer. What a waste. My parents sure loved his music. It saddens me too. Friday, around this time, Doctor Williams, of William's clinic, calls to confirmed June; and of all the days, he said the twelfth. My baby is due exactly a year from our wedding day. How weird. I can't wait to write Warren.

I thought I would feel pregnant. I don't. I am gaining weight slowly and hardly noticed 20 pounds had crept on… not careful, soon ten more the doctor said. There is nothing much else to do. I sit and eat. I wait for mail, send my love letters and think about what to name my baby.

When Minerva, who's talkative, gets home from work she and I go on and on about old times: her teaching me how to smoke, that boy I was so crazy about, her 2 year old son

The Store

Paris, and me being friendly with her two sisters. The oldest, Kathie, and Jean both look alike. Minerva is the baby and the most attractive.

Warren and I became buddies with Kathie. It was at her place in Hyde Park, that I got the diamond ring I'm wearing. Someone had pawned it to Warren at his store. Kathie also taught me to knit and frequent resale shops. I had never been to a second hand store before. Now, I learned to take scraps and create masterpieces crafting. Every day, creating dreaming of what's to be, thinking I have plenty of time.

Late one night, near 2:00 a.m., I was curled up in bed, not sleepy. I get interested in a movie on TV called, *"Les Miserable."* Then I heard it, the young girl's name in the tragic film was Cosette. I first thought first of naming my baby, 'Claudette,' but I know that if I have a girl, I'll name her "**C o z e t t e**."

***

After two months with Minerva, I regretfully leave. Daddy doesn't like me staying in that basement: he thinks it's too dark, damp and drafty. He secures a one bedroom apartment, right down the hall from his, and signs the papers. The place is at 740 E. 79th Street and it's ideal, where most of my decorating skills can shine. Everything fits nicely and I arrange it perfectly.

I try to explain "everything" to Warren, because he and I live for the mailman. Although his penmanship and spelling is deplorable, I understand what's in his heart. I purposely remain upbeat in whatever I share. Seldom do I mention his mom, my mom or what they're saying. He doesn't mention the family. I assume Warren writes everyone he loves.

Mrs. Fain and I seldom talk, but I hear from Warren's sister, Charlotte. The family feels helpless and Charolette laments every time we talk that she has to take over for Warren. Little Miss. Charlotte doesn't like that.

I have complete control over his monthly allotment check. I have cut all my pennies in half, mostly by eating with relatives and whatever else it takes.

***

I have fallen more deeply in love with Warren, a thousand times while sending and receiving love letters. But, I'm truly miserable. I send no pictures. My pretty words paint them. I am glad Warren is far away, 'cause he can't see me. Dr. Williams says no sugar or salt, because my feet are swelling and my weight gain is out of control. I have been so skinny all my life, now I can't believe I've gained over fifty pounds.

Claudette is picking me up. I eat at her place often and I am trying to be on time. I hobble down the stairs and wait in the vestibule searching for her car through the glass door.

Swish! All this water down my legs and into my shoes! Nervously, I ramble-duck-like, back up the stairs; as fast as I can, to my bathroom.

This is awful; I'm a sloppy mess! It's –it's too early!

I scream into the mirror, "You're here, I am having my baby!"

***

I'm scared, sitting on two bath towels, leaking profusely as Claudette is flying down the highway in pursuit of St. Bernard's emergency room.

The Store

My sister is too quiet. Normally we chit-chat about girl stuff, today is different. I know she's as surprised as I am. My baby is coming.

She blurts out: "Cathy, we're having a baby shower. For you! Tonight! Cathy, what can we do?" she pleads. I look at her trying to keep us on the highway while she's screaming at me. "You won't be there!"

I try to laugh at our situation. It's that funny, but the more I laugh, more water gushes.

"Cathy, the baby shower is a surprise. I've got everyone there waiting with food and so many gifts. My apartment has been decorated for days."

"Ok. I don't know what to tell you. I've got to get inside this hospital. It's not hurting, just this liquid pouring out of me," I remind her as she pulls up to the main dock.

***

I push as soon as Dr. Williams tells me to bare down hard. Everything happened so fast. My legs were still up in the stirrups as the doctor lay the sweetest bundle on top of my sheet.

"Ahhh," I sigh again and again, "A girl." It's instant love! I am exhausted, but, now a mother.

The whole world has changed. The grass, I know is greener, and the sun, coming from outside the windows, is brighter.

Friday, May 21, 1965, Cozette Yvonne Robinson is here! She weighs in at 4 pounds 13 ounces after me gaining all those pounds. "Ahhh " Why she wanted to arrive so early in this cruel world, only God knows.

The Store

I find out she's too tiny to take home. She has to be at least five pounds.

I'm heartbroken, disappointed and angry too. I can't breast feed or hold her, it's hospital policy. She's placed in a high risk ward for newborns. I pace the floor crying. I try to contact the Army again, but their policy, is to keep me from talking to anyone. Mother had rushed to the hospital and sat with me all night.

I don't know if anyone called Mrs. Fain or contacted Warren's commander.

Saturday morning my phone rings.
"Cathy?"

"Warren!" I scream, recognizing his voice.

"It is you! Sweetheart! I've been crying for you. She's here and I can't have her!"

Trying not to sob, but sounding pitiful said "It's the policy of the army and the hospital. I am sick of policies."

"Honey, sweetheart, my darling, I got the news last night. But what's the matter? What are you talking about; that you can't have her?"

I tell him everything: her name, her weight, eyes, mouth, fingers and toes… and she looks like you!

***

The hospital calls saying I can have Cozette by Friday.

The longest seven days of my life.

Claudette and I walk up the stairs into the waiting room. I sit over against the door of an office trying not to look nervous. I am.

The Store

This isn't like me. What if I don't have a clue: taking care of her, feeding her, seeing her breathe, what if she cries, she doesn't know me. How will Cozette understand that I am her mother?

"Mrs. Kathleen Robinson." I jump up!

Immediately unwind from the trance I'm in. "Yes, that's me!" An important looking woman comes and looks right at my face.

"Do you still have your hospital band on?"

"Yes, someone asked me not to remove it."

She holds my wrist, checks the name and date. Then puts my arm down and tells me to come with her through a hallway. But that's not where I left my baby.

"Claudette?" my sister looks up from a magazine she's reading and nods her head.

This lady takes me to an elevator and we step in. I say nothing. I don't smile or look in her direction. I look at the floor number she pushed on the instrument panel. The oversized doors slowly close. I keep my eyes directed down at my shoes. My thoughts are racing...I look a mess. I have awful brown oxfords on that I tried to polish but didn't have any. My hair wouldn't cooperate. I had nothing to put on this morning. Clothes thrown all over the place, nothing matched.

I want to look exceptional to pick up someone new and so special.

I am lead into a nursery. I am handed the most beautiful baby in the entire world. I can't explain it.

I'll never be the same. I have totally changed from the inside out. I am responsible for this infant girl that doesn't open her eyes or cries or wines or nothing. She's perfect. I

The Store

don't concern myself with anything for days. I look at my baby and tried for the life of me to breast feed her.

It's not working. She latches on! It hurts like a knife is cutting my nipple.

What in the world is she doing grabbing me like this? Jaws of steel, on this little thing, and she won't let go! "Wait a minute. Let's get another position. Come on!"

I end up with cracked nipples. There isn't anything I can do.

I have people talking about me, even my close friends.

* "Girl! That's nasty, letting her chew on you like that."

**"Give her a bottle. What are you trying to prove?"

And the nastiest one yet, that has me angry, every time I think about it.

***"Tits are for your man honey. Give that baby a bottle!"

Since, I have changed, and I know I am not the same person, I have to be a good mother. No, better than that.

At Cozette's first check-up, an army doctor tells me about a wonderful author: A book about baby and child care by Dr. Spock. I devour it from front to back because he tells me what to do, and how to do it at each stage of Cozette's precious development. But, in the quiet hours of the morning, it is just Cozette, and me. I am her mother. It takes months to realize it. I stare at her. I dress her, feed her, and then take her on long walks in her stroller. I'm proud of what I have made.

We made a baby, come Lookie, Lookie. People would stop me to admire Cozette. "Can I see your baby?"

Then it happened. That nasty woman touched Cozette's little hands. I cringed. I don't have the guts to say, "Please don't touch her hands." It is simple, too simple. Open my mouth and say something that Cozette can't say. Over again the same thing, stupid people touching her and each time I feel awful.

Cozette's mother is a wimp. I am so weak. God is teaching me a motherhood lesson of Pain-Reinforcement. I am Cozette's mouth. I will open it for her. Protect her, while her daddy isn't with us.

I do get better every day and say something. Guess what I came up with?

"Touch her clothes, not her hands." That simple turn-a-round statement helps me go forward. I am giving people permission to touch her, but carefully directing them.

Months creep buy. I send Warren a crunch cake so it gets to Korea for his birthday by the 9th of September. I have so much fun packing it along with other gifts. I want to be like no other. He gets "something" from me at "MAIL CALL" every time.

Counting months until Warren comes home drifts into counting weeks. One at a time I cross off each day on my big calendar.

Chapter 35
One, two, don't skip three

The letters stopped. All the promises were over. I counted hours: he'd walk through my door; hold his daughter and then he'd make passionate love to me. I'd dreamt of nothing else.

The most wonderful chocolate, taste and see, day came!

I cleaned the floors, polished the wood with a gleam that should have been there at the beginning. The window sills, the kitchen counter cleared off and the cabinets de-cluttered. I washed the linen, changed the bed covers three times. Now it's perfect!

I did my hair in his favorite style, Cozette in her prettiest dress with shoes and socks to match. I even put a bow in both our hair.

Mrs. Fain picked Warren up from the airport. He called from San Francisco and we talked, not caring about the cost. He keeps saying how much he loves me. The sound of his voice is a thousand times better, coming through the receiver, than his letters conveyed. "Never stop" I keep saying. "Never stop loving me!"

"I missed you." I whispered. I keep saying sweet things, peppered between his sweet responses. We're meaning every word. He tells me I'm sexy: he loves the way I move, talk, my eyes, skin, hair and most of all, make love. He stammers as he tells me of all those private moments: His dreams of us; I wonder…

I'll fall from this pedestal he's put me on.

The tap on my door… my heart does flips, then stops.

The Store

No one will ever have a way of entering my space – the way he does. I fell in love with him, and it is a "total surrender" for life.

His bags drop when I open the door. His face is perfect. The way I envisioned him for months comes true. Mini-moments I'm inside the embrace I've been longing for. His steel arms enfolding me, lifting me high off the floor as our mouths find each other, and then tenderly melting our lips. I am in his domain again. I can't remember how long I stay inside his arms as once again time stands still. We both don't come up for air. Every part of my face, neck and shoulders are kissed. Our threshold held us captured. His body is delicious with the fragrance of him. We never realize he has not stepped through the doorway, still in the hallway making love.

He looks so marvelous. He's smooth shaven, his hair cut close to his head and uniform is sharp and pressed. I move my hands and finger each seam, button and feel his muscles even his heart beating. Boom, boom… boom… I can't believe this handsome chocolate man is here with me. Forever!

As Warren slowly carries me into the apartment, he lovingly glances over the place, his big eyes land on her crib. "Yes, sweetheart she's waiting for you."

Warren immediately holds out his arms, hoping Cozette will reach up to him. He walks over and tries again. "I'm Daddy!" She doesn't smile nor show she's pleased. Her eyes search each part of his face and every button on his uniform. Cozette rocks firm in her crib holding the railing with clenched fist. She turns her little head; let's go, then flops down, and then turns her face towards the wall… reaches for her bottle and several minutes later is asleep.

I loved the way Warren didn't grab Cozette and make her kiss him. Warren came back, leans down next to his

The Store

daughter, and then puts his knees on the floor, reaching to her level. He stays there for the longest. Watching her must have been prayers answered. He winks up at me. I have tears in my eyes. We are his girls.

One light is coming from a floor lamp in the living room. That supple illumination makes our apartment seem even dreamier, cozier. Everything seems perfect and he can't keep his hands off me. He adores our new home as I point to each piece I'd lovingly purchased, each one was only thinking of our nest together. With his favorite dinner fixed: He sits there stuffed with, fried chicken, mac and cheese, candied sweets, corn bread and string beans all made with its aroma competing with my cologne.

Our first night with daddy home —Cozette has to miss me. Her bedtime routine includes: splashes in soapy water, plenty of kisses, and then hugs with her softest towel. The room is saturated with the fragrance of Johnson's baby power, and then I lotion her from head to beautiful toes. She drinks her warm bottle, while we sit in Mommy's rocking chair, next to her crib. I cuddle her in my arms, back and forth, the two of us, while I always sing: *Rock-a-bye baby in the tree top. When the wind blows the cradle will rock. If the bow breaks, the baby will fall and down will come baby, cradle and all. Jesus will bring Cozette's daddy home. Yes, He will. Yes, He will. Jesus will bring Cozette's daddy home.*

After her favorite Mother Goose pages are turned, I say sweet prayers to bring Cozette's daddy home. "I'll stay in his arms, never to leave, when You Sweet Jesus, bring Cozette's daddy Home."

Korea stole months from us.

The Store

***

A tray decorated with chocolate candy all around the plate, stumbles a bit as it comes through the doorway of my tiny kitchen. Eggs were fried, toast buttered –he moves toward me, apron and all. Hallelujah! I know my days of not being pampered and petted are finally over.

Sweet thing, he wants to serve me breakfast in bed already! Trying to delight all my senses, the aroma of coffee, bacon and buttered potatoes, are delightful. My eyes feast on the array of choices as I peek from under the covers. Like Mrs. Fain's fancy dinner table, more is always better!

I don't spoil the moment. I rub my eyes and sit up to examine all of it. My oooh's and aaah's are music to his ears, he says. He kneels at the side of the bed. His prayer is authentic but most of all thankful. He reminds the Lord how blessed we are.

We share the feast he's prepared. He feeds me bits of egg then lays the fork down. My thoughts go through the roof when he places the tray aside, and pats my lips to hush. A pink tiny box, with a lavender ribbon, comes out of the apron pocket.

I must open a gift. His eyes tender, he looks down at mine. I pull the sheet up over my breast again and sit straight in the bed. My hair bushy all over my head, I placed my hand over it to pat it down. My makeup ruined. Why couldn't he have waited for me to look beautiful? I thought as I close my eyes, then pop one open, as though it was Christmas morning. I whispered. "I thought I opened them all last night."

"You did."

"What are you up to? You're all…"

The Store

"I'd have you open a gift each morning if I could –you and Cozette."

"You'll be my gift each morning sweetheart."

The kitchen, strange to him, but, I guess he found everything. But strange things are happening by the second. Cozette isn't crying! She had to be changed and fed.

My thoughts quickly turn back to his advances. I tear open the box, and laid the ribbon aside. –A gold heart on a chain – I picked it up and held it for him to fix around my neck. "I love it!"

We finished feeding each other laughing and having our fun. The sun shone through the windows over the bed as we made it.

I brushed my teeth and fixed my face, as I gazed in the mirror; the sparkles of gold in the chain's heart are twirling around and matched the sparkle in my eyes. I'm the happiest woman alive. There is so much love in the apartment. The mist of it, is falling on to the floor, running out the door, and the aroma of it, fills the air.

Chapter 36
Knit two, pearl three

Mrs. Fain is on the phone. She compels us to come over. Customers are pleading for his presence, she says. He tells her, no problem, we'll be there.

We have our short time together before Cozette needs her morning agenda. I change her diaper, smiling down at her as she coos and laughs up at me. She doesn't mind her daddy coming over to welcome her to a new morning. He stands behind me smiling at her as I tend to her needs.

Down the hall to my father's apartment I skip, my insides are racing... I can't believe my day has started like this. Remembering, being at this very spot, yesterday. I had excitement thundering through my veins. The heighten anticipation of Warren coming near me. What I'd do, what he'd say? It never came close to my dreams. I am never disappointed! Warren gives love and it always over flows in miraculous ways.

Knocking on Daddy's door I say, "Good morning Pop!" I neeeeeeed him and ask for his help. "Wannah do something? ...Watch Cozette?"

***

Mrs. Fain seems surprised to see us without the baby. She looks around as if we're hiding her. She smiles, first at her son, then gives me a wink and waits on three customers before she is free to greet us properly. We go from end to end of the tiny store without much fanfare. I notice her shelves are filled. By his demeanor Warren seems relieved when he stays in the back and sits down, leans back in his favorite tattered chair.

The Store

"This place looks great!" Warren hollers up to her. Mrs. Fain's husband and her daughter, Charlotte, "They do all the running around," she tells him.

"I missed you real bad. No one can operate this place like you, and you know it." She echoes over to him, as if to put a 'guilt trip' in his heart. It seemed her main goal was to keep the little store running until he returned.

"Hey! Can you take over this register?" Mrs. Fain is asking him to handle her next customer as if he'd only been absent overnight. But that wasn't what he came in for; she was disappointed he's not in uniform. "Come on, get up." She had a surprise for him later.

He hesitates, and then goes over behind the counter. "Hey, I haven't done this for over a year!" Apologizing for his awkwardness, Warren grins at Mr. Wesley. He finds the correct keys and finishes doing what he does best.

Mrs. Fain announces she is going to parade Warren around the neighborhood. "Everyone will be excited. My son, my soldier hero!" She says real loud over and over, laughing. She wipes a tear from her eye with the rag she was proudly waving over her head.

It is a crude "speech" written out on a handmade poster.

He will tell the throngs of people he was glad to serve his country. The post he held was hard work. Everyone appreciates letters and messages from home. He wants the American people to know how much he cared and the war was still going

The Store

on. Fighting men deserve support... and that's a done deal.

He is home now.

Mrs. Fain practices it again of what she wants said. If anyone was there to hear, she'd go on some more about his tour and his meaningful work for the United States of America!

That's what her son would say, she said smiling broadly … if all her customers were there to march with them. It is early, 7:32 a.m.

From the apartments upstairs, over the store, only one man bothers to come down when he hears her shouting. And he is the janitor.

Warren walked around the aisles for several minutes looking at everything. Mrs. Fain reminds him of all his great ideas; sound maneuvers; interesting concepts he had always made to her in dealing with her business. Even all the compliments, and suggestions and more he made to his mother, inside letters while in Korea. "I just did whatever you told me to do." She said. When he got her attention, he compliments her on various new items she was carrying that he had nothing to do with.

Warren's future plan was to expand. He constantly fed Mrs. Fain with dreams of teaming up with her. That was over!

Mrs. Fain helped her brother's business. It largely grows under her watchful eye and now she wants Warren to stop over there and see how nice it looks.

"It will do you good to see your uncle's store before you leave." She says adding a wink. "I've tried all your ideas there too."

The Store

"We better get back home, by now Cozette has Cathy's dad frazzled by tearing up his immaculate apartment. She'll have both her parents to handle her now. We'll see Uncle William tonight at the dinner." He said all that smiling at his mom, and then he grabs my waist.

"Mrs. Fain, we must …better hurry back!" I chimed in with more liveliness to back him up. I am so thrilled, just flattered he held me in front of his mom. He reached over to kiss me when he mentioned his little Cozette. Mrs. Fain noticed everything. "Warren stop! Hasn't he become a big flirt?" I say meaning; I loved it.

"You're coming tonight by six-thirty aren't you? By Mrs. Fain's tone we knew it was a big thing. –The Homecoming Celebration Gathering! "Yes, for sure!" We both sing out. "Warren can't wait to see everybody tonight. Especially Charlotte!" I say that to reinforce something I know nothing about. His sister was a 'thorn' most of his life. But he misses her, she did a great job in his absence. "Bye for now." I hollered out glad to leave and not too late for Cozette. I had told my father we'd be back early.

I thought out loud. "I have never seen Mrs. Fain so jovial towards me."

Warren opens her door and it squeaks closing behind us. He holds my hand walking to the car. The morning air still crisp, birds chirping and several pieces of glass shine like diamonds on the pavement under my feet.

Warren waves at some lady across the street coming out of her court-way building. Then he yells, "See you later Mrs. Jackson. Okay?"

"I see you home boy. Is tat your wif?"

"Yes ma'am, you'll meet her soon, glad to be home. Thanks."

The Store

Warren opens my door and I slide in. He is proud of me. I have to sit close and rub my gloved hand over his thigh when he's settled. The engine starts. He looks around at his old neighborhood through the windshield, seeing it for the millionth time. A quick glance over at me crunched close brings a delicious smile across his face. Then he closes his eyes. I know he's saying a private prayer. I know too he notices my breast were larger than ever. What a gift.

"Cathy." He pauses several seconds.

"You'll never know how much I ..."

I snuggle up closer. "Bett-sha I do." Then he whispers, "I m p o s s i b l e."

He kisses my lips so tender covering them completely.

***

Warren drives slowly, savoring the Woodland area, like he'll take it back with him in a bottle. He remembers everything. I linger at the same things, to see it as he does; learning to love what he loves. There are dilapidated houses and patches of dirt in front of tall weeds mixed with debris and broken glass all over. Down the street where he lived for years, he pauses often next to every other house. Yes, the buildings on upper Dorchester are the same, he says. From the quiet oohs and aahs he's enjoying memory lane. Then he starts to bustle a tune I don't recognize as more guttural sounds pour out.

"Where is?" Oh, he sees it. He questions the missing businesses, the houses that are abandoned and the ones with all the extras added: new porches, siding and fences dot the homes he knows so well. He is really enjoying being back, just surveying his old stomping ground around the 'Southside.'

The Store

Our neighborhood is new to him on 79th Street. While lingering in the vestibule he sees the mail slot where I picked up his mail. The high ceiling can cause echoes and also the distance I have to travel to retrieve his love letters. He closes his eyes and instantly soaks my route. Down. Up then down, then up. Whatever, it was in the past.

Pop has Cozette in her walker. We made it by 9:00 as promised. She knows my voice before I reach the door. Her eyes question mine, like, who is this man always next to my mommy? "We're going to get used to this man, your daddy!" I tell her. "We're a family." She enjoys the tone in my voice. Playfully she scoots off in another direction. I have to keep an eye on Cozette at daddy's place, she's trash it. Quick.

I light a cigarette and Warren does too. "What's cooking? I hover near his little kitchen. "It's Liver and onions, Mac and Cheese! Got enough for us?" I holler out to Pop. He's occupied getting ready for work. "Yes, go ahead, help yourself." He yells back from his bedroom.

I offer a bite to Warren. "Honey this is Mac and Cheese!! Your favorite, better than mine!" I say as he opens his mouth cute, like a baby bird. Cozette looks up at us, and then he gives her some from his lips. Cozette looks at her daddy while slowly chewing, frowning her cute nose. Warren is thrilled. For the first time she giggles at him and doesn't stop as Warren keeps feeding her.

"She's the cutest, isn't she?"

"Yes, and she's all yours. Whew! Boy'ee, does she need her diaper changed!"

"Pop we're out. Thanks for your vitals. We didn't eat them up."

"You can have all you want. Hey! Welcome home Soldier!" Pop enters gleefully to greet his son-in-law with a handclasp and then they embrace.

The Store

Warren looks like a guy with two left hands changing Cozette. I tell him how to pin and where to put the soiled diapers.

"Honey, I don't have Pampers. Mrs. Fain supplies a service that comes twice a week for the pail."

"Where's the pail? Oh, What the _____?" Ammonia fumes knock him over! "Wow!"

Chapter 37
This is family stuff, just that

We are not going to be late for Mrs. Fain's dinner! But, I don't have a thing to wear. Warren's comments didn't help when he brought Cozette back through the door. She is high on his shoulder grabbing his head with her fingers spread over his temples.

"She looks like she squeezed your head off, holding on for dear life!"

"We went for a walk."

"Did you run instead?"

"Why?"

"She is holding your eye socket too. What did you do to my baby?"

"She loves it. Wants more! Hey, I can change a diaper too!

We laughed and he put her in her crib. She held his arm firm as she reached over to take her blanket from off the railing. Next time I looked over at her, she was asleep.

"You wore her out. Do you always treat your girls that way?"

***

We do get to Mrs. Fain's dinner party late.

I didn't believe one word of Warren's observations about how I looked. His family hadn't seen Cozette since she was born. But my dress is too long, wide, and floppy and women, know what I'm talking about. I looked like I was

The Store

going to church. So I changed. I thought to wear a navy checked jacket, a red skirt with black pumps and gray stockings. My hair is awful, Warren had ruined it and my shoes don't match anything, but Cozette is a doll. She's in a wide pink eyelet dress with ruffles and bows; I saved it for her daddy's home coming. Exhausted, I had changed clothes completely three times. Warren agreed as I modeled before him that I had on the perfect outfit each time. My mirror said, otherwise.

The entire dinner at Mrs. Fain's was wonderful. She enjoyed us the minute we stepped inside her doorway. The music is loud. Blues and a few jazzy tunes were heard throughout the night, and everybody danced and sang songs, played cards and enjoyed the food on her banquet table. All Warren's favorites.

Mrs. Fain's place is clean and neat. Her style of furnishings is traditional, a bit stuffy, nothing to write home about with plastic covering the sofa and two chairs to match. Drape swags covered the window out of the same fabric. I hadn't developed a style of my own. I didn't like hers.

The door to Warren's old room is tucked over in the corner off the living room at the front of the place. I had forgotten how sloppy it was, it looks the same, and no one occupies it.

Hoots and pats on the back, for a job well done, as each one greeted Warren with gratitude, for serving his country. Warren walked around amazed at the attention he was getting. He was the hero of the family. He wanted to cry several times but held back the tears, dabbing an oversized handkerchief to each eye. His family does love him. Everyone showed up. All his uncles, their wives, his school buddies and neighbors.

The Store

Cozette at 8 months is the star. She looks at everyone and pleasantly enjoys her blocks on the floor next to the couch I had brought to keep her company.

Off the entrance was the dining room where another table was adorned with plenty of food. Walking down the hallway from the dining room I passed the bathroom then Charlotte's bedroom and Mrs. Fain's room is in the rear opposite her kitchen.

I met friends of the family and cousins, then more relatives arrived later and the introduction starts again showing off Cozette and everyone staring at me, as Warren's new wife. I wonder if Mrs. Fain's depiction of me held up to what she said a year ago.

Charlotte makes a grand entrance with her new boyfriend. She dresses like a movie star. She might have felt compassion for me as to how I looked. Her eyes told me she did. No, I didn't look like she wanted me to. I didn't want Mrs. Fain to know I wasn't having a great time. The gala was for Warren not me. I tried to hide my feelings by keeping a grin on my face. Happy-go-lucky me.

Cozette searched the crowd for us a few times but her daddy and mommy were seldom far.

Warren enjoys his mom's cooking. He walked around with a plate in his hand as he greeted everyone with wild stories that grew more exciting by the end of the night.

All had their favorite memory of Warren, his interaction with Mrs. Fain, her store and Charlotte. They laughed hard when they shared them. I loved the way they showed their warmth but Charlotte didn't think the accounts about her constantly harassing her brother were funny. She pouted a bit and that was it. She never got over his un-attachment to her feelings anyway.

The Store

Listening, I found out Warren wrote to his cousin George. They are close in age and became like brothers. I think Warren wrote his buddies too, but I never asked.

Warren wanted to be the last to leave. Cozette was already asleep and he used that excuse to say his good-byes. He didn't fool anyone but himself. He had had too much to drink.

When we got to our place Cozette was still dead asleep on daddy's shoulder. She wasn't used to late night adventures ending at four. Now that he's home things will be ah changing.

Three weeks later:

When I start my morning routine with Cozette, Warren stays in bed, dog-tired. He was never a morning guy. I get dressed and then finish Cozette. It takes me over an hour to get out the door. If Cozette was a boy Warren would be dressing our son, I thought.

I didn't want to complain. I would never nag. Never bother my husband with what I could do. I learnt that from the families I was forced to stay with; every thought, filtering through pass experiences. I saw mistakes. I wanted love. I have an attentive husband and manageable daughter. I want my marriage to be different. My life: like the soap operas, and romance novels; it's going end happily ever after.

Warren starts work as a truck mechanic using his army training. Mrs. Fain uses him on week-ends and after work in her store. I got a job with a I-Deal Personal Employment Agency downtown. I interviewed applicants for various corporations seeking clerical positions. I screened them: typing skills, dictation, and appearance. Although I didn't type, I had a desk beside a window, phone, note pad and felt important using what, perceived, professionalism I could muster.

In a couple of months we moved to the most adorable 3rd floor apartment. It was nested in a court-way building in my old Hyde Park neighborhood. The trees were greener there and the sky above shone through fluffy white clouds. Each building down our street was kept and manicured. The joke was: to find a piece of paper you had to throw it down yourself.

I use my mom to babysit Cozette. Mom swore she had quit her latest loser, Manuel, and then she was back again under his spell. It's hard to say if he was her "Waterloo" but he just might have been the straw that broke her. I loved my mom and wanted better for her, but she was stuck on something. We all knew she was in these crazy love situations and couldn't break free. She would run away to my place for a couple of days, said it was over, then run back and be found with the bum again. I could NEVER do that. IF my man went out on me I'd leave and divorce him so fast it would make his head swim. I sure didn't want to be the apple on her tree. Falling, God forbid.

I had several positions during those early years, raising Cozette, before Annette was born: A dental assistant, an office worker, an Airline as a telephone reservationist assisting people to their destinations all over the world, and finally an Oldsmobile dealership. Of course, some positions I left, some released without notice. Warren didn't want me working. That angered his sister Charlotte and maybe his mother, Mrs. Fain as well. Folks couldn't understand what made me so 'special' to Warren, that I couldn't help support us.

My longtime relationship with Janet Wells continued to grow. My sister and I thought Janet, at age twelve, was the most precocious young lady we'd ever met. She made sure, each visit, she gave us a shock treatment, with her sexual comments that made us blush. She came over Aunt Eleanor's apartment to visit her daddy, Thurman, who had married my aunt after she divorced my Uncle Ross.

Janet lived in the pocket, that area of the city which Mrs. Fain's store was located. She worked Mrs. Fain's little store after school while attending Hyde Park, H.S. During Warren's early courtship with me, Janet kept the secret from Mrs. Fain that she knew me. On that famous New York Excursion, who knew, we had ears there listening. Janet's account of what Mrs. Fain said when Warren stole her brand new Bonneville is priceless. She said the woman exploded right before her eyes! Her language wasn't fit for human consumption. By the time I married Warren Janet knew more about him and his family than I did.

I don't blame Mrs. Fain. I didn't ask Warren to steal the car, drive to New York and alter our lives forever. He had that notion from the Lord, and then carried it out with his two crazy friends. God's Plan made sure I'd turn around in my tracks. That trip altered the course of this book. I'd be in New York working with an Eastern accent, sipping colas on the train back and forth to Jersey.

Janet came by after work to see me when I lived on Bennett shortly before Warren left for the army. She came up the stairs and had this tactile look on her face grinning from ear to ear. Her thoughts were to have our utopian situation for herself as she viewed our place front to back.

Warren had sparked a "new" era. The entire "bad boy/bad girl" taboo of living together was dissipating in America. Now, Janet knew two people that were enjoying themselves. She saw my entire apartment, 'Doll-house' style and it looked right.

The Store

Janet married Jack Wells after I got married, and then they moved into her grandmother's apartment. For some reason she kept up with me.

Chapter 38
It's not finished yet

In 1968, I'm deep into reading the book: "Gone with the Wind," off towards Memphis, Tenn. Warren's quest was to meet his biological father.

We carve a space for Cozette in the back seat amongst our bags. Long car trips aren't pleasant with three year olds but we had no choice on our budget. Rob has this entire August 18th week off for vacation. It's our first long motor trip and Warren is doing all the driving.

Mrs. Fain has set us up to stay in Hernando, with her best friend; the local sheriff, Ade Baldwin. Her home is tucked off a back street down a winding dusty road. When we get to Memphis we didn't stop but went straight into her driveway. She is a handsome brown skinned woman, loves men and knows everyone in town. She has laughing eyes, with constant sweet words for family and friends pouring from her lips but tuff when she has to be.

"Have I been waiting for you!" she grabs my husband and acts like she can't release him. Our car door couldn't open fast enough when she runs over to us as her breast flaps under her uniform with each jolt of her gait.

"And, this must be Cathy, your beautiful wife." I got out of the car and walked around so I could approach her properly. She is warm, and wonderful. All remembrance of wanting to use her bathroom left with the thrill of her warm southern greeting.

"Sweet Jesus, Lord, you made it safe." She said.

"I haven't laid eyes on you since you were this high" Her hand went lower to the ground than he could ever have been. Warren never says a word. He sits his case down to hug her and move his sleepy daughter up in his arms.

"This be your child?" Ade beams at Cozette with delight.

"What's your name sweet thing?"

"I'm Co-Cozette" as one of her hands rubs her eye but she manages to say her name intelligently. "Give me some sugar." Ade forgets we are tired. (The 18 hour trip was exhausting.)

"Miss Ade, can we use the ladies room?" I asked looking up at the beautiful home she has. From then on, she pampers us with her words of endearment and makes me feel like a queen.

After dinner she takes us around the one street in town to meet everyone. Several people swear Warren is dead ringer of his father, including Cousin Ade. "He looks spit like him." And another would comment, "Sure nuff!" It only heightens our interest. The mystery of son meeting father and vice versa, and is there really a likeness? From then on and into the night we wonder; could Warren and his father be that much like twins. But soon we were going to find out for ourselves.

Come morning time, close to seven o'clock, Cousin Ade be in her kitchen fix'n grits, eggs, sausage and ham. Homemade biscuits were steaming from her oven too. Rob was in paradise. The aroma of her food filled the house and she just started. "Dinner fix'n at my house, just might knock your socks off," she said. She loves to cook for guests. I found myself learning bits of more Southern Hospitality. She had her grits creamy, a little salt and butter and I loved the taste. Warren puts sugar on everything but I never put sugar on rice and grits. Hey! The North won!

The Store

"How did you get your grits to be so smooth like this?" I begged to know.

"I puts cream in them grits while they boil, child" she smiled. Her star gold crown tooth showing.

"Oh, I like your grits a lot. It makes them soft too" Right then I vowed to copy hers and treasure the idea forever.

She had other suggestions for me. All along she'd mention what she did in the kitchen, making the beds, picking herbs, greens and peas from the garden. She boiled her things with ham hocks and smoked bacon. Much like I learned from Tracey's kitchen.

"Just a pinch o' sugar Miss Cathy, on most things you fix. Your husband will be eating your draws honey, trust me!"

Later that afternoon, after the hot sun left the sky, we all get ready for Memphis, to finally meet Warren's papa.

"Are you two excited?" She said as she got us all situated in her big white Cadillac, with its shinny rims polished to match the interior's gleam. I had to mention all that, she's so proud to own it.

Chapter 39
Tie a knot in it

Cars lined both sides of the street near the charming home where it's told for days the big reunion would take place. People are stuffed in a tiny house all wanting to see our family, up from Chicago. We are let out in front of the curved driveway to the humble home while Ms. Ade tries to find somewhere to park. We don't know anyone but they all greet Warren as if immediately he's known all his life. Warren keeps that famous grin on his face, as he sees the attention he's given, and also to his wife and daughter, Cozette.

The spread of food from one end of the table to the other is stupendous. Baked ham, Turkey and Dressing, Chitterlings, Bar-B- Q Ribs, and Fried Chicken are in abundance. Louisiana Gumbo, Ham hocks and Greens, Corn on the cob, String beans, Cabbage and Carrots. Then there's the gravy, potato salad, mac and cheese, tomatoes, and pickles too. Everyone has their plates piled high as they are chewing, laughing and reminiscing of what was and could have been. There was more gold in them grinning teeth than in Fort Knox. No one put out their hand. You got a hearty grab, and they do nothing short of it.

Listening intently, the Toliver family: amiable, strong, handsome and resourceful, married into the Robinson family: progressive, and a bit more intellectual. Many years ago there were more of the Robinsons. All together they still call each other cousins, first and second removed, over into their third and fourth generation.

We didn't find anything like 'Chicago' in Memphis. We came to discover Warren's roots and amend a strained father-son relationship; mission accomplished. I noticed

The Store

everyone's ample lovability, and lots of charisma. We'll have to bottle them up and show northerners how to live. And each and every one seemed to adore me too.

My relatives, on both sides, came up from Memphis. It was called the 'Great Migration.' I don't remember much as a child. I was traveling by automobile with my parents, and Big mama sat in the back seat with me. This had to be in the late '40s. My daddy helped his mom, poor thing, as she hobbled out of the car. Then she stepped over into some bushes on the side of the road. She pulled up her huge dress to squat down to pee. I do remember that. I pee'd in the weeds along with her; everybody did. Of course, I didn't know we couldn't use any public toilets near where we were going.

The time comes, and sneaks up on us, that we've all anxiously been waiting for. I am the first to see Mr. Robinson Sr., a small figure of a man, (I don't think he looks identical to Warren) appear in the back doorway of his sister's home and just stand there. He has a yellow straw hat in his hand. He surveys the room and then smiles, sits down on a kitchen chair, and then gets back up. Warren distracted, looks towards the doorway when someone shouts "There he is!" But he couldn't see his father's face for everyone screaming and running to reach his daddy.

Mr. Robinson is graciously lead by his hand straight over to his son. A brief awkward moment takes place. They stare at each other, stiff like, in amazement right there in the middle of the crowded room. The likeness of my husband and his daddy was striking they thought. Years of cynicism melt away instantly.

Hoots and hollers roar like thunder. "This was all worth it!" someone shouts over the noise. Both men's lips start to curl. They laugh; warm tears swell their eye sockets.

The Store

"Hey, Mr. Robinson how ya like your son?" A gruff voice made it known that this is what everyone came for.

"He's here aint he? Warren's father said grabbing his son by the shoulders hugging him as if he were gold as tears rolled down his cheeks. Then he pulls out his man sized handkerchief and wipes his head beading with sweat, "My son is home!"

Warren and his daddy were strangers no more. Mr. Robinson around the dinner table recalled all his memories: a red wagon, boxes of unopened toys, that's still up in his attic packed, forever waiting. He also noticed instantly a scar on Warren's chest and remembers too well when his son, fell off the porch. They lingered on into the evening out in the backyard. Warren sat on the bench next to the rose garden. His daddy standing over him with one foot perched on the side. They talked and shared their serious men stuff I guess, drinking cans of beer.

Warren and his father have the same coloring: dark brown, and the same shaped eyes, nose and mouth. Mr. Robinson, stockier than Warren, two or more inches shorter, shared even his cigarettes. Both men are of few words but they made up for lost time, with unanswered questions answered, maybe even solved. "Your mother? No, she sure didn't want me. She left to go up north for Chicago and that's the last I heard." He went on to share his bitter lifestyle and all the vices, he regretted most, the women, the booze, gambling. "Son …there's 'bout 20 years of history. You can't take it all in now."

Warren meeting his father and aunts proved life altering. I believe it anchored him. If he was a 'tiger' before; now he's a 'Lion.' We kept up with our new family remembering who, went with whom, for the longest.

On our last day Warren wants to give me a nostalgic tour of the place that he shared with his grandparents. When

The Store

we drive up I see, up through an overgrown path, a three room shack with a broad overhang, spanning the front of it. "It's still the same," he says, wide-eyed, feasting at his boyhood memories: broken down porch with a swing hung on rusty chains …the pot belly stove, "Weathered wood has charm too, just needs paint, inside and out." I smiled at Warren as he slowly finished touching treasured moldings, the basin tub and even the walls. "It's hard for me to picture living here, so small, but she kept it spotless," he whispers. Everywhere you look around outside, the grounds are mile high with weeds, shrubs and broken down trees. We walked, after coaxing Cozette from the porch swing, all over and around and up some dusty roads. The day is sunny and crisp, not too hot and Warren wishes he could stay, and find some more rocks to take back home.

"I remember granddaddy always taking me to pick cotton up over there," he points to a field in the distance. "Early in the morning we'd be ready to ride." Warren keeps talking about that cotton and the tale takes a little more time to tell this time.

The sun is long down. Cozette sound asleep and cousin Ade is off into town somewhere. Warren takes advantage: the moon is high, crickets permeate the bush, and the summer breezes blow the curtains. That's what they do down here on warm evenings. It's rumored that Annette, our second daughter, was conceived right there in Hernando, Mississippi, in Ade Baldwin's spare room. And she never found out we enjoyed her place that much.

Act III

Chapter 40
Absolute Surrender Absolutely

July 7, 1969 at 6:40 a.m., the phone rings.

From under the covers, Warren reaches out for the receiver.

"What!"

"No!"

"No!"

"What! O God no! How did it happen?"

Mrs. Fain is on the other end and she meticulously tells him all she knows. Warren's black skin beads with sweat as he listens for several minutes to every word. The sunshine peeks through the blinds painting stripes of gold on his tear stained face. He groans then hangs up the phone, then slumps back over the bed, staring wide eyed at the ceiling. He understood fully what he'd heard. With both hands over his face still wiping tears from his eyes he sits up. Then he looks down at the mess of shoes and clothes on the floor under his feet, and then kicks a boot. Seconds pass and then he slowly says,

"Cathy, …my uncle was shot dead."

"Which uncle?" I said, reaching over to rub his moist back pushing the covers away from his body. "Gosh, honey what happened?"

I keep questioning him as he leaves the bed to get dressed. He stays in the bathroom the longest time.

I found out slowly it was Mrs. Fain's favorite brother, William that has the grocery store on Woodlawn.

The Store

Cozette wakes up. She heard us talking.

"Did we frighten you, honey?"

"Mommy?"

"We have to get dressed, go get your sister's bottle." I said as I moved the covers to conceal me. "We've got to go somewhere, hurry up!"

We've been in this third floor one bedroom apartment over a year. I love our charming place but it has become uncomfortable with the birth of Annette three months ago. I'd hoped to doll it up but couldn't seem to get my priorities straight. My colors were going to be bright and cheery or one day we'll move to a larger place. A beautiful house: with a white picket fence, green grass all around and a recreation room, plenty of comfortable furniture, with two bathrooms and … I'd raise my girls with stability and never let them "feel" displaced.

Now, I am running around looking everywhere for something to wear and nothing is clean. I planned on staying home all morning washing clothes, then taking Cozette to the water park. "Hurry Cozette mommy needs you!" Her makeshift bedroom is off in the rear next to the kitchen. Annette, still asleep, has her crib next to our bed.

Warren had been out until the wee hours of the morning. He gets paid every other weekend from his position at REA Express as a truck mechanic. We had just finished making love when the phone rang.

***

There is an unusual silence from Warren all the way down to the vestibule. Annette is slumped over my shoulders and Cozette is busy counting each step she takes. Warren has trouble finding his car key by the time we walk over to the car.

"Did you leave them on the kitchen counter?" I said rocking the baby. She is getting heavy and I wished he's find them before my arm breaks. He is looking in every pocket after the other. He pulls out papers, receipts and even loose change. His eyes look tired. Still, no key. I never have a key loose but on a ring. It's so easy to misplace it. My keys have twenty seven things on the ring.

"Glad you don't have to run upstairs and get mine." I said while sliding into the front seat when he found it inside his shirt pocket. Warren secures Cozette. She's so excited about going somewhere and I also bring books so she can read to me or play make-believe with her doll. I entered her this summer in a new idea of learning for pre-scholars called 'Head Start.' Her school is not even five minutes from our apartment. We don't mind walking our tree lined streets with her skipping along picking up dandelions.

I roll down my window to let some air come through. Annette is still asleep. My mind wonders. I don't hear Cozette's questions as to where we're going.

When did I see William Toliver last? I wish I had known him better. Warren rolls down his window to let the hot air escape but continues to have nothing to say. He turns the key. Sometimes the engine stalls. This red Chevy II had taken me to work several mornings after I dropped off Cozette at Delaney's Day Care on 53rd street. Then, I would rush to my position at the Oldsmobile dealership as an office clerk. I was teased there by the mechanics as, The Mrs. Robinson, of 'The Graduate's movie. Several men sang to me every morning. *"Well, Hello Mrs. Robinson, Jesus loves you more than you will know, Hey, Hey, Hey!"* I loved the popular song but hated the reference to Dustin's old nag.

The Store

I know our old car is temperamental. Warren knows all about them, so whatever it does, it does. With me not working since the baby, we can't afford another one.

I don't tell Cozette where we are going. My thoughts are wild; thinking all sorts of things about the family I married into. Mrs. Fain didn't let Warren have that place but sold it to her brother. Hmmm, I remember William Toliver, the more I think of it. Yes, at a family outing in the Wisconsin, Dells. Can't understand what happened. He was tall, handsome and friendly. He had once complimented by baby's curly hair, and how pretty Annette was. His image was pleasant but nothing more. Like the rest of the family, I really didn't know him.

Warren's eyes lay straight ahead; he weaves in and out of traffic like a wounded animal seeking shelter. I have never seen him this way. I'm scared to say a word. A million things must be racing through his mind. He hasn't shared one with me. His jaws are sucked in. Nothing is on the car's radio. I don't dare turn it on.

It's a clear day, like the promises of lazy Sunday mornings all summer long. Not even a breeze to disturb anything. The sunlight filters through the trees as we seem to move so fast, yet in slow motion. At Woodlawn, Warren proceeds down the loneliest street. He finally ends at his dead uncle's store and parks under a tree. He's motionless, off in a daze; then he leans back, takes a deep breath, like he's filling his nostrils with ammunition as if contemplating shooting someone. Both his fist hold the steering wheel. He stays for the longest, deep in thought. I wish I could read his mind. I don't move anything. I'd stop breathing if I could. Cozette is silently turning the pages of her book. The baby is asleep with the bottle still in her mouth and cool air is coming through windows. We seem to hurry to get here and wait.

The Store

People conjugate around the iron gates, shifting, listening, puzzled as to what happened, that their store is closed.

Warren turns his head, and then stares off in the direction of, The Store.

***

He thinks he hears in the distance, Mrs. Fain's voice.

"Jr. Go up the street, take my car, check that corner store on Woodlawn. Is it still there for sale?"

Warren is remembering every single detail: so vivid, less than 10 years ago, when Mrs. Fain asks him to check on this very store that he falls in love with.

"Yes, mama, I mean Mrs. Fain. I'll run and check it out." He says dropping the boxes he'd gotten from the wholesale house. He was going back out the door, tripping over another box he had left behind. Before he could say anything else but "Excuse me," he is out the door. He loves driving his mom's car every chance he gets. He drives up the street, three blocks and pulls over.

He watches both ways, then crosses the street. The entire corner is barren. He straightens up his collar, and then slowly walks towards the large rustic building.

A brilliant reflection off The Store's front window gives the place a glow. Coming near he sees a 'For Sale' sign and placed beneath it is a hand written phone number. While pressing his moist forehead against the window he uses both hands to cup his eyes from the sun's glare. White sheets of paper cover the panes of the dim interior that conceal its treasures. He searches for a crack, any slight opening to view her beauty for himself.

The Store

Sparse shelves, bare floors, and cluttered papers thrown around the counter leads him to investigate. Why is she abandoned? Immediately he knows what he will do when he owns her. She'd never look like this again, all empty and alone. He sees her shelves filled with polished can goods, and the meat case, lined with choice meats and luncheon deli delights. She's painted, petted and primed for business, of the downtown 'North Side' kind. Her proudest sign says: 'Open for Business'

He memorizes the contact number. On second thought, he pats his clothes for a pen, and scribbles the number on his palm. 555-5555.

He must be affected deeply by his uncle's death and going near this store is tearing him up but he has to do what he came for. Warren breaks some trance. Then he slowly lights a cigarette and inhales a few deep drags then hands it over to me. I look at him. He says he has to go up and console his uncle's wife, Helen.

He opens the door, checks on Cozette. Then says, "Let me get this over with, I'll be back." He walks across the street then stops at the building and walks over to the glass and peers inside, cupping both hands to block the sun. He's told me too many times how he loves that store. He remembers when he whispered long ago to The Store twice out loud:

"One day you'll be mine! One day you'll be mine!"

He spreads his palms wide with an entire hand print on her window. The Store feels his hands. She counts between her whispers.

"Rescue me... Rescue me....aahh, Rescue me." Warren swears he hears her voice again. He looks around. *This store is alive!* Who would believe me?

The Store

I watched him slowly leave The Store's window. He glanced back over at us, knowing I'm wondering why he stayed so long looking inside the window. He nods to a few people standing near the entrance of his uncle's apartment, and then goes right pass them, up the stairs out of my sight.

Three cigarettes later, the car is hot but Cozette isn't complaining. I use one of Annette's diapers to wipe my forehead. I turned the radio dial, nothing on worth listening to. My hair had wilted from last night and I look horrible. I lower the rear view mirror to check my face. What's the use; I am not staying here I'm going up there too. Determined, I open the door. "Honey, we're going to get daddy." I held Annette. Cozette grabbed my skirt and we reached the curb.

The neighborhood is bustling with people crowding around outside. It was long past time for The Store to open at 8:00. One by one they had gotten the sad news, from others standing by, that the owner was shot dead, earlier that morning. So many people were bringing cards and flowers to place on the iron bars. Some customers stand there crying. Everyone had something nice to say as pockets of whispers and networks of news spread to a new batch of onlookers.

"It's so sad. ... Did you hear?"

"Yes, it's true!"

"I never knew anyone who was nice that had been shot dead before."

Chapter 41
Absolutely, I say it twice

William Toliver had been found shot in the head sitting in his automobile just a few blocks away. He lived over his grocery store with his wife, Helen and her two teenaged sons. He was greatly loved by his customers and the community for six and a half years.

***

Helen was awakened at 4:14 a.m., by two policemen banging on the front door.

"Who is it?"

Helen yells from the top of the stairs as she leans over the banister. She can see through her tiny opening from the top of the stairs. It was dawn and the sun was up by the time they got her attention.

They shout through the door. "Ma'am, we want to ask you some questions. May we come up?" She leaves to get her robe, and then suspiciously creeps down to open the door.

"Are you Mrs. Toliver?" the taller officer asks.

She quickly says, "Yes, sir." She wants to say something else, through the cracked door, but thinks first about it. *He's still not home. I know something happened.*

The officer continues: "Ma'am, may we come up?"

After both officers get inside, the shorter one, looks straight at Helen and says, "I'm officer Murphy and this is my partner, Officer Brown. There is something we have to tell you." He hesitates. "It's about your husband." Helen puts

The Store

her hand over her mouth, bites her lip then turns slowly to go back up the stairs. The officers follow her. When she gets into her kitchen, she sinks down in a chair next to the table, looks at the dull linoleum and pushes her head from side to side. She wants to pay attention as officer Murphy takes off his cap. She knows. In the pit of her stomach, she knows something is wrong.

"It is about your husband not coming home Mrs. Toliver." Officer Brown tells her part of it, then officer Murphy continues, but not that her husband was found dead. Back and forth they exchange information as she sits there stunned.

~~~~~

William Toliver was found at 1:19 a.m. in his black Oldsmobile parked at 69** S. Drexel. There was a single shot close range in this left temple. Mr. Toliver's car was still running with the horn blowing as he lay slumped over the steering wheel. It could be robbery but the window was down and his wallet was found on him. They are taking finger prints and an investigation is under way. A passenger, who was with Mr. Toliver, may have seen something. She claimed she was in a house visiting her mother's boyfriend along with her five year old son, when she heard what she thought was a gunshot. She was still being questioned.

None of the accounts with finding Mr. Toliver's body is relayed to Helen in the kitchen. The officers want her to identify the body. A social worker will, if necessary, disclose more information and take over if she needs sedation.

***

The Store

"Ma'am please get dressed, you have to come. Come to the station." He says with pity in his voice.

She leaves the room, removes her robe and nervously buttons a dress over her tiny 49 year old frame. Weak from the anticipation of what the officers will tell her she gathers her purse, glasses and walks back towards the kitchen. "I'm ready." She bravely says. "Thank you Mrs. Toliver, we'll follow you."

~

Sitting in her kitchen recalling all that was done, Helen was feeling relieved. She had been to the station, and did everything they asked of her. It was traumatic for her seeing his body lying on a slab in the morgue. Officer Murphy held her up as she identified that that indeed was her husband. They had cleaned his body of all the blood, she said.

***

As more concerned souls were coming inside Helen's small apartment asking, "who could have killed Mr. Toliver?" it was hard to find a place to sit. I didn't know anyone. They tell me some of these folks were friends. Most were overly concerned customers that had never been into the private quarters of the man who owned the grocery store. People were everywhere, even sitting outside on the back porch and on the steps at the main entrance.

The first thing I see approaching the top landing and rounding the stairs is the tiny kitchen with Helen seated at the table. Her youngest son, Bobby, a stocky handsome kid, is standing over her with his hands covering her shoulders.

I don't know what to say. Warren must have disappeared with Mrs. Fain into another room. "Helen, I'm so sorry…" I blurted out softly. She looks up with redden

The Store

eyes then acknowledges my sentiments with a nod. We don't go into her kitchen but walk pass several people standing around the hallway. I am holding the baby securely on my hip. Cozette is not far behind me. As we push our way through the crowded place, I keep my eyes straight ahead. The smile on my face might be the only passage permit that clears a path into the next room. "Excuse me, excuse me please."

Noon sunshine ignites the apartment. It is hot and airless. Other people are fanning themselves profusely but still no one leaves. I stay put in the living room area, but restless, I try to find some relief. With every window lifted we would all welcome a faint breeze, if it tried to flow through. I had made a sorry trail over the entire cramped apartment saying "excuse me" to everyone a second time, then a third, keeping Cozette close and it was beginning to be stressful on me and the baby. Relatives are in Helen's bedroom, the dining room and in the second bedroom in the rear of the apartment as they keep coming up the stairs. Aunt Betty is crying over on Helen's bed with her two cousins around her. I want to get Annette's wet diaper off before Warren gets us out of here but there isn't an empty spot in the entire place. I might just have to return to the car to change her.

I see Warren and get his attention as he looks up from conversing with Mrs. Fain and I motion to him. "The baby, she's tired. I'm tired. Honey, we'd better leave." I say it sweetly gesturing towards Annette fussing in my arms. This is the first time he sees me since he left us downstairs.

I whispered, " I wan-tah go home." Looking at my baby's face again. "Mommy wants to take you home." My heart is downcast, looking at the wooden floor planks with worn linoleum that is in much need of care. I lean against the dark brown wall, just to rest, impatiently waiting for my husband to finish his with his mother.

The Store

Beyond the dining room is a living room. It is full of smoke and everyone is sitting there in disbelief. Every single room around me has ornate moldings surrounding the doors, over the windows and ceilings, and it all spells O-L-D. I notice every crack, all the dirt and the gloom.

Cousin Frank is leaning out of one of the six foot windows overlooking the corner of the street. A customer hollers up from down below on the sidewalk. "Let me up there honey." She's holding up her bag of goodies for him to see. "I've got chicken 'n biscuits for your family." Frank tells her to hold on, as he will have to fight his way through the crowd. I am told this was a sample of what went on all day at Helen's small apartment. Each one of Mr. Toliver's customers, in some way, extended their love and compassion well into the night. All I know, I want to leave as quickly as possible and not come back for a long time.

How could I know the entire place, I think is so awful, will be mine soon, forever.

Chapter 42
Yes, it's true

Helen Toliver arranged an elaborate funeral for her husband. She had so many flowers, and well-wishers, and tears, all giving him tribute and testimony. In the brief time, William Toliver was owner of the grocery store on Woodlawn, he had so many customers mourning his lost. Cars, in single file to the cemetery, blocked traffic for miles.

Although there was a handsome reward given, no one came forth. None of the leads panned out to solve the senseless crime. The family and Warren were left in the dark as to what could have happened. Why he was at the place of his death with another woman.

***

Helen Toliver thought long and hard. After conferring with Mrs. Fain, she gives a concrete decision. Sell it.

Helen's relationship with her husband wasn't ideal. Because of the nature of his death she doesn't want to live near the place one minute longer she moans.

Helen really wants to give everything to Warren. She offers him the same deal Mrs. Fain had offered her husband years before, only better. If he would take the business off her hands she was more than willing to work out a deal he couldn't resist. Although he was only twenty six, he had every qualification needed to step up and operate it. His work ethic was impeccable and Helen knew this would satisfy Mrs. Fain's original desire to have Warren own and operate it, plus repay the favor. It was a unanimous decision.

The Store

Warren comes home late again. I have missed him nightly after work since the death of his uncle. I know something is different, something unusual is going on. I don't have a notion what's been discussed with Helen, Mrs. Fain or any real possibility of owning anything is in our future I say, "How was it?" As he sinks on the side of the bed.

"Not good."

"Where have you been?"

"I've been to the bank first, and then made some other important runs."

"Honey, don't wear yourself out."

Warren was feeling miserable because although Helen had offered The Store to him, it wasn't enough. He doesn't have a dime to acquire it. His dream of ownership will go right down the drain. I see the man I married, crash before my eyes, when he falls backwards over the bed.

If you want something, get it.

If you don't get it,

You must not, have wanted it.

I see something come over him. He smiles, and then roars.

"I know you can tell me something." I say with a roar to match his. He leans back against the pillow of our bed, and then he says after a long pause.

"It's going to be fine." I laugh and he does too, while we're roaring at each other.

"Come over here … give me some loving, and you know it's going to be fine."

He grabs me to fall on top of him. He's made up his mind.

The Store

It's going to happen.

***

Each day stock is perishing. They start this frantic effort to get The Store reopened as soon as possible.

Helen calls. It's 4:44 p.m.

I see him lower his voice and talk quietly into the mouthpiece. I leave the bedroom and start washing the dishes, give Cozette her crayons and let her mark on her art board. Putting away some pots inside the oven, there's Warren peeping around the corner. I scream. "What are you doing?" His sheepish grin says he's teasing me with his eyes.

"Okay, what did she say?" Just then he yells: **"Cathy, she wants ME to have, The Store more than I want it!"**

His palms are covering his ears, as if his head will explode!

"She says she will hold off, as long as I need to get my bearings." Warren is out of breath and control.

"…and in the meantime, I can open The Store on 'faith' that I'll have the money!" He takes two more gasps for breath!

"Furthermore, she ain't worried!" He starts to scream! "Yo!"

I am witness to a dream coming true for my husband, over a single phone call! He keeps yelling all over the apartment. I have never seen him act crazy like this! Never! He's skipping around and lifting me in his arms. Cozette is scared. Annette starts crying all the way from her crib.

The Store

He walks in and The Store is dropped in his lap: As if on a silver platter.

Now, that's one more miracle I see happen in front of me. First, I have a complete heart change: I love the ground my man walks on, I marry him, and we make babies that I know changes me from the inside out.

Now this!

***

While the girls are asleep, we lay without a light on, neither TV nor a sound from the outside world. I am cuddled secure in his arms, so safe and reminiscing about my day: the puny dreams, about fixing up the apartment, what colors to choose, battles with the baby not sleeping and Cozette's reading score going higher and what is to be done this coming weekend.... He breaks my babbling and says.

"Honey, 'No Matter What' we're going to make it."

"OK." I look up towards the ceiling. My thoughts are trying to stay in the moment. "Oh, Okay, yes." I desperately want to see our future with a grocery store in it.

"Honey, my washing machine is ..."

"I want you with me, Cathy ... but if you're not ... I'm going in alone." Warren says this, matter-of-factly... even as if he's thought about it for the longest.

That 'no matter what' statement people use to act determined. I remain stiff for the longest time staring at my walls then up at the ceiling. *He'd go in without me? It's a jolt to my heart and hurts my spirit. ...without the girls too?*

I want to hide for the rest of the long night. Every scenario possible filters through my mind about The Store.

The Store

What trills Warren saddens me now. Leaving this apartment will be the test. I bet we can stay here! He's not talking about leaving our place. I know it is going to be ruff if I have to move over into that place. Living in that dingy space, well it's impossible!

I squeeze my eyes dry; say a prayer as I wipe them. "Lord help me." What does he mean, 'going in alone' Lord?

Nothing else is said. After Warren falls asleep I finished with the kitchen. I had made chicken and rice with a few leftovers of greens from the night before. This would be Warren's third night skipping dinner.

I've got a little more growing up to do. How?

If he's going in it, alone.

***

Although Helen has given him the ultimate chance to own his dream, he has to find the money. He wants The Store, but now to find a way to step in with dignity and own the place he's always wanted with his name plastered on it. So much for me and the girls, I know he doesn't ever mean leaving us for a store.

Warren's conferences with Helen are frequent at first. As a couple of days go by their talks trickle down until there is nothing more to chat about. He secures Helen's trust and the deal was made that first day. He is counting the hours when he can officially call the business his.

***

I'm upstairs with the kids visiting Helen while Warren is downstairs with some friends and workers counting every can and item on the shelves. He makes it clear that before the end of this year in 1969 prices can rise. And he doesn't want the sale to be higher than the grand tally for: inventory, refrigeration, appliances, fixtures and the brisk business that comes in the door each day. Warren knows all the money has to be transferred over or a "promissory note" given to Helen, before he can fully take over.

I believe with all my heart, that she gave the entire grocery business to Warren. The Store is a powerful entity. Helen, by years of experience dealing with her husband's involvement with it, knows something we don't.

Meanwhile, Warren handles the business in its earliest stages. The first day on the job, The Store is more than willing to have him at her beckon call. No one knows the deal that was made between Warren, Helen and The Store. Not me, Mrs. Fain nor Warren's so called 'Partner.'

The Store fell in love with Warren, the minute she saw him, years before and yearned for his ownership. She set out to have him that very day he placed his palm on her window, and now they are in cahoots with each other.

The Store swears by the bricks she stands on, to take care of all Warren's needs, my needs and his entire family, no matter how many children are born to him, generation after generation.

Furthermore, The Store set out to make, Warren, the 'hero' of the neighborhood.

The Store

All the promises she will keep over the course of his lifetime, and they enjoy a love affair, that will never end.

***

My overworked husband has been operating The Store for over a week when Helen, comes by to take her last things from the apartment. She seems somewhat friendlier today, as she packs each box. She looks up occasionally and gives a faint smile. Her two sons help tirelessly and that alone, makes her life tolerable. She is a widow and serves the reality of it, well, on a plate of sorrow.

Helen tried to share who she thought The Store's personality was, while I am getting to know her. We stand in the kitchen talking over several cups of coffee. Warren hears my footsteps, down below, every time we walk across the bare floor. Cozette loves stepping behind me, as the empty apartment's echoes throughout. Helen fingers Annette's curly black hair and she adores Cozette's brilliance, when she reads her favorite books, about flowers.

"Everybody's different." Helen says, packing a big brown box, her son will take out to the car.

"What do you mean?" I come back wondering, why she mentioned 'everybody?' "You and Warren, being so young, coming into the grocery business, might make it. I wish you well." Now, I really don't understand what she means.

She continues. "I didn't do well being the wife of the owner. The Store fought me going and coming." She comes over closer then murmurs.

"I was jealous of this store." Her eyes are dead in my gaze and I widen mine. "You are … you were?" I search her face, wondering: What! Is she a nut? Jealous of what? How can she be? She means she's resentful of the involvement her husband gave his business, maybe. But she can tell I don't have a clue to what she has just confessed. I shake my head and try to empathize. She knows I can't see it.

Helen Toliver never says another word about what happened the years she stayed over the business or the apparent power everything had over her.

An hour later, I follow her down the stairs, with Annette on my hip. She kisses the baby and goes into The Store's rear door to say good bye to Cozette, who is counting candy for her daddy. Warren leans over from behind the counter and whispers something into Helen's left ear. She turns, gradually looks back through The Store. Glances towards me, winks, then the door closes behind her.

Helen walks away. She hands the care of The Store, the neighborhood, the customers and Warren's involvement in the business over to me.

Now, it's too late. I am trapped. In a period of two and a half weeks, Helen has intentionally left the picture, never to return. She said her tearful good byes upstairs in the apartment. It's obvious to everyone close to the situation, and no one thinks otherwise, she acted like she couldn't leave fast enough.

The Store is now Warren's.

Chapter 43
No way of escape

By October 1, 1969 we settle permanently in the apartment over The Store. I have no idea what I am headed for. I slowly become aware of my new address and status as Warren's wife, and a reveal about The Store that is made over a period of two years. There is no Grand Opening since he's already been opening each morning at 7:00 and a formal announcement is useless!

The expense of having balloons, signs and give-a-ways are out of the question. Our deep prayer is that we'll be successful these first months. Warren is visibly excited and in total agreement with each prayer between us as he goes down the stairs each morning. He greets his helpers that are waiting outside and opens the door wide with his biggest smile.

We have invited our close friends over so they can buy something. Most are happy for us.

It's Mrs. Fain that comes over often.

I try to help, with Annette behind the counter in a mechanical swing, while waiting on the customers. The regulars get a chance to see Warren's family as Cozette is not far away. I have already checked her into an Elementary school only a couple of miles away.

Warren remembers the prices of everything in The Store. I can't keep the cost of common things in my head, like peas or apple sauce to ring up on the register. I'll forget the price of apples per pound or cigarettes or even diapers and lemons.

I holler out often for Warren. "Honey, what is the price of this size loaf of bread?" He has to tell me again. It doesn't matter if it's a large loaf, either brown or white. Then there were different sizes of cereals or cartons of milk. By the third time I had forgotten the same item … that's when he looked over at me with 'That Look.'

I don't remember how long before my husband asked me to stay upstairs. All I know, I am relieved of my duties as his cashier. I think he's jealous of my pleasing personality and the way I laugh and talk with his customers. He can't compete with me. He wants to be the only Big Cheese in The Store. That's what I think.

Our friends don't understand how we can afford to start a business. Warren's buddies and our mutual friends, his friends and mine, and in fact both our families, are curious. I hadn't worked since giving birth to Annette. We have no concrete explanation and it stands as a mystery that remains unspoken. Judging from several conversations and encounters; we are the talk of the dinner table.

***

Several weeks later, Warren doesn't come up for our usual dinner after I put Cozette and the baby down. We say our prayers for the night. "Dear Lord, bless Daddy and Mommy, all our friends and keep us safe. Amen." There is nothing else to do but wait. Eating together is our special time. I fixed one of his favorite meals: Smothered bar-b-q ribs over rice, gravy and corn on the cob, collard greens with corn bread.

Thinking about it I decide to creep down the steps. The Store has been closed for over an hour, put to sleep with the lights off. Warren's body is in silhouette against The Store's background.

"Honey, your dinner is" He doesn't notice I am behind him, I can tell he doesn't hear me:

The Store

A woman's voice, is softly whispering in his left ear. She is discussing what the day was like and about a few customers that came in. That man with the brown cap stole a can of corn and Mrs. Sarah Millsap put some chips in her bag, thinking you didn't notice.

He doesn't forget how she takes care of him. He has an ally. He can keep on top of the riff raft that curse most places.

He appreciates all she does because sales are soaring.

He's listening, looking at her shelves for the longest time. He notices everything about her. Then he says softly to match her tone, "You know I'll live right over you always and I'll talk to you and give you all I have."

The light from her meat case cast a faint blue hue over the floors. I notice immediately the faint aroma of fresh mint. His chin is lowered against his folded arms as they lean on top of the meat counter. His eyes are fixed on the heavy laden shelves before him. The Store's conversational tones are clearly evident. Several refrigeration motors hum mimicking musical sounds off in the distance. The atmosphere is as a misty vapor hovering over a restful lake at night.

My eyes soak in the loveliness of this moment. He is so peaceful and serene after a hectic day. I wish to share this time but hesitate several moments. I back up and quietly leave, choosing not to disturb him.

Back in my harsh apartment, I mentally compare it to what I witnessed downstairs. I long to return. I felt something wonderful and can understand how The Store can put her victims under her spell. I reach the chair next to the kitchen window to sit. I can't get that mystical experience out of my mind. *What was that?*

I do not believe this. Another hour passes. Warren is downstairs standing at the meat case listening to The Store as she communicates what she wants. My husband is enjoying the sensations she gives but still I can't blame him. I am drawn back down the stairs again but know in my gut. I'm not invited.

I have washed all the dirty dishes and the evening news at 10:00. Channel 5 painted a sorry picture of The President's state of the economy and I turned it off.

I hate it up here and feel Rob does too. We have accumulated so much stuff. Can I put the living room together? Then there is the stupid kitchen and the baby's crib location in my room, or should it be in with Cozette? Anyway, does it matter? It isn't easy to place anything in an attractive manner. How did Helen and the boys do it? Almost six weeks now. I have not liked this apartment since day one. Warren chooses not to be upstairs with me tonight and I wonder if I should return back downstairs to be near him?

I never intend to question him about the several hours he spent in the dark store ever or what Helen confessed about it. The generous attitude The Store and Warren are showing me; I have everything I need and more.

I keep all these things tucked in my mind. Every so often, for the next month or more the influence of The Store's vital presence in our lives comes up in my mind and it bites me.

Chapter 44
I hold on tighter

Warren crams everything he offers in his grocery store on a little white business card. **ROB'S SPOTLITE FOODS**: Hours of operation; days of week open, address, owners new name, his meats are choice, vegetables fresh and he delivers to your door. Next, he opens a business account at the Hyde Park Bank and gets these long designer checks that he's so proud of. The various vendors take his checks and its several days for their money to delete his account. Later so excited, he prints weekly sale flyers to distribute around the neighborhood to advertise The Store's new name and latest 'draw-in-hook'.

Immediately Warren wants everybody calling him 'Rob.' It has a great sound that he likes a lot. "**Rob**!"

The phone rings off the wall as customers dial, 773-667-9542, and asks for "ROB!" He says "Yo!" each and every time.

The most colorful person working for Rob is the butcher, Joe Daniels. He is soft spoken and greets anyone with a smile as he cuts bacon slabs to perfection. He's a cheerful alcoholic and the two of them go out drinking after hours.

Female customers with the exception of a few loves Joe's charm and how he keeps his quarters behind the meat counter clean and polished. When you shop on Sunday mornings you'll get more of what you came for. Like, if you're looking for slab bacon? You'll leave with bacon and sausage and everything to go with it.

At first, I am envious of the business related attention Rob gives exclusively to Joe. I'm upstairs in my window. I

The Store

can't imagine what keeps them together sitting in the car so long. Are they discussing what kind of meats they will order from the wholesale house the next day? That only takes only a couple of minutes to discuss. But I notice Rob isn't inviting Joe to stay downstairs after closing. He wouldn't dare share The Store's ambiance because that's their private time.

I hate to complain, but I wish my relationship with Rob would grow. I'd like to have mundane chit-chats connected with The Store's grocery needs. I'm not stimulating enough and what do I know about exciting interaction with customers and business?

I end up asking Rob for a special baby food for Annette or worst, some variety penny candy Cozette prefers. Then I beg him to order the exact panty hose for me in the colors and size I'd like them in; extra tall, coffee or off black.

Rob's pairing up with Joe is constant. Joe this, and Joe that. I am feeling stuck upstairs, compared to The Store's intriguing interactions. I can't compete. Wiping up after Annette, doing homework with Cozette, cooking breakfast, lunch and dinner, cleaning, ironing, back and forth to school and stuff like that is boring domestic stuff. I listen to the radio because there no time to sit in front of the TV. I feel left out, isolated, abandoned and almost abused.

Rob with his gregarious personality laughing so loud I can hear him through the floor. The customers are stimulating and he's enjoying them more than ever. Since he's secure in the neighborhood he has few things to worry about: only sales and other promotions. Then he grabs them with his charm like a hook on a fishing line.

He's in The Store all day but changes to like a hermit when he comes upstairs. He acts tired, and never mentions what goes on. He finds a beer in the refrigerator, and gets comfortable in his favorite chair beside the bed, kicks off his shoes and turns on the TV.

The Store

I holler from the kitchen.

"Rob! You hungry?" I mention what I fixed for the kids and me. He doesn't have strength to holler back. Just as Helen predicted; Rob's involvement with The Store becomes serious to the point I am frantically jealous. The closer he attaches himself to her it makes me more determine to wean him from her and recapture my husband's affections.

During a series of circumstances beyond my control, I lose some battles, but trust me; I will not lose the war:

Number one: The Store's influence is everything Rob wants.

Number two: The Store is Rob's means of giving me everything I want.

Number three: This is the weird one. I don't fully understand what The Store is. Would I feel the same way if she were miles away and Rob had to get in his car and drive twenty miles to open her? I am fighting a losing battle with myself but I don't know it. It's simple to realize how wonderful Rob is. He has given his heart and soul to me. That is evident.

But I take everything for granted. If I have to share Rob for any reason; that's where I part company with all logic and fail to compromise.

I want to separate him from the best thing in his life and he isn't budging. If I will just jump in and rally around his involvement with The Store he will, maybe, act differently. Rob wants The Store, his family upstairs, his outside activities and me to go along with the package and he isn't going to give anything up.

Like a roaring lion, I see Rob take a bold stand.

***

The Store

Cozette thought she was a big girl helping mommy shop for food in daddy's new store. She counted those stairs up and down many times. I ran out of sugar, bread or eggs, as I prepared food or made lunch. It was exciting at first, for both of us having everything we needed right down stairs. Dinnertime we ate together, as my family did when I was growing up. Forks and napkins go on the left of the plate, a knife and spoon to the right as the table was set.

"Honey, mommy needs milk. Ask daddy to give you a quart."

She listened as I told her exactly what to tell her daddy.

Her Daddy has everything, she thought, as she told him the two items she remembered to say.

I seldom walked through The Store. Some mornings when I needed something I always sent Cozette or as the years went by any one of our kids to get the desired thing I needed. They all became accustomed to running downstairs to get something needed for upstairs. Rob was up and gone before they dressed but always near. The kids learnt to depend on his presence. He kept watch over us constantly.

Rob's heart became attracted to the new love of his life more each year. I didn't notice the gradual change at first. Soon everything revolved around The Store. We never left as a family unless The Store was taken care of first. One day she took first place over our lives. I wish I could tell you the exact month, time or moment. Each night I had my husband next to me but I wasn't loved like I had been loved before. He didn't listen to me and that's what I missed. I had a life too, upstairs. But it was dull compared to The Store.

Living over The Store was beginning to be serious outside too. Our front door faced a twelve unit building directly across the street. The people in the building were strangers, all potential customers if they weren't already. I felt those tenants staring at me and the kids, wondering what

The Store

we were doing, where we were going every time we left. Upstairs the apartment was drab, lifeless and boring. I hated it. Downstairs, The Store was foreign. I didn't belong anywhere. A major adjustment had to be done inside my heart if I wanted to stay married to a grocer that had The Store on the corner.

Chapter 45
Upstairs / downstairs just steps going nowhere

Rob does invest time in his family as much as possible and he searches for little ways for me to help him. I think the customers pump him with ideas and he tries to use most of them. He also makes time for interesting trips. Some are long out of the way over into Indiana or up in Michigan. Most of our trips are short excursions around Chicago's north side. Distance isn't a problem to get away and enjoy the family.

During the week our first days, weeks and months starting out in our new store were exciting learning the neighborhood, and our role in shaping the area. Week-ends are Rob's favorites, and I looked forward to them too.

Sundays after The Store closes at 4:00 the kids are anxious and ready to go. Restless, they like going with Daddy. I pile them in the back seat of our station wagon and we wait for Rob to finish locking up. I have taken them to Sunday school and attended church and the concluding afternoon is our time. Rob is exciting so fresh to be with. His energy level is high and the kids and I never know where we're going. That's the surprise.

I had the opportunity to sit back and let Rob drive and encouraged the kids to keep quiet, read a book or play car games. It's my chance to get comfortable and casually observe diverse scenery. It might be green pastures and little farm houses dotted along the landscape or tall buildings overlooking Lake Front. Quaint ethnic neighborhoods that are foreign but interesting may come into view, it all depends in which route Rob takes.

I smile at the notion of being with Rob enthused with anticipation. I touch his hand while it rests on the seat. Most times there is silence between us as The Store, customers and its business affairs are far behind.

The roads are crowded or deserted before us as Rob is set on his planed destination. Depending on the season of year and his big revelation with his choice of recreation we get there as usual.

Meanwhile we have a good time by listening to the radio or singing songs. The kids give us plenty of excuses to pull over but I have a potty in the rear of the car for them, just in case.

Rob draws attention where ever he takes us. It is his posture, attitude, mannerism or countenance that give an impressive appearance when he walks into a room. I believe, on more than one occasion, people think he's a celebrity. I do. The final treat is a famous restaurant to enjoy before we head back home, some eatery different than our local area offers on our South Side.

Rob is beginning to be my hero. My love for him is rich, deep and committed. He makes little miracles happen and he likes most of all to give surprises. Over and over again he does them for me, his customers and his family. The Store gives him a platform to implement programs that otherwise would be difficult. He keeps an idea before it materializes for he must have been at it for days, weeks or even months. No leader tells all their secrets.

I know Rob loves me. I can feel it and seldom question his abiding affection for me and the kids. If the change I notice in Rob were instant it would slap me in the face. But this change, however subtle, is something quite different.

There are periods when he misses dinner, then goes out with the 'guys' and he is somewhat distant although he isn't someone who chatters endlessly.

The Store

The change is subtle and has the slowest drip. I since it started with the acquiring of The Store and his close involvement and secret negotiations to own her. I expected him to be missing long hours at first. The business had to build momentum. During the course of a work day he comes in contact with shady people, which want more than groceries.

Helen told me something and it gnaws at me. She was jealous of her store, something that can't move, but stands there and waits for someone to operate it. Like a priceless violin waiting for a master to pick it up and play it.

It's like Rob is married to The Store. I am his mistress. But lately there is an unpredictable development in this scenario. Various women Rob comes in contact with, since he's become owner of The Store, have noticed him and they refuse to leave him alone.

Rob is never shy about his affection towards the opposite sex. He likes them brown, black, tall, short, skinny, fat, young and older than dirt. As time goes by he finds that some attractive women make eyes back at him when he makes eyes at them. Now his big brown eyes do get him in trouble and his body goes along with it.

I didn't have to work in The Store. Rob handled the entire operation by hiring his relatives.

Mrs. Fain's sister, his Aunt Louise, we called her Mrs. Johnson, who had helped his uncle before he was murdered. Now, Mrs. Johnson worked the morning shift from opening to 4:00, until the kids got in from school.

He also used Mr. Baker, his favorite uncle, Mrs. Fain's brother, who stood watch over the kids. He was mean, barking at them constantly.

Joe or his cousin George Walls, Mrs. Fain's sister's kid handled the meat case.

The Store

Rob hired teens after school, giving them testimonies that he gave them their first job. Male or attractive females, rich, poor, young or old, he always found them a job to do. Then he had our home designed workers upstairs from the time they were born. He taught them well.

Downstairs was great and improving daily.

I didn't have anything to do with how The Store was decorated. Rob had visitors daily and enjoyed showing off his efforts. I didn't realize the deal I had made staying up stairs. I must have been comatose. Once it was set in stone the upstairs was mine, Rob came out the winner. I didn't have adults to talk with. He had every opportunity with so many avenues of growth all parading through his door. New ideas and concepts bombarded him daily, which afforded him a royal education naturally.

Upstairs I was miserable with the floor plan of our apartment, and its 6 foot windows. The two bedroom apartment should have been reversed. I never liked the awkward arrangement as you entered from the hallway up the stairs.

Next year, maybe, I will carpet the floors, get new furniture to sit on, and upgrade all the appliances. I had complete control of my space. Wanting it charming, but having too many kids, it didn't materialize as fast as I wanted it to. I seldom wanted anyone to visit. I'd meet them at their homes or at a hotel lobby, restaurant, anywhere but my place.

I had the kids and that was it. Up by eight, wash, brush teeth, and braid hair, cereal for breakfast, down the stairs without falling, then pile into the car. I did see an adult now and then. I wasn't able to converse though, too busy being a full time mother. Not complaining about that, but it does drag you down. Then, those lonely nights.

The Store

The first Christmas after we moved in nothing had changed upstairs. Rob and I had everything exactly as Helen had left it. Changing the dark brown wall paper was my first assignment mentally. I screamed at the walls each morning. "You've got to go!" I had to change the décor of our apartment:

One evening watching, Channel 11's Auction extravaganza, we won a bid of leaf patterned wall paper. With so many rolls of it, Rob hired a guy to paper the entire apartment twice over. That was a start. The floors were another challenge; chipped linoleum with flowers and stripes had to leave too.

The second Christmas; I became more comfortable and determined to explore any possibility of making a difference with the decor. I solved it by getting a King sized bed. It changed our love life back to the beginning when we first began having fun with each other. Oh, did we love that bed. I was excited with all the room that bed gave us.

My Christian walk became decisive. I didn't want to straddle the fence any longer. I wanted to be a bold follower of Jesus Christ even though I fell on my face constantly. I was a horrible specimen of a believer.

***

Every woman falls in love with Rob it seems; for one, he's the owner of the grocery store. Second, he smiles, and always knows who she is, compliments everything about her, what's in her purse and how much she's going to spend. He loves them young and pretty, middle aged, wise and wonderful, old and sweet, and even the ones that can hardly walk or come with a cane or walker. He'll have a special chair set out so they can sit while he runs around getting whatever they came in for. Rob makes everyone think they

The Store

are the most important person on earth. And they are. You are too.

Rob's female customers would get a tiny red sticky heart during each Valentine's Day season. His hearts were memorable. He'd place one on your coat when you came in The Store. It glowed, and quite noticed from across the room. Your eye went right to it immediately ensuring miles of smiles. It was a LOVE symbol. That one act of endearment said he cared and that you had contacted "the giver."

"Where did you get that heart?"

"This guy at The Store placed it on my coat this morning."

"You mean Rob?"

"He is so nice, isn't he?"

"Every time I go in The Store he remembers me."

"That's Rob!"

The Store paraded so many beautiful women for Rob to get excited about. They came in the morning before work. They came during the day cooking for their families. They came in the evening after work. Between that, they came just to come in. My husband was no man of steel. He flirted and I knew it. Just how far do you go? I loved to flirt. Bus drivers when I was going to school. I got off and winked. They had to stay on and go to the next stop. I didn't. What happens when you flirt with somebody and they are in your neighborhood? They know where you are and you know where they live?

Little old ladies were a special delight to Rob. He'd take food to them and sit a while over their kitchen tables. Greens, ham hocks and corn bread would come back to The Store in a foil covered plate. Madness. The cooks became younger. The dishes different, more spice, maybe some hot sauce. There are a million stories in that neighborhood.

***

The men Rob knew had nothing to do but bid their services.

"What can you do man?"

"I can nail, paint, and fix anything."

"OK, I need you to fix that shelf over there. Can you do it tomorrow?"

"Yes sir. Mr. Boss, Yes I can."

They call that future 'Craig's List' information. Then he could get a cheaper quote too. He had wide connections. They trusted him, and no one ratted on Rob. He had the food stuffs, the transportation and the money. Time off was his only downfall.

At the end of any hectic day, Rob would grab a beer and then head for his retreat in the big bedroom. Something was going on in his mind as he sat there alone. I thought something or someone in The Store was bothering him.

The Store had begun to nurture him in a way I never could and he acted as if he was coming down from a drug. I was so busy, in gayety, starting to adorn the apartment, getting used to having two kids, and one on the way. I didn't notice that his focus had seriously turned from me, for he hadn't totally changed.

At first, The Store was a novelty but the fun of having things downstairs got stale, for each time I entered his territory I felt awkward, even unwanted. Soon reality set in. A very important part of my life was slipping from me. Like

The Store

a toad slowly boiling to death in the middle of a pot, and not jumping out, my entire marriage had flipped.

Warren was this wonderful golden treasure slithering from me. Then picture me grabbing for anything to recapture him; then see him melt, impossible to keep. Something, someone had captured his attention. I wasn't number one and I felt its sting, enough to make me shiver and shake. The more I grabbed hold the more he seemed to run in the opposite direction. He stayed out later, almost to the breaking of day but he'd come back, not to me but The Store he had to open.

I had discovered him and when he blossomed before my eyes, too many others were waiting to pick the sweet spot that was reserved only for me. He shone like a diamond and I couldn't stick him back in my private box.

My plan, I didn't want to look like I lived over a grocery store and had so many kids. I was angry I liked only the "good" costly stuff. My taste in clothes matched the magazine adds soliciting my attention, Rob would notice if I had the LOOK.

The '70 Chevy Monte Carlo was a delight with the newly introduced racer green color that caught my eye. I rushed home to share the idea with Rob.

It was exciting to drive that sports car and seldom did I ever need to get on a bus.

My body was coming back from giving birth to another girl. She's beautiful and I am happy she's healthy, not my son I craved but delighted that I am back to my original weight. I was interested in my appearance mostly for vain reasons, my husband's affections other than in bed.

I conceived marvelous ways, short of stealing, to get the clothes I craved. I'd post clipping of fur coats, fancy dresses, and designer garments everywhere. Then I kept very busy

The Store

sewing only vogue patterns. Claudette had had the Bug so she would entice my higher calling of a 'Duchess 'n Rags' by sending me lofty ideas with patterns, pictures, and swatches. I longed for years to look like I didn't belong in my area but on the pages of magazines or walking the streets of Paris. I had something on my wall so I'd see it as I passed or washed the dishes; a fur coat; raccoon on a beautiful model, stuck prominently where I could dream it hanging in my closet. I shopped, searched and browsed the high end stores. I no longer ate what the kids left on their plates but let the trash receptacle have it.

But now I was ensnared by erroneous thoughts. This is what I envisioned: My education held me somewhat stymied. I didn't mention my lack of schooling to anyone. I didn't feel I had money, although Rob gave it to me, it was his money, I felt. The feeling of having to ask for a tube of lipstick bothered me, having it doled out like I was a spoiled child. This ever gnawing reality; I didn't have Warren Robinson. Not like before. That man I married vanished and an imposter took his place. Under the sheets he made love regularly. That's what kept me fooled, the nightly affection.

Rob became attractive to women and I could see he had become even more delicious to me. He had spoiled me and I thought for the longest, he was all mine.

I was imprisoned in my mind. I couldn't have him and that's what I set out to do. It consumed me and each year it grew to be an overwhelming desire to reclaim that man that filled my face with kisses down to my toes. My out going personality over ruled most days but when I was low, I hit rock bottom. The bargain I had made with him, that first day I decided to tie the knot, feeling I'd have complete control of him forever, went Poof.

The Store

So on the outside during the day, I looked happy, content and satisfied, and if he went out and stayed late, I crashed.

***

This 'home' dwells within; I decorate it every day in my mind. Disillusioned with everything around me, to hide my dark thoughts; I shifted from my dull apartment's décor to enhancing my body's image. I became conceited. Rob made sure I felt pampered, but that wasn't enough, I wanted his affection.

Rob paid for my indulgencies using The Store to supply my greed. I needed someone to assist me with the "upstairs" I was never interested in.

I found a girl named, Carrie. She went to South Shore H. S. She had long blond hair, glasses and slightly crooked baby teeth. Her trademark: Genuineness; it glowed in her smile and laughter.

The first day she came for her interview, she casually said something I took to heart and never forgot. "Your kids are happy."

"How can you tell?" I asked, surprised when she volunteered that observation.

"Your house looks like they have fun."

I hired her on the spot!

Carrie helped: wash, fold and sort the kid's clothes, set the table, wash dishes, put the kids down and even told them their stories before I took her home.

There were other things Carrie helped with. She gave me a break. I could leave or stay home, it didn't matter. The

The Store

kids adored her, since they didn't play outside, they played games with Carrie.

There were other amenities afforded me in the daily operation of this upstairs apartment. Along with having Carrie as a mother's helper, Rob sent men to mop my floors, and wash my windows.

As the months melted into years, I had money doled out for luxuries: hair appointments, expensive clothes, fine jewelry, furs and leather purses and shoes. I knew every inch of Marshall Field's, Carson Pirie Scott and Chas. A. Stevens. They all were favorites of mine, as I searched all their departments. Then there were trips around the country: Texas, New York, Tennessee, Wisconsin, and Michigan to name a few. So there wasn't a problem getting out, exploring what other females were doing.

But I was missing something in all this: Rob was busy with The Store. I had a problem so huge. I know about Eve, she had everything but concentrated on the one thing she didn't have. It cost her. You know the story. Rob thought he was giving me everything affordable. I had tasted his apple. I had "fallen" and I couldn't get up.

I wanted my husband back.

Chapter 46
"Can I go out?"

I sit in the window and think where does my marriage go from here? Why do I stay in my thoughts about what I had so much? The streets are deserted. I'm smoking too much. She came by today and I knew what she's about now. Mrs. Fain lost Rob's devotion to her and her business when I came into her middle class idea of The American Dream. I don't know how long it took, maybe months, weeks, or days, for her to discern a difference in his commitment.

Most men are habitual. I should have been with Rob long enough to notice 'anything' different and question it instantly. When his name changed, he went from 'Warren,' who honored and adored me, to 'Rob,' who became fixated on something or someone else. I noticed the slight difference that crept into our relationship but I attributed it to his life's dream being fulfilled.

Now, I'm beginning to realize what Mrs. Fain must have felt. She couldn't offer what I was designed give him. Neither do I have the means to compete with The Store. Rob's love interest wasn't a real breathing thing I thought. I can beat bricks, and plaster with a little dab of lipstick. Wrong. I was married to a Rob, who petted, adored and almost worshiped The Store.

I don't know the 'Warren' I fell in love with anymore. The one who worshiped the ground I walked on.

"I'm not feeling you care bout my needs like you did last year." The Store's voice as a seducing woman would say as she whispered in his left ear. Then Rob would scramble to tell her he was working on it. No one was more dedicated to The Store's needs than its owner. He never took her out to dinner but several times I actually saw him bring food in. He'd offer it to her as it fell over on to the floor. "There's

The Store

something on the floor, don't step in 'It!'" he told me, and Rob didn't pick it up either, as if he was sharing it with her.

This is what bothers me now: Thinking 'bout this scenario gets me every time.

After closing The Store, shutting her down and putting her to bed, Rob would go out.

"Honey, where are you going? My voice high pitched and questioning innocently.

"Out?" He said, not to mind what I thought about it. "Can't I go out?"

"Where?" I asked, really wanting to know.

"Why? Can't I go out?" The tone sharp and meaningful. It hurt.

Silly me. He had to get away from it: The Store and all that meant. Of course he could go out. After working hard all those hours, he sure could go. But where? With whom, what for? He could share that the mess was getting to him. Couldn't he say that?

My kitchen windows overlooking 72nd Street began to sting on nights alone searching for meaning. They became legendary, not for reasons to raise blinds for the southern light to shine through; rather they stood for arduous hours yearning for Rob to return. I waited stationed on the bench surrounding our table, crying, and then praying that this helplessness I felt would end. While spreading the yellow curtains, I'd be watching, and then peeping through the night that his car would appear. By two o'clock I had abandoned all notions Rob was innocently at the pool hall, gambling or at some house party. This is when I'd spitefully go down the steps, and direct my way around the dark store. I knew where the Winston cigarettes were. I'd reach up take a pack out of the bin, and then zip off the cellophane wrapper. The fire from the lighter illumined my sickness as I inhaled a long

The Store

slow drag. I was going to hurt him. It was getting close to four o'clock. I was there to relieve the pain but immediately I'm reeling. I leaned over the counter coughing, choking.

I was disturbing his store. Her motors were humming, all her lights resting. She had a day's work behind her and she wanted some peace. I blamed Rob for this agony I was feeling; soon I would blame The Store that I was stumbling through.

***

See this is what I suffer with now, my dark thoughts. Nothing is cheerful when Rob leaves me helpless, crying, and pitiful. I only long for the sunshine coming through my windows. The light: the night, the long hours. Hurts badly. My chest only grabs small breaths at a time. My lungs can't be filled.

Rounds with quitting smoking, and then the pitiful window experience; my sickness with watching, waiting, praying … has become my norm, of grabbing cigarettes all night.

The kids knew I struggled. Everybody knew. Okay, I tried to hide them. That made it worst. The stench of them on my breath, in my clothing, going to church wasn't my idea of victory in Christian living. I had my doubts if I could reach Heaven; my puny prayers weren't getting pass the ceiling. Those cigarettes were powerful. If I went anywhere I'd stink. "Lord Jesus, help me!"

I was after Rob now, a total reverse; he taught me well; I wasn't giving up.

Where was he?

Who was he with?

The Store

I was caught upstairs overseeing kids, and downstairs keeping watch over his store while he played the streets. I didn't have anywhere to go in between, and no one to ask. I tossed in bed. My relationship with my husband had twisted over and upside down. I lit another cigarette. Now I was desperate. Rob came up missing too frequently. My husband was distant. I blamed The Store and then Joe, then back knowing it was The Store's fault. I didn't know where to turn. My clothes, my figure, my new found lifestyle, nothing worked. I can't say how many months this went on as a year came and … one day, I looked up and I had had enough.

Chapter 47
I don't feel what I am supposed to feel

"I have to leave." Making a statement was my ploy to get sweet attention. I had said nothing audible to him up to this point. My mouth got me in a corner. I said, "I want out." In my mind I had said it a thousand times. I had found myself creeping down the stairs into the back of the dark store. Rob was leaning over the meat case starring at the floor or something ahead of him. He turned around, because I seldom disturbed him. I would wait patiently upstairs and we'd access the immediate situation. Either he was going "out" or staying in, depending on his whim.

I had put the girls to bed.

My statements didn't have weight before. Nothing did.

"Where are you going?" this was my famous line and getting me nowhere.

"OUT, can't I go out?" It was his all familiar line having me 'feel' at fault for asking.

There it was: My dilemma. I felt awful and didn't know how to fix it. Rob being the hero of the neighborhood and The Store adoring him as well, and me, asking him another question, the same question I'd asked for the longest. "Where are you going?" And he had slaved for me and the kids; how cruel could I be?

I thought to myself, what's the big secret? This is where the sickness would come over me and I felt 'sicker' even asking him to stay and be with my dull situation upstairs. Heck, I wanted to get out of it too. Maybe that's why I would run to the stores all day. I was sick of diapers, baby bottles and what ever he thought being with me meant. I knew I didn't like the status quo and why in the name of Heaven

The Store

would he like it. Someone had to "watch" the girls. Me. It was deemed my job at closing. No, matter what I had on, smelled like or said.

So, I'd ask again a little sweeter, just a bit better.

"Where are you going?" But the same response came back, firm like.

"Can't I go, Out?"

One thing I begged in my heart to say and I do mean this. I longed to give: "Yes, you can go out and have a nice time." That sentence was my quest. I longed forever to say it and -mean -every -word.

What I did, repeatedly, in gesture – *No way can you go anywhere without Me* – with steel eyes that could kill.

Then, what seemed like forever; the horrible decisive silence; as I stood my ground; -staring, -steaming, -exhaling hot fumes of vapor.

He looks at me. It's my turn to grieve at the window all night waiting, with the pattern of turning it around. What in the Hell am I dealing with?

He always came back to her. I was beginning to think she's too powerful. He would come back to The Store.

~I am reduced to nothing. Maybe tonight will be different. I desperately wanted to have something substantial from him. Having him physically present before me wasn't enough. A woman knows. I found myself there waiting for him to say something. He was quiet, as before. I only heard the hum of the motors as they moaned. Then breaking in, I said.

"I was going to ask you something else." Now I'm really 'dying' inside, fighting to take another breath.

The Store

"I know The Store has you trapped." Then she let go of his gaze and let him respond to me.

"What's the matter Cathy?"

"I am feeling very lonely, -disserted and I want to leave. Rob I have to go."

Is silence golden? Well I wasn't buying it this time. It was awful and he took forever to speak. My mind was racing. I had painted my picture and signed the page. I wanted him to grab me in his arms and carry me upstairs, drop me in our big bed and make passionate love all over me right then. Convince me. I had seen the whole thing in movies. He would love me and no one else. The Store wasn't even on the radar. You asked me what I was thinking those arduous minutes that he held me captive with his silence. I was forced to say something. It was killing me.

I looked around at the empty store. Her florescent lights were switched off and motors purring that gave this melody of calm. I could understand Rob not wanting to break her spell. Her beautiful polished shelves were done. The floors swept clean and the counters wiped with Windex. Only the light from the meat case reflected back against the window pane. Someone passing The Store could have pressed against the glass for we wouldn't have seen them.

I gently inched closer. His arms were folded under his chin and he didn't move a muscle as he stared straight ahead. I mirrored his stance and buried my face in my folded arms and my mouth muffled my voice. "Do you still love me?" It was different and I longed for his response. I would abandoned all thoughts of leaving – if only.

I thought I had said the magic word. "Leave." This alone should, would get him to tell me to "Stay." Our things were going to be special. They had to be. I felt I was at his mercy.

The Store

A total reversal from our days when I held the cards and kept the deck, and now I'm reduced to begging.

My worth depended on his response. It did, I thought. Right then I wanted him to affirm that we were in love. Everything was RIGHT between us. But something was WRONG. I knew it and hated to face it. The Store and what she represented, our livelihood and living over her had come between us. I hated her. I hated The Store. I couldn't say I hated him. "DO you love me?" I had dropped off the "still."

***

I just wanted you to take me in your arms. I only wanted you take me in your arms. Over and over I kept saying that in my pillow after he slammed the door and left.

He opened the door not even coming upstairs to eat. Same old -same old games of putting the blame on me and I was going to Leave and run as fast as my car could drive, far away. I had to. I had played my cards and came up losing the biggest game of life to a man that I was reduced to fighting for.

He thought I had come downstairs to accuse him. Maybe of false abandonment and stale affections.

I had nothing. He had made a move and he was out the door. I thought him cruel when he was fighting too. I never thought of his side of getting away wanting some space, and peace. My sweet spot had turned to pricks and they were hurting both of us.

By 10 o'clock my pillow was wet. Midnight I would stare off at the ceiling and I knew each crevice in it. 2 o'clock, I was up pacing the floor, staring at the bathroom mirror, looking for someone I'd lost. My mascara was all over my eyes and I resembled a bear that I saw at the zoo

The Store

taking the girls. Panda bears are adorable but I wasn't, that lady was ugly.

This stranger couldn't sleep. She was sicker than ever before. I didn't invite her to stay but she lingered all night. 3 o'clock she whispered in my head. He would be back. He had to open his store. He wouldn't leave her. I stayed at the window, watching, waiting. I tossed and hit the pillow again and paced the floor then back to the window. It's no use.

I heard the door open and close. Footsteps up the wooden stairs. The upstairs door opened and I sat up straight in bed then fell over in pain. He was back.

He walked through the living room over to the bedroom. Closed the doors and sat on his side of our bed. I was furious, my heart racing, pounding. He had not parted his lips about his love for me before he left. It was 4 o'clock and I hadn't closed my eyes. I had to make breakfast in hours and he would be sleep in a matter of minutes. He took off his shoes. One at a time I heard each hit the floor. Then he came out of his pants and took off the shirt as I watched him. The city lamps outside gave me his image and this demon inside me, helped me rehearse. Where was he? Who was he with? The joints had closed hours ago.

He parted the covers and grabbed his pillow from my side of the bed. I lay there. He turned over and put his arm over my body. I lay there. He strove closer. I lay there breathing deeply, frozen. He buried his head in my neck and kissed it. I lay there. I knew he loved me. I knew he cared. He was sick with something I knew nothing about. He rolled over and made love to me.

When I was sure he was asleep. I searched his clothes. I took everything in the bathroom light to see if I smelled something. Any tale-tell sign of what happened and where he'd been. I smelled his feet and checked his breath. Nothing, I couldn't find anything. I let the stranger tell me what to do. I had created the monster and she took over. I was helpless under her spell. She was sure something sick was going on and I went along with the chase. One day I'd find out.

***

I left Rob, The Store and everything I have and don't have. This time, my plan: to stay with my mother. She's constantly begging me to come, see where she works as a live-in maid in someone's mansion in Orchard Lake, Michigan.

The girls are with me in the back seat. Its night and the car is packed. Cozette starts reading a story to Annette from the dome light and Paulette is asleep in a cradle propped up on the dash board. I end up smoking every cigarette in my purse driving all night, 237.8 miles, by God's Grace and safely park in mother's massive driveway.

Mom, happy to see us gladly helps unload the girls. I hand her the baby and crash into her bed exhausted as soon as my eyes survey her place.

Her quarters are charming. She's in a one room spacious place downstairs from a beautiful rambling home settled right on the lake. The bath area and kitchen are on one side and her comfortable looking double bed is hugging the wall on other. Large sliding patio doors overlook vast grounds leading to a pier. Mother cleans and maintains the huge house above her while the mother-in-law of the family cooks. Mom would never be hired for her culinary skills.

Mom had fled there six months ago running away from another loser. He was much younger and physically abused her several times. What troubles me are two cigarette burns on her face and black and blue marks still over her arms and back. I've swung at him several times when he came around

The Store

my Hyde Park apartment. I wasn't scared of his threats. But she was. "He said he'd hurt my grandchildren," tearfully telling me that day. "You believe that creep?" He was a true coward but she couldn't see it. God gave her a new start in this place far away and she vowed to "Live for the Lord" the rest of her days. No more men! That's what she told me over the phone.

Mom raised us going to church. My life doesn't manifest Jesus taking over, but I pray to Him constantly, I tell her when we talk.

The next morning we all go to mother's new church. I hadn't found one yet. After service an elderly woman that's beside me offers her hand. Her face is kinda nice and she smiles. "What's your name child?" seeing how sad I was rocking Paulette in my arms, I ended up telling her my life's story, ending sharing that I have my longings to have a son and my husband loving me again. She says something in my ear I'll never forget: "Honey, why don't you ask the Lord for a boy, a son? He'll give him to you. ASK." I mulled over everything she said all night.

The next morning it's still inside my heart. Just ask? No one ever said it that plain before. Ask! Why hadn't I asked? I was having baby girls, wanting boys, every time I got pregnant. I also asked for my husband's devotion and his relationship with the Lord. We'd be a family living over that store. Oh, Dear Lord. You know my heart.

I put down a fleece. Like in the Bible with Gideon's plea that God would show him he'd win a hopeless battle. I asked the Lord to show me: Lord, if I have another baby and it's a boy, then You will save my husband. Now, if I have another girl baby, then Lord, my entire situation will remain the same. I go on and on as to what I personally promise the Lord to do. I finish: to be the spiritual head of our family, memorize scripture, go find a church and get off the fence and more and more rattling's on. That was my conversational prayer and fleece given to the Lord that morning. That was a warm feeling at mother's church, speaking with that sweet lady.

I do know I can't stay forever with Mom. This is the seventh day, and it's murder. She can't take care of me and the girls, and feed us too. She has her own tragic situation she's running from.

Mother understands my pain. She listens to all I confess; of my side, of Rob's, and The Store's. She can't give motherly, sisterly, or a friend's wise counsel; poor thing, her life is a mess. How can she help me? She has made so many mistakes with men. But I am proud of her re-dedication to the Lord. She vowed! No more dead beats! I guess, until the next one shows up. I tease her. But she's emphatic, says it is different now. I'm praying my situation is somehow different too.

I packed my suitcase. I pulled around to the front driveway and loaded my girls. Kissed mom good-bye several times and she passed her sweet kisses around to her three granddaughters, twice over.

I turned the Monte Carlo in the opposite direction and headed home to Chicago full of hope, with a resolve for CHANGE.

That mesmerizing drive from Orchard Lake, Michigan back to Rob that night convinced me; I could not reverse anything, I was hooked, line and sinker. I loved my husband, Warren. I even loved a grocer named "**Rob**." I thought hard and long about my bargain with the Lord too, and what I would do when I got back. I listed them.

I'll do it!

Getting to the Illinois Stateline; the familiar streets remind me I have minutes before I'll be home, doing it.

The Store

Pinching my face, I am not a new person. I don't feel different. I just want God's revelation to prove something with the commitment I've made. Things don't have to be so-so anymore. Having no place to stay scared me. I have to make it work. "**If just for my girls!**" I scream.

The Monte is parked, the key stops the engine; one deep breath, then I make another. So thankful; but in tears. I blow my nose. Make a wish. I can't say it was a prayer, I am crying too hard. I have disappointed the Lord many times. *I wish my husband missed me, would love me, instead of The Store. That's all. Love Me!* That's what was in my simple prayer-wish-hope, petition.

The girls slept through my mayhem. I blow my nose, and then lower my head, my eyes closed for half a minute. "LORD this is serious. I am back and can't keep running like this. Help me –I'm ASKing." Then I repeat the 23 Psalm from memory. I say the 4th verse twice. *The night sky looks so beautiful. A soft blush from somewhere illuminates it; a burst of moon shine maybe? I don't understand the heavens unless; God is telling me everything is going to be all right.* "It's You and me from now on Lord."

The cold air is seeping inside. I must stop this procrastination, release the stirring wheel and go upstairs. I fall back. The thought of lugging all this crap.

Ten thirty. Rob closed long ago, the corner deserted. "Wake up Cozette. Help mommy with Paulette's baby things." I leave everything behind. Paulette is on my hip and Annette is impossible to wake up so she walks up the stairs, one by one, to the top landing. "Don't stop there Annette, go to your bed honey." I tell the sleepwalker. I don't know what I'd do without Cozette, my little angel. Always wants to help mommy.

Yes, I'm brave to walk back into this apartment. I take Paulette and lay her in her crib. Dirty diapers are still in the

The Store

pail. I search around with swollen eyes. Everything is just the way I'd left it: kid's toys, clothes on the floor, our dog had pooped, empty juice glasses on TV trays, movie ticket stubs, dirty towels in the bathroom, and dishes in the sink. Rob didn't do simple things. Will he help me tonight?

Rob is sitting on the side of the bed counting The Store's receipts. The TV is blaring; startled, he looks up, then reaches over and uses his left hand to turn it down.

"Hi honey" I whisper –I don't want him to hear me.

By his sad eyes that never leave me, wants me near him. I look awful from driving for hours. Cozette has gone with Annette. They're both quiet, hopefully asleep. I'm leaning up against the molding to our bedroom. Pitiful and scared I stay motionless. "Rob, I have nowhere to go." I start crying and burry my face in my hands.

"I feel lost."

"Honey, don't cry. Come here." Rob reaches for my waist and pulls me over on top of him. I fall in his arms backward on the bed sobbing. He holds me, squeezes me, and rubs my face, as if I am cherished. He attempts to wipe my eyes with his fingers. "Don't cry."

The scent of his cologne smells good along with his strong arms folding me in an embrace. His head is in my shoulder, and then he kisses my mouth, my ears. I wasn't the cleanest but Oh, God, oh, I am taken over by his touch in all my special places. The very thing I said I wanted: in bed with wild funky love, like we did at Mrs. Web's, saturated in thunderous throbs, so passionate and tender.

I didn't want to say 'no' to something I craved more than anything. Gosh, he's my man; I had sworn to love, and to obey. I also promised, Oh, Lord Jesus –just hours ago, to stay for the life of me.

The Store

***

    I am sitting at the kitchen table and nothing has changed. He always loves me to my bones. The thrill of last night's love making buzzes through my brain. My blue ashtray is almost filled again. The dish water in the sink stinks and my coffee is cold. The sunlight shows up the mess I have to clean. I've been thinking long and hard about what I could have done. I searched the ceiling last night, after Rob fell asleep, knowing I'm not crazy. No one was willing to feed us and house all of my kids. I can't; I have nothing, and totally depleted. The girls and I have grown into monstrous eating machines. Rob's little store downstairs has to support us. No one else will.

    I've cleaned up the kitchen and start on breakfast. It is early Tuesday. I've sent Cozette downstairs to get some milk and bread. I have plenty of eggs and we'll have French toast and sausage for our first morning back.

    Sunshine pores through my kitchen windows, over unto the floor and even the cabinets and walls are gleaming. Mornings are glorious. Silently, prayerfully, I whisper to the Lord all my cares. They try to get beyond the ceiling and out into the blue sky, up into the Heavens, where My Lord can hear them.

    "I will work it out, first in my 'cotton picking' mind. I have to!" It isn't cute talking to myself. My girls always think I'm asking them something.

    I set the table for Rob but I know he can't come up. The girls and I finish our feast and Cozette helps me wash all the dishes, again.

    The start of any new day has its guarantees. There's a Promise waiting for me. I asked.

The Store

My cigarettes are beside me. My blue ash tray will be packed before noon.

A change? Has anybody changed! How can I remain carefree and spontaneous, happy and full of surprises? Rob begs me to be that same woman he married June 12th last night. O how I told him; I long for the lover, the attentive man I had before we came to live over The Store October 9th.

The Store is definitely the third party in my marriage. I could see her slowly take over. She demands more of his time, energy and talent than I do. She ran out of milk. He has to find milk. She is low on heat. He turns it up. He keeps her clean, mopped and smelling good. All her machines are serviced regularly. Rob has her hum, humming. I don't like the new tricks she is playing: flyers, new checks and business cards, vendors of every kind. She takes what she wants. And she is never satisfied. Rob's Spotlight Foods is alive and well. Nope! She isn't going to seduce me.

Rob thinks he runs The Store but that isn't what I see. Friends and customers come in and make several comments on how nice The Store looks. She becomes vain. She has to appear better stocked than before. She has to compete with what any customer might randomly say, and she hears everything: **"I saw a little store over on the North side, Rob; it had a vegetable bin that would spray a fine mist over its shelves."** Oh, did she get green-eyed with that comment. Now she wants her vegetables watered regularly too.

Each week Rob has the audacity to have me fix her up. Ugh! It's nonchalantly mentioned while we're cuddled up in bed that he needs something from me: A large sign to advertise her sale next week. The meat case has to have signs all across saying **Fresh Grade A Chicken .49 lb., Loin Pork Chops .99 lb.,** or he has me designing sale papers; **Sale ends Labor Day!** Even drawing her warning signs,

The Store

"No Loitering! No Credit -- We're crying too. If you don't see what you want, ASK for it!" Then Rob came up with his famous slogan: **Big enough to Serve you, Small enough to know you.** Okay, I do it all!

    I do know Mrs. Fain became envious of The Store as it prospered. She comes over often to check on her son. Meaning, how was The Store fairing; comparing its sales to hers. Location didn't matter. Mrs. Fain was bent on finding out what made The Store so popular with its customers. Surely it wasn't the décor. It had wide isles, clean shelves and each can good was faced front and center. Rob had hired workers that fell in love with The Store the same way he had. You loved The Store or despised her, there wasn't middle ground. Where she lacks, there was always someone around with something helpful that noticed, and then quickly made up the slack.

    The Store had constant request to do impressive stuff to make her look, feel and smell better. Tape, scissors, markers, glass cleaners, pads, mop, broom, rags and heavy duty detergents were always at her beckon call. She offered those things for sale too. The Store was on display and she knew it. She had people admiring her from a distance and she got them coming in regularly by her charms.

    There were too many noises in The Store during operating hours. I notice her conceited attitude more at night searching through her shelves looking for clues. She has a humming sound and motors running under each of her units that kept her contented during the night. They purr a lullaby, coaching her to sleep and leave her boss, Rob alone.

    "Please leave my husband alone." I'd say audibly creeping around headed for the cigarette rack. I really hate her 'hums' when he'd come away from petting her and leave at closing to pet someone else. I thought for a moment... I

The Store

am not even the mayonnaise between two slices of bread. Oh, but Rob is the Ham!

Rob opened his store everyday like clockwork for years.

By 7:15 I would have each one of the girls, Cozette, Annette and Paulette, one at a time sit on a low stool. As they sat between my legs, I would carefully comb their hair, and then tie the braids with ribbons. When, breakfast was finished, by 8:45 I'd drive them several blocks to Pirie Elementary school on 83rd street. I fixed a delicious dinner, waiting for them, by the time I picked them up from school. They bounced in our station wagon all excited about the wonderful things they learned that day. We'd sing or listen to the radio all the way home. My 'day-time' hours were entirely spent on my kids.

***

My daddy had moved to an apartment on 75th Cottage Grove over a liquor store. When he became sick, I'd visit often. I remember that's when he began to slowly confess what really happened to their marriage years before. Some bad things about Mom, as if she was a tramp, dishonest and selfish. He went on about an affair she had with the butcher. I didn't want to hear it.

I remember the feelings I had not being able to tell people to stop touching my baby's hands. I remember my sick helpless trashed feeling in my gut in the Gardens.

I was grown woman now, and couldn't tell daddy to stop the trashing. I'd sit there and listen to him tell the same story over again too many times and none of them were good, as if he was a Saint. I was tired of listening and still stayed too long. This must have gone on for weeks.

The Store

"Daddy… I have to say this today" *Oh, I was dying inside.* "I can't listen to you anymore." *I felt sick and my eyes watered. I had to continue or my foot would have gotten stuck up my butt for sure.* "I never want to hear you talk about my mom again."

He sat there, looking at the kitchen floor. I got up from the table and pushed the chair back in place. I left him there and walked to the front area of his apartment. "Daddy I love you." I hollered before closing the door. I got in my car crying and drove home.

I grew up that day speaking up for myself. I became an empowered woman.

There wasn't anything I said that moved a mountain, but a mountain moved. I stood up to my father.

I never had to tell him again.

***

Finding a church to go to wasn't easy. I had to get serious with my Christian walk. I was on the fence: one foot in the world and the other trying to serve Jesus. I had to keep my promises, but where do I start?

Grace Conservative Baptist Church was in walking distance on 75th and Ellis. I was drawn there and found several people that seemed committed. The service wasn't long and I pondered: is this where God wants me? Later, I told Rob, "I've found it!"

Each Sunday was a delight getting ready. With Rob's assurance, I settled for this charming group of people that welcomed me.

I enjoyed the messages on Salvation, the precious hymns that entered my soul; like refreshing water for my thirst. I'll forget the message but never the songs. I needed that body of believers, because God knew, "The Potter" was about to start. I needed all the help I could get, it was going to hurt being changed and molded and designed as a pipeline God could use to His Glory.

Okay Lord, I've got my seat belt tight. But do I have to?

***

As the years went by I was aware that my husband was unfaithful. My prayers were deep and sincerely pitiful. I cried out to the Lord for mercy and relief because of the loneliness I endured some of the time when The Store closed.

I did have my doubts at first, because when he left he seldom changed his clothes. He would leave by finding an excuse or refuse to give one.

My pain grew, as I became closer to the Lord. I listened to only Christian radio and had my Bible and study notes with books and things around.

We were both holding on and defending our firm positions:

"Your Christian sainthood, it's going to come between us Cathy" he reminded me, one afternoon, leaving to go back into The Store.

"I believe it's going to bring us closer Rob!" was my reply.

I remember in prayer meeting, crying to the Lord one Sunday.

"You are my husband Lord." I had struggled all night before wondering where my life was headed. I lost weight. I was smoking like a chimney. I brushed my teeth and spread lotion all over me so the people at church wouldn't smell the stench. My life scripture came over me. I wanted to post it everywhere.

Trust in the Lord with all thine heart, Cathy. Lean not to thy own understanding, in all thy ways acknowledge Him, and He will direct thy path. Proverbs 3:5,6

I taped this verse all over my kitchen. I had excerpts of it over the sink and on the refrigerator. **Trust in the Lord,** on the stove. **He will direct thy path,** on the mirror over the sink. These verses reminded me constantly of God's Word. All the time my bones were torn in pieces. My husband was actually going out on me with someone else, my gut told me this.

My thoughts were mean and resentful. The Store was in on it. I knew this. The Store was the reason my man was after someone else. I was in so much pain. I thought I'd feel better if my arms were ripped from my body. It couldn't have hurt more. I sure wanted to die. I leaned over in agony, holding my body, so it would stop trembling.

My eyes were red and I looked in the mirror just to check if I was still this ugly person. I was. I'd read my scripture and wish it were so. Trust God no matter what? How could I do that and keep on living in Hell?

Someone that comes in, laughs at the thought of me, and then parades around for him to wish for. **Lean not to thy own understanding**. How can I know that verse is working for me? These are pretty Words that someone pinned down for fools like me to read and trust in. I can't do it. **With all thy heart,** I know that's not true. I'm giving all I've got.

I had to find help. I ran to Grace church and talked with anyone that would listen. It was in my mind. I was entertaining demons; of doubt, hopelessness, and despair. The more I searched The Store, the more I found.

The Store

***

Mrs. Fain came all the way upstairs purposefully to see me one day. She seemed as a "Power House" and I was more pitiful than I'd ever been. I was at my lowest. She had been talking with her son all afternoon, about me. She came up the stairs and stood next to me while I was standing in my kitchen. I thought it strange until she opened her mouth. "So you want to die?" she softly said in her lowest voice; but I heard her well

I didn't know it showed how miserable I was. Maybe Rob had shared my mental state: I had been making his life miserable with accusations, tossing pots around the kitchen and refusing him in bed. I had been making my life ridiculously unbearable. I was into chain smoking, had stopped eating and totally sleep deprived. The circles under my eyes were dark and puffy.

I melted in front of her and slipped down unto the floor. I kept shaking my head in disbelief. My soul was naked. I dared not look in her eyes afraid I'd see no compassion.

"Cathy! Are you alright?" she said with a tone of tenderness I'd hadn't heard ever from her.

My eyes stayed closed. I dared them to open. They were dripping in water but my cries were silent. I wanted to depart this life on the floor curled in my misery. She didn't touch me nor hand me a tissue or anything. Towering over my weak body she stared at me for the longest it seemed. My new found 'Womanhood,' crushed. The pain was unbearable.

I got up off the floor half crawling to the MERCY seat against my window. I pulled myself up and sat down but kept my eyes directed on the linoleum under my bare feet. She came up to help me but I wasn't available to respond. If

The Store

she was a "friend" I didn't hear her. I couldn't forget how we started. All I knew she won. Gosh, I know she's gloating.

I grabbed for my cigarettes. The pack was empty. Any other time, I'd run downstairs pass Rob, reach up and get some from the rack. She saw me needing a fix crunching the cellophane between my fists. I whispered, Lord help me!! I was desperate for Him to answer my prayer right then, please, why is she seeing me like this? Mrs. Fain stood at the spot she found me. "Come on, Cathy, you have so much to live for." She continued. "Why let yourself down like this and quit?" She never cared this way before. Why now? What made her come up to talk with me?"

"I've had pain too, like you... I have wanted to die and I'm a living witness it doesn't last long." She said, lovingly, a total reverse of her stand.

"You have to help self; don't act like this ever again." She continued.

"Rob's father was up to no good when I left him. I wish I didn't. I could have forgiven."

Mrs. Fain knew my pain, she had had it too. The Store had my husband's days and someone, something was taking his nights. All I knew I wanted him back.

She told me slow and systematically how to do it. But, I was hopeless and couldn't quit feeling sorry for myself.

"Can't you see what you've got: the license, you've got the status, you've got the kids, the money, the car, knock out clothes, furs and a body to go along with it. So don't throw it all away for a cheap thrill Rob thinks he's getting. Honey Child. Please hear me." She said leaving.

"Come talk to me later. I have other things to share. Half a man is better than no man at all sweetheart. Don't trash him yet."

The Store

O how I resented those words. I wanted my husband, just like the beginning.

Now, like she said, he made sure I had everything. Just leave him alone.

Well, I wasn't buying it. I wanted more.

***

Rob left. Kids were asleep. Leaving the window, I'd creep downstairs for a pack of cigarettes. I'd see interesting things: notes and numbers spotted in odd places, then other ones, under a shelf, some inside the register; Rob's counter area was beginning to be a place of mystery and suspense. The stranger in my head told me to stay longer, and probe deeper through the mess of papers, cards and pictures. The Store didn't seem to mind me quietly searching from beginning to end that day's activities. I was comfortable in the dark, learning my new found craft. It became a habit. When Rob said he was going out, I said in my mind, me too.

***

"What -are -you -doing?" He slowly said.

I had no idea how long he'd scrutinized the sorry scene with me behind his counter… as he'd come in early.

"I'll be right up Rob." I was taking a firm stance with the tone of my voice, fuming and he knew it.

He left my pitiful position he found me in. It was after 3:30. I deliberately lit another cigarette. I took my time up the stairs and walked into the kitchen. I grabbed a glass from the shelf and slowly sipped some water. I took another drag on my cigarette and walked to the bedroom where he was sitting on his side of the bed. I didn't say a word. I was caught. Learning to keep quiet, I took off my things one at a time and threw them on the floor.

"So what did you find?" He said as I slipped in under the covers beside him. "Whatever you left behind." I could have kept my mouth shut. Five solid moments seemed like eternity and then he said,

"What do you want to find Cathy?" It was 4:34 in the morning and he had had a long day with The Store and left soon after he closed. He didn't say another word. He had a hum when he slept and that turned into a purr. I did the lifestyle searching for what I didn't want to find while he slept. I smoked three cigarettes before falling asleep cradled beside him. I hadn't found a thing.

Another day another dollar. The Store continued plugging along each year with more of her demands. Rob invested into her shelves that kept her running like clockwork. A customer never left wanting something The Store didn't have.

Hamburger would be ground daily and she had fresh caught catfish on Thursdays and Fridays. Normally I would prepare what Rob brought upstairs. He influenced me to cook like his grandmother's southern ways. They called it "cooking from scratch" without measuring. I'd throw ingredients in a bowl or pan using my eye to gage it. My creative talents dominated my kitchen. My dinners were delicious. It was hard not to go back for seconds and thirds and very night we'd sit around the table having family time laughing and enjoying the meal. But Rob couldn't join us. The Store wouldn't let him.

With The Store having everything anyone would want my waistline was in jeopardy. There was another thing called "will power" I had to master. I could have easily gained 300 pounds that first year we opened. I had to keep my weight

The Store

down to keep my husband interested, and did quite well getting pregnant so often.

I also made a declaration to stay well. I realized there was no one to take care of my kids. Mom had to work. Mrs. Fain had her duties at her store. I could do everything possible upstairs while Rob worked hard providing everything downstairs. He couldn't see about me and the kids with The Store and customers begging for him. I had complete control of everything: kids, and the décor of the apartment, even what music played on the radio, so it should have worked perfectly.

Before daddy died I called my sister to get here from Houston.

"Claudette, daddy isn't doing well. When can you come?"

"I can't come now. Maybe next week. Is that ok?"

"You do what you can. I just wanted you to know." Then I added. "He's your daddy too."

"Pleeeze, tell me what's he like?"

"Claudette, daddy is dying."

"I'll be there."

I picked her up from O'Hare. She looked like a model. Her clothes coordinated like she was going to a staged photo shoot. I didn't want to look pregnant but that wasn't possible. I was ugly, pregnant again and had picked up tons of weight.

When we arrived at daddy's apartment he was home from the hospital. Claudette surprised me and everyone. She changed her clothes and mopped daddy's floors, and then talked to her aunts who were there keeping an eye on their brother. She stayed overnight doing what she could.

The Store

I start spotting, only six months into my promise of a son. I call my doctor at Christ Hospital. The girls look so sad seeing mommy hold her tummy going down the stairs. They look over the banister saying, "Hurry home mommy." Daddy is waiting in the car. Rob had to close The Store because I am in trouble, my doctor wasn't responding.

Rob in desperation rushes me over to Chicago Osteopathic Hospital in Hyde Park. I lay there in a cold room checked in 'emergency status' and it doesn't look good. Eleven thirty the baby came but didn't make it. Alone and scared, some nursing staff try unsuccessfully to comfort me. I cry uncontrollably.

Rob and I are together holding each other the next day as a nurse's attendant wheels in the dead baby. We both stare at that image for a long time. Sedated, it's all I remember; seeing our son in an acrylic crib wrapped in a striped towel. Rob noticeably upset, kisses me then later has to leave me that long night. Privately, I don't know what to think. God has answered my prayer. Should I have asked for a baby that grows up to be a man? That's my fourth time being pregnant, with three girls, should I keep trying?

***

My children got to share, somewhat limited, in The Store's camaraderie. Unlike me, they worked the register and waited on customers from the time they were tall enough to reach over the counter. Then, they thought it fun. As their innocent years matured, working in The Store turned into a true hatred of living over her by the time they are youngsters. It makes them resentful of The Store's popularity, for everybody knew them but she and their father both kept them safe and out of trouble.

The Store

***

I tell Rob I am pregnant again before he leaves our bed. My belly gets bigger as my disposition plummets. We aren't even mildly celebrating this revelation like before. My prayers aren't making it.

The Store thrives making money handily for us; chugging along very well, thank you. She tries to tell me often, with our bank account, she loves me too. I must not be hearing it. In anticipation I contemplate what's ahead of me. During the day I'm a Happy-go-lucky individual. The sun always comes through my windows giving a spark to my hopes as I sit with the last drop of coffee. Boy or girl? I'm anxious to wish again.

Over the next seven months I stay absorbed with my girls and stay busy with all sorts of things at Cozette's school. Annette, barely four, tries her best to keep up with her sister's academics. Paulette my toddler cries and complains but we sing her happy songs to confuse her. I do have great friends, Gwen and Janet, and we enjoy kiddy birthdays and outings at the beach.

Surprised, I happily connect with Mrs. Fain. Rob and I have to attend all her parties she has at her new house on Dorchester near 87th Street. We go on family outings and she loves the Dells, fishing for smelt on Lake Michigan with a boyfriend she has since her husband's death. She teases me often that what I'm bringing home is another girl. She's satisfied with Charlotte's 6 year old son, Dwight, who she enrolls in Pirie School with Cozette and everything else my kids are involved in; Dwight comes along.

When the time grows near for me to have another bout with the maternity ward, I'll say this pregnancy was a piece of cake. I fear some discomfort and that's all. Cozette learns to catch the bus to school. It's frightening for her on public transportation but somehow she manages, although eight, better than we thought. I'm just too far along... she's got to do it.

Tonight there's this cloud over me. My husband leaving out makes me sour. It's crazy but that's the only time I'm blue. Days are sunny; nights are horrible. Something else that I must take care of while waiting for my due date: The Blues. They have poured into the days. The more immobile I am, my internal cares multiply: personal appearance, disposition, spiritual commitment, and then trying to act like I enjoy life. I don't have the energy to do anything. Carrie starts doing more when she comes to assist me. Rob spends more time away from me. This is me. I'm feeling so sorry for myself. Pre-baby blues? I pray that's all I'm beset with.

Having a son born to me should have given me the thrill of my life. Yes, I felt great seeing the penis on the baby when the doctor laid him on my sheet the second he was born. But, I wanted Rob to hand out cigars in The Store and proudly share the news of Warren Isaac Robinson III, being in our lives on June 2, 1973. He didn't. I was tired of getting pregnant, losing my waistline, so I had them sew me up, against Rob's wishes, while still recuperating in the hospital.

Rob sure didn't mind more babies and he seems like he would have kept me pumped, pregnant every year if he had anything to do with it. It made no since to me. He never complains about my pregnancies, not excited, but he goes along with it. He knew The Store promised to take care of all of them, no matter how many. I wasn't going to find out. Not me. I'm through. I had my son and thankful. I got my baby the best of everything: Crib, toys, blankets and boy clothes, nothing with bows and frilly ruffles again.

***

The Store

My father was my first experience of losing a family member and my second experience is horrible. Jeff drowned. He was only 21. He visited Mom in Orchard Lake. Her employers had two teen sons that enjoyed their lake front property, especially when guest came. One late evening, they all went swimming off the pier. I got a frantic phone call: a swimming accident, something about a cramped leg after a meal eating Mom's beans.

I loved Jeff like a brother. In his own way he made our lives exciting. He had his view of the world studying history. I accepted this tall sensitive fourteen year old when Mom told me about him. He's rueful she married his mother's brother when Paul relocated her briefly to Buffalo, New York. Initially, Jeff seemed sensitive about Mom living away from her two daughters.

Jeff longed to meet us as much as we wanted to get to know him. I learned to love him deeply as Mom did. Long distant phone calls were expensive, but we made them every chance we got as he kept up with all the places we moved. For the longest he regretted letting us to know he was gay. I didn't care. Every chance he got he visited me over the years and I knew I'd see him in his manhood. His death robbed me. The ache never stopped.

During our last meeting, Jeff bounces up the stairs from visiting The Store and conversing with Rob. His face glows. Knowledgeable of classic fashion trends he forgives my appearance immediately. He nods with approval of my white long sleeve T-shirt tucked into my bell bottom jeans. He had traveled to Europe; romping through it with friends and he was so enthusiastic to give an account of his trip abroad. Sitting alone on the couch finally; it's our time, for we had plenty to share between us.

First, I wanted to give him something deep and lasting: The Roman Road to Salvation. He's attentive as I go through each Bible reference, turning the pages: Romans 3:24, 5:8, 6:23, 8:9, and 10:8 and 9. I tear a few times; but I have to know for sure, that he is a Christian. That one act, sustains me now: making sure I told him plainly, without reservation about Jesus, and that he accepted my faith gladly.

Jeff had a wild time in Europe and kissed a stone or two from the adventures he recalled. We talked an hour or two and ended up with him thinking my kids were cute. Gobbling what I fixed him for dinner and then to visit Mom, out into the night, he left kissing me good-bye.

Mom doesn't stay long in Orchard Lake after losing Jeff. She moves back to Chicago and lands a job working at the Rust-Oleum paint factory in Evanston. She has a terrible commute from where her rented room is; far south on Lake Shore Drive.

Chapter 48
Love never fails, that's what they say

Circle Y. Ranch is the name of a unique Christian Bible camp, settled on a beautiful lake in Bangor Michigan. She takes urban kids off the streets of Chicago and Detroit for a life altering week during the summer. Just imagine, these youngsters existing without a TV, radio, or comic books. Oh, they can bring pillows, teddy bears, note books, pencils, swimming gear, blankets and of course their Bibles. The kids enjoy the best chow experience, three times a day, mingled with nature hunts, breathing fresh air, team sports, tramping through sand, table games and learning to swim. They are told about Jesus during nightly meetings or bond fires. The participating staff adults are dedicated individuals and I am the camp's craft director, dining room hostess or cabin counselor during some of the weeks of July through August. When I am assigned a session, my kids have the golden opportunity to be at camp with me for a couple of weeks, but in their own cabins. Rob adores the camp, often visits and on one of the trips, buys a CJ-5 Jeep, that was located on a farm, near the camp grounds. He is so spontaneous and I thought he wanted some of his days in the army revisited by that purchase.

At the end of each summer season the camp would host adult Bible Conferences. During one of their conferences, Ezekiel Hemphill is captivated by my mom who often attends with me. He's an elderly gentleman in his 70's from Muskegon Heights, Michigan. This man is totally old-fashioned, unlike anyone Mom has ever let near her. While seeing this guy, in the interim, Mom is driving ridiculously long hours trying to make a living. She is popular with her JESUS signs around her work station along with handing out religious tracks to coworkers. Lately, she's been asking the

The Store

Lord for relief; reminding Him how tired she is on her commute.

"Mrs. Herndon, would you come to my office?" Her supervisor says.

"Yes, sir!" She lays down her tools and follows him.

Mom proudly seats herself in his office when she sees a chair. Another coworker is seated to her right. The supervisor continues: "We have come to notice …;"

I'm in my sunny kitchen; with its southern exposed twin windows, washing last night's dishes. Cozette and I are verbally agonizing back and forth over her homework assignment. Mom shows up in our archway. She had walked silently up the stairs, opens my door and stands motionless, smiling. Shocked to see her, I shout. "Mom!" She unpretentiously announces something our entire family will never forget:

"Praise the Lord! They fired me!"

I wipe my hands on a dish towel and cautiously sit her down. "Mom, what happened?" That's all I say. She tells me the entire painful experience of what happened in detail.

"…my services were no longer needed, he said, and my station closed, then, I was asked to remove my JESUS signs, and clean my cubicle."

They fire her… Her positive reaction revolutionized our family's treatment of any news; Bad or Good. It was so contagious.

Then later, we find out what's really going on: A plan, thought out during those arduous hours each day crying about her life's choices. Plus, she wasn't looking forward to another brutal Chicago winter.

The Store

"I'll move to Houston. Live where it's warm." This phone call was from her bedroom at the rooming place where she vowed she'd stay for good ...at least a year.

"How are you going to **live with Claudette**!!?"

Now, anyone knows to get fired: with no income, and I sure couldn't support her and I know my sister wasn't, baby that just wasn't something to Praise God for! But it changed the course of my life, and who knows, who else was affected? For several days she recounts her audacious plan to anyone who would listen. She's firm with regards to relocating, but one person that hears the feint... didn't like it one bit.

It's expensive coming to Chicago each weekend, but Houston was just a tad too far! So smitten by Mom's charms the old gentleman, Zeke, makes a hasty decision.

"Marriage! Mom! Do you really think you want to get married ... again? Mom!"

"He asked me last night. I said 'Yes!'" Her sly smile told the story.

Ezekiel Hemphill, with cap in hand, came in a couple of weeks to whist Mom away to his quaint place far away in frigid Michigan.

Claudette, so relieved about the wedding, flew up from Houston. And she brought her three daughters: Nicoya, Charmion and baby Meka; and with Cozette, Annette, Paulette and little Robbie, they all round out the crew, that piles into my station wagon, for the sweet drive up to enjoy Mom's big day.

Zeke had planned the little church wedding, and their unpretentious reception. We stay around to wish them well then tour her new community. Seeing her surroundings proved interesting: Trees and more trees, stuff and more stuff, house, side driveway to the garage, plus a cellar full of

The Store

treasures only an antique hunter would appreciate. Mom never worked another day in her life. He's loaded.

***

Jealous women do crazy things to get attention. I'm number one in that department: So jealous. I cried tears in my sleep and woke up more evil than ever when I see him run to get yet another item for The Store. She's never asked me to take a shift or learn the register. I knew The Store was only after Rob.

To get wisdom, I call my sweet Uncle Ross, my mom's brother, and my favorite relative in the world. He can tell me something tangible, other than this malarkey, Mrs. Fain told me. I need a man's point of view. Uncle Ross does come over. But he talks to Rob downstairs for hours.

So, would The Store be their main topic? How well stocked she is, how clean? Rob tells him The Store makes all this money, and she has the unparalleled fame of the neighborhood; on and on, to what she does. I could hear them laughing. I listen from over the banister; and I am sick and unable to stand it. Sounds of their gayety reach my ears and I don't believe it. No! O No, Uncle Ross is hooked too!

Lord, is there anyone that's able to escape her solicitous charms?

***

I've wanted my own house from the time I was set out from the Gardens. A stable lifestyle located in a good neighborhood, to raise my kids, with dogs and cats, maybe even a monkey, horse or mule.

The Store

Living from place to place must have affected me because the thought of Rob, ripped from me, sends me into a sicklier 'Panic.' There isn't anything or anyone that has changed my heart; I only have eyes for him. Once I decided to love Warren, marry him and have his babies, the game was over. I vowed on June 12th, to stay in my marriage until death.

The thought of not having a home of my own still scares me not knowing in subtle ways, it was from my earlier pain of abandonment. Those impulsive 'desertion' thoughts go out of control when I see Rob leave. Weather it is The Store downstairs, Joe, George or another woman. In my mind, he has discarded me, when he stays late somewhere. How could I leave? Live in a shelter? Fully knowing what that experience did to me as a child? I can't. **I love my kids too much**!

I am paralyzed now, so many doubts. What looms is not good to mention. I wished I had the strength to grab him with my hands; barring the entrance to the streets, and tuck him back into my web.

Nothing I have been through during my marriage compares to the worthlessness I felt that day I came home to my things set out in the streets. Ever since that day, I have pretended all my life to be deliciously happy. Success or a failure in school, what did it matter? I was forced to enjoy the rejection-ship ride, and scrupulously hide my feelings. They are hidden so deep, even I can't uncover them. They try to surface and I push them down at all cost. Only Rob knows.

Now it's me that let the crap that is around me snuffle out any simple life that I have left. I make a rut, then crawl in and get comfortable. As my daddy would say "Don't waddle when you fall, get up, dust yourself off."

The Store

Then terminating my education years ago, settling for what Rob thought I should or shouldn't do, instead of what I knew to be true for me; robbing myself of 'me' one drip at a time, jealous of everything because I didn't play smart cards, when I had a loaded deck. Now, I am paying for taking the easy way out.

Rob loves me I know that, but I don't love me, how could I, when I'm so horrible, not even Jesus wants me.

Rob never raises his voice, raises his hand or threatens to harm me. He constantly tells me he loves me, by showing it. But I refuse to understand or comprehend it. He waits on me, breakfast in bed and makes passionate love. I never had to fear being on the brunt end of his hand when he pounded a hatchet on the meat counter tenderizing a steak, the precision deliberate and sure. But his same hand caresses me and holds me at night when he's home. Is that love? Then why does it hurt?

***

Rob's nose, that I hated when we first dated, had a shine that never leaves. It tries to out glare the glint in his brown eyes that grows deeper shades of beige as he ages. His hard kinky hair that was once so thick you couldn't see his scalp is thinner. Gray hairs mingle through his head and it only gives him a stately mature look. Go figure.

I dye my hair a lofty blond to hide the balding that I fear will soon take over my scalp. We both have gained twenty pounds plus, enjoying the countless restaurants he takes me to. He swears he loves my cooking but doesn't want me slaving in the kitchen.

Annette graduated from Whitney Young High School and excited, she enters the University of Illinois at Chicago and checks in her assigned room.

The Store

Finally, desperately trying to leave Rob alone –where's he going, who he's been with or whatever, I've joined an Image Consulting Business, called Beauti-Control Cosmetics. It absorbs my time. I recruited everyone I knew, even my mom in Michigan. I've made her look more beautiful than she already was. Just a little make-up and scarves positioned around her 'communication zone,' from her shoulders up, and she's a knock out.

Rob buys a brand new '89 white Lincoln Mark VII and I am using it exclusively. It has a phone inside and it's impressive driving to my consulting positions in various homes and businesses.

During WCLR's radio promotional winnings, Rob and I had traveled first to Las Vegas, then Hawaii all expenses paid. I had the direct number to the station because I asked for it, when the D. J. answered the phone; I complained I could never get through. He graciously gave me what I asked for. I didn't have to dial the 555 the masses used. If I was the correct numbered caller, it made me the winner! I was blessed with everything from movie tickets to lavish holidays. Using my blessing, my buddy Janet won a car!

Rob and I have gained our privacy for the first time since moving over The Store.

Paulette is off to Texas Southern University close to Claudette. I am so proud of her. She seeks a degree in Physiology. She craves better grades so we practice using "Where there's a Will, there's An A" as Rob and I drove the Lincoln to Houston on highway 10, for her first semester. She competed with her two highly gifted sisters, all her life. Although Paulette was brilliant, she couldn't keep up with them academically. But we all knew she processed excellence somewhere inside her. She still fights with Robbie. Both have graduated from Hyde Park High School

The Store

and when Robbie enrolled in the same college, TSU in Houston, Paulette balked.

Annette does well at the University of Illinois at Chicago and stays in the dorm there on campus. She was glad to graduate from the prestigious Whitney Young H.S.

Yes, my children are successful and Rob spends all his reserves on them. We don't have a savings account, 401K, life insurance or stocks. We seem to invest in the kids, his business, needy customers and friends. God was faithful over the years. We have no injuries or hospital stays, nothing major happened that wiped us for a loop, for any of us.

I seldom hear from my sister like before. She's in a beautiful home in Houston, attentive husband, two daughters, and a cat, situated among fantastic neighbors and a marvelous lifestyle. I'd once thought about sending my daughter there, supposedly, Cozette was involved with some rift-raft in our neighborhood. I was thinking Claudette's pristine surroundings were better. It wasn't. I'm glad Rob kept Cozette with us in Chicago.

Chapter 49
Life 101

One morning at four o'clock I was alone. I am 49years old, had celebrated over 25 years of marriage, but it was a mess with my suspicions behavior tormenting Rob.

Mom gets over her third husband's death quickly but still lives in her small town in Michigan. Zeke was: a rock-in-his-chair-back-and-forth-sit-on-the-porch kind of guy. He played musical instruments of all kinds and sang her dull tunes that drove her crazy. For over 15 years Zeke tried unsuccessfully to clip Mom's wings. She dreamt of warmer climates; maybe out west this time, in California, where her daddy wanted to live.

Mom gets an invitation:

"Paula? Hey girl. This is Inez... I'm so sorry to hear Zeke died. Why don't you to come and see me?"

"I'd love to come. When? You still live in the same place?"

"Yes, girl, I live in sunny California!"

Mom gets a plane ticket, packs her bags faster than a jack rabbit hops to the next carrot. While there, sipping lemonade, Mom phones me for advice. She wants to stay an extra day. "...If I leave tomorrow afternoon, I can go to Inez's church."

"Yes, Mom, I would stay if I were you, and really enjoy California."

She stays, has a wonderful time, and even enjoys the sermon. As she leaves the sanctuary, she's introduced to a Mr. Johnson, who couldn't keep his eyes off her. Much to his regret; she's heading back to Michigan in hours. He offers to take her to the airport.

"If you don't mind, I'd like to get you to the plane on time." Flattered, grinning ear to ear, she tells him "Yes" and on the long ride, gives the man her number. He contacts her minutes behind placing her bags down in Muskegon.

"When can I see YOU again?" He says assuredly. "I can come next ... " Then he pauses seconds for her response.

Mom calls me as soon as she hangs up. She tells me word for word all that this handsome man whispered. She finished by saying, "His name is George and he's in love with me." That phrase is all I remember.

Mom had found another man, but I was hurting so badly I couldn't listen or breathe.

Before The Store closed, I did the "unthinkable." I had placed a tape recorder inside our Lincoln. I would push the button, before Rob left, on his perceived rendezvous.

Chapter 50
Still stupid and it hurts so bad

It's going to be painfully difficult to share what happened but it did happen and I'm sorry.

Rob and I passed each other as I'm leaving the garage; the device set on record. I watched him get inside the car, and back his way out of the garage. He looked over at me. I said nothing. I'm so nervous. I hoped I pushed the correct button.

All evening and into the night and on into the wee hours of the morning I sat at my window praying nothing will be on that tape. My pain is the same, but I feel justified. Soon, I'll have proof my husband wasn't out with another woman.

The thought had festered for weeks; the idea came from desperation. I have to know if I am fighting someone besides The Store. That night became my longest. I want Rob to come home and I longed to know for myself.

3:36 I see Rob's car. He slowly drives around the corner. I stare as his red tail lights that indicate he's stopping. Rob hesitates again, as the garage door rises and he drives inside out of my sight.

I listen for his key. Instead of coming up the stairs, Rob goes into The Store. Five minutes go by before I hear the door reopen; he creeps up the stairs. I stay in position at the window with my blue ash tray filled with the stink of hours of lit cigarettes.

He looks at me with a twitch of his head. His eyes are sad. He moans under his breath obviously, I'd been at my post all night. I keep my eyes on him as he turns, but instead of coming inside the kitchen, changes his mind and goes into

The Store

the bathroom. I get up, dump the ash tray and go closer to the door, and I put my ear to it.

I hear water running. I quietly slip back toward the bedroom and sit down in the chair next to our bed. I lean back to wait. I want this ordeal to end. For the first time, I have a motive for him to quickly fall asleep.

When he walks into the bedroom I could tell he was tired and wasn't ready for accusations. He shook his head and said. "You've been up all night again?"

He only took off his pants and laid them over the foot of the bed as he lifted the covers to slip inside. Before I could answer back, he whispered so I could hear him.

"I love you Cathy."

Why does he say that? I keep quiet. I surprised myself, but I have a good reason to stay silent. I want to get that tape and the only way I can hear it, is if he is asleep. Nothing is said. I light another cigarette. My throat is dry. Rob fluffs his pillow, beating it several times before it is just right. Soon he'll be in dreamland. I wait.

By the second cigarette, I have my reward. I hear the purr in his breathing. He is finished with his day and mine is just beginning.

I start on my quest to retrieve the tape. It is time.

My plan is to go into the garage by the rear door through the back yard.

Every light is turned off.

I open the back door. There is nothing about black darkness to frighten me. It has been my friend too long.

I close the door behind me testing the knob and lock so I'd get back in. I start slowly down the steps that lead to the garage. I peer inside and see the car and touch the hood. It's

The Store

still warm. I sit inside where he'd been all night. The ceiling light illuminates the interior and I reach for the glove compartment. It pops open and the precious tape recorder has stopped. I push rewind. My hands began to tremble uncontrollably. Something is about to happen. I stop, take several breaths, lean back and pray.

"Lord, I've got to know."

I get out of the car and tip-toe up the stairs into the apartment to the bed to check if Rob is still asleep. He is just the way I left him. I have the tape recorder under my arm. I go down the stairs, to The Store, as fast as I can. I hoist myself on Rob's counter to sit. Push the play button, ... then listen...

For several minutes the tape has nothing on it. Rob seldom turns on the radio, but if he had, the tape would be useless. Any sound would drown out everything I want to hear. I get up and start pacing the aisles. Everything is dark. Nothing shines except the street light's glow piercing the windows, begging to come in. I don't want a light on. I have to concentrate.

I hear something on the tape. I'm so nervous, I start to shake. The sound is not clear. Someone got in the car. It's Rob's voice welcoming an intruder. The meeting is obviously planned. I hate the casual tone of his voice. My heart is pounding out of my chest. The Store finally can hear what her owner has been up to when she thinks he's upstairs with me." We both listen intently. I can't believe it. I start to scream! **"You knew this was going on!"**

I have to run! I fly up the stairs like a mad woman, crazy with rage and I don't care if I wake Rob. I don't care about anything but myself. I am a wreck going somewhere to happen!

The Store

I find the car keys. I have to get away as fast as I can. What else can I do? What could I have done? **"I have nothing!"** I scream.

The Store and this witch both have my husband!

"Why does he say he loves me?" I know it isn't true. He loves The Store I see that daily. Now this? **"Oh, God. Why?"** My thoughts are wild; it makes no sense.

I, miraculously, open the garage, get in and start the car. It roars like thunder. I zoom out of the garage thinking of nothing but Rob's lies.

I don't remember driving all over the city crying. I drove until I found myself at the lake and prayed over again and again. **"Lord please deliver me! Let me go. Let me live without the pain. Lord I don't love Rob anymore, Lord, or let me love him less. I have got to be released from this agony."** The Lord answered me.

"Love him more!"

"No, No, No! I can't do that Lord. No, I can't do what you ask."

I see the sun come up over Lake Michigan as it split open the sky. I am at The Point, an area along Lake Shore Drive, where countless boulders are laid against the shore and the waves, crash up with billows of foam dissolving the tears of its onlookers. My tears are out there. Some have evaporated in the wind and the rest of them are crashing over the rocks and thrashing the shore line. I sure don't have the nerve to walk close to the edge. But I do want to die. I am not thinking straight but this morning I have something more important to do than kill myself... No, not kill Rob but hurt him deeply, run away to Michigan to start over with my mom. I will live there forever. I want to leave the entire situation and never see Rob and The Store again!

The Store

I light a lot of cigarettes. I sit for hours arguing with the Lord. Over and again He tells me what to do and I can't do it. I couldn't love Rob more. I hate him!

I creep home after The Store opens. Rob is tending her needs and her morning customers and doesn't notice me sneak in, pack and inconspicuously drive off.

I'm on auto pilot and know how to get to Michigan. I haven't closed my eyes in over a day but I am determined to reach my mom.

I left Rob. I am thinking of the last words he said. "I love you Cathy." He is a big liar! I keep screaming to myself inside the car to keep awake. Yes yelling, like a crazy woman, shaking my head, pounding the steering wheel. Screaming as loud as I can;

"Rob! You big dirty liar! I hate you, I hate you! I hate you!"

Chapter 51
Run, run, run but where

I'm almost fifty years old in less than three months and I shouldn't be going through this pain. I want my life to be a piece-of-cake, but in reality, it sucks. I am driving away from what I thought was love. And I am homeless!

A few things, mess up the scene I experienced last night. Something else serious comes to occupy my mind. Unlike The Store; she walks, talks, breathes and makes love to my husband. I know it's over! Rob. The Store. Now this voice on the tape and it's all down the toilet! I am crying horribly and I'm almost sick.

"**Oh, God deliver me**!" I blow my nose and swipe my eyes with the same tissue. I am sick.

"If what I'm going through is labor pains, the birth of a new marriage, then there will be a joy on the other side. Not my will Lord, my puny desires, but Your Will Lord, may this, *%#@#, bring Glory to You!"

"I don't know why I am praying all this. Something I heard. A sermon somewhere? If only my prayers will work, and reach up to Your Heaven."

My mind is racing every-which-way.

"It isn't fair! This is not really happening. All my fears were true! I don't have a husband. I divorced you in my heart last night Rob, because you ain't mine."

The highway is smooth. My eye lids are lead. I punch the radio knob and search the dial. It doesn't help; nothing makes sense, all mumbo jumbo. Maybe a CD? Roll down the window for air? "Something has to keep me awake." I slap my face and do it again, harder. In the mirror, my face looks

The Store

awful. Swollen from crying, my eyes are red. I haven't brushed my teeth or eaten.

My foot presses the gas pedal to the floor: 80, 85, then 90 miles per hour. Scared I slow down. My gauge says empty and I'm out of cigarettes. I pull into a gas station, lock the car and walk over to the counter. I'm so accustomed to running downstairs. I forget cigarettes cost so much. I ask for "Winston's please." Indiana's prices are lower by a dime. I fill the tank of this Mark VII. **"Rob will find I took it! He'll never see the Lincoln or me again!"**

I contact Mom from my car phone at 7:30 my time. She's out shopping and wishes I had better news. She says, "…the front door is open."

***

"I made it. Now the difficult part; confronting Mom with the rest of my story – that I am here to stay!"

"Thank You Lord! If I could, I'd fall on my knees" Oh, how I am sobbing, blowing in my tissue … "if I could, You know how weak I am" driving three and a half hours from my place to hers, I sit, fill my lungs with air.

Mom stands there waiting. I leave my stuff and think of nothing but getting into her arms. I almost trip on the sidewalk and carefully go up the steps.

She looks vibrant, so fresh, smiling at me sweetly. I appreciate her cheerfulness, but, she has to let me rest. She has to. "Gosh, Mom! I am so sorry, I think you'll understand." She hugs me and gently moves me over to the couch. I flop down. She grabs a cushion for my head.

"What in the world? You look sick." She tells the truth.

The Store

"Mom, I am sick." I don't want to share all the crap I've done; baiting Rob with a recorder. And Mom, what I found on that tape is Rob lying about his love for me. What did I do? I left him for good, Mom, that's why I've been up all night. I had to run away, to you. That's why I look half dead. It's deep and I can't do it. The sickness in me, I had to leave. Mom, I am too sleepy to go on. Can I crash on your bed or upstairs?"

She carefully sits there and listens to me ramble on then takes my shoes off, pulls my jacket down past my shoulders and leads me to her bedroom. My eye sockets are hurting, I am wasted, and her bed looks so comfy. I might forget about my pain.

It's near 3:00…

I forget where I am. Oh, yes, this is Mom's room. Oh, God, I feel it; the memory of the tape recorder burns me still. Mom knocks. There she is. She hands me a big bowl on a fancy tray of homemade soup with a few crackers floating on top. She smiles.

She was just on the phone 24 hours ago telling me about this new man in her life. While I am sipping her delicious soup she confides she's in love. I'm not surprised. I tell her as I start going on and on, that I want to stay with her forever and abandon my marriage.

She doesn't mind me staying with her, but she has other plans. That's when Mom says something that put a bummer in my situation.

"Cathy, I'm moving to California. George is going to ask me to marry him. Honey, you are so welcomed here … have my house if you want."

Ever since her father told her his dreams of moving to California, now she wants it too. Her eyes are wide and she's delighted about the prospects of finally getting there.

The Store

"Tape or no tape, give Rob the benefit of the doubt, sweetheart." She says, as she fixes the covers over me, removing the lunch tray. Now she thinks 'love' conquers all!

"Mom, thanks for lunch." I half smile at her efforts. "I'm hurting Mom. I am …"

I'm still talking out of my head as she leaves the room, closing the door behind her. I sink back down in her pillows, pulling the comforter closer to my chin. Ahhh! "Who will understand me? Rob is doing this to ME!"

Chapter 52
Leave all to Me

A week later, I don't think I'm going to enjoy staying in Muskegon, Michigan. I tell Mom not to follow me everywhere I go. I can learn my way around her town. But, I think I hurt her; I know I did. Mom tells me the place to smoke is out back in the carport. I can't dump any ashes in her trash containers inside; under the sink, or in the laundry room.

"That cigarette odor permeates the entire house."

"Don't park on the street past 10:00. Drive into the carport."

I am up with Mom every morning by 6:00 to have Bible reading and devotions; often with heated discussions about the Apostle Paul's ministry on Grace in the New Testament. Later I'm assigned kitchen duties, then house, yard, laundry, and several other important things she wants done in her over stuffed house.

Mom's so funny. She's acting like a school girl talking to George; into the wee hours of the morning, hearing her through the ceiling, giggling. I can tell her marriage to this man in California is imminent. I'm upstairs crying, contrasting her joy to my soon …D i v o r c e! There I said it!

I ache every night to talk to Rob on the phone; to argue about my life with him, what he's done to me, how I feel and what I know I'm reduced to. When we talk, Rob shares what he's thinking, still denying everything I accuse him of. He lovingly says 'nothing is wrong' and stays with the same stubborn "going out" position I left him for.

***

The Store

Mom seems so full of it. She's is in a dream romance.

I want Rob "To COME for ME!" Show up and tell me lies, that's it's all a mistake.

I am plagued with unrealistic dreams. *Head lights are coming down the street and it's Rob's car! Coming to take me back to Chicago!* Several nights go by and another dream: *I open the front door and Rob's there on his knees, with my favorite flowers behind his back, in one hand, candy in the other. He's begging me to come back. He stands there waiting for my answer –blowing kisses.*

***

One month and two weeks pass.

Michigan is so beautiful in autumn; lofty trees hang over the streets: Reds, so many kinds of oranges, yellows; every fall color imaginable to take my breath away, as I go back and forth on my errands. Mom is bustling around preparing for her marriage to George. November 27th is their target date. I am more miserable and she is deliciously happy, singing to herself and telling all her friends she's moving to California.

I try to get into Mom's excitement but I need a job if I'm to stay here. I search the newspapers. I need my GED and go to the Muskegon Heights Adult Education Department and sign up. I meet several people and share my pain with a special Co-Dependency group, and start attending their meetings every chance I get. I find so much comfort, how to forgive myself, accept my situation and create legitimate boundaries. I wait in line for the free health clinic to get examined.

The Store

Cozette is working in The Store, for her daddy full time now and we talk often about my new lifestyle. She says she misses me.

"Does daddy mention me?"

"No, Mom, he doesn't. I'm sorry."

"Don't be sorry honey. That's your daddy and he does what he wants to do."

She didn't want to hurt my feelings and quickly tried to change the subject by mentioning the dirty apartment.

"We need you around Mom. I hate to tell you how bad the place looks."

"Hey, I understand if you can't tell me what's going on." I didn't have a reason to enquire about what her daddy. I knew the demands of The Store. Cozette loved us both and the separation, and pending d i v o r c e, has hurt her and the kids.

"Mom I miss you." She said as our conversation drew to a close.

She mentioned hearing from Robbie and Paulette battling it out at T S U .

"I talk often to, Paulette, Mom. She's fine and adjusting well with her baby brother bothering her."

"When I talk to Paulette she moans and groans to me about her brother being there." I said, trying to sound cheerful.

We both forced a good laugh, knowing how miserable Paulette must be. Having Robbie there was anything but comfortable. He could check on her more than my sister ever could.

Robbie was having "Store-I-est" being away from The Store for the first time. He wasn't able to run at the drop of a

The Store

hat to get his favorite treats. I hated to hear him bemoan the idea of leaving his dad on our weekly phone calls. Working in The Store was Robbie's passion but he was adjusting well to school. He seemed to adapt better than his sister had two years ago. He wants a degree in marketing, a goal to take back to The Store. Who knows, he's bound do better than his father ever did.

***

    I've been in Michigan three months. I'm constantly listening to my favorite, a CeCe Winans CD. My cigarette habit is out of control. I spend lonely week-ends sitting in the carport outside, smoking and praying, feeling sorry for myself.

    As I take a long drag on the cigarette, I rehearse the tape. I think I should stop torturing myself with the recording, just playing it over and over again, when I go to bed at night. Her first words confirmed my opinion of her. It replays in my mind. "What did you bring me, Rob?" she asks in a familiar, expectant low tone that really sticks in my gut. Then a Whitney Houston song comes on and she turns up the volume, so I can't hear them after that. Instead, I am tormented by the lyrics to, '*I'll Always Love You.*'

    Mom is in high spirits. Her fiancé is coming for an extended weekend next Thursday. I volunteer for the task to help make her house immaculate from top to bottom. She even throws out a few pieces I thought she liked to de-clutter the place. Mom uses my artistic talent to make a "*Welcome George my* Love" sign; that's posted on the front door. Mum plants in six quart container pots are placed up the front steps to compliment the entrance. After a few more touches we both agree the house is ready.

The Store

Mom's long awaited day arrives; I finally get to meet her handsome guy. She brings George Johnson home from the airport. Her arms are full of flowers and she has a box of candy. A gold charm bracelet adorns her wrist and it's obvious that he's crazy about her.

George is a charming: he's a medium tall elderly gentleman with sharp eyes and wit. Later, Mom grins across the dinning room table as she explains that the bracelet signified their first kiss. *This is sickening ...I wonder when they'll pick up her ring?*

Mom had me fix smothered chicken, hot rolls and apple pie for his special welcoming dinner. After he was stuffed from eating everything on his plate, the two of them go into the living room holding hands. How sweet. Mom shares every picture she has collected in her family albums over the *years, while they listened to Lawrence Welk's latest rendition of 'Moon Light Bay.' I am in the kitchen alone, washing dishes. I'm thinking how she's boring him. No, use. I hear her famous giggle and he is laughing harder than most men do at his age.

Mom has told him why I am living with her temporarily and he and I get along fine, initially. I watch them leave to go out dancing, sightseeing, to the movies and to any community event Mom thinks she can drag him to.

Every night, she takes George to the Motel 6 off the highway, checks him in, then rushes home to talk with him again, by phone 'til dawn. Mom says she's never felt this way; she exists on pure love and doesn't need any sleep. *I never used to be like that.*

I've had no word from Rob for a couple of days. I am delighted we do argue, if we didn't I'd be loonier and I am twice as sad listening to Mom brag about George for hours.

George is well educated, invested wisely, and widowed from a long-term marriage. He has no children and his curly hair and caramel complexion suit Mom just fine. I have to be happy, that she's finally found the love of her life-time.

Since that morning fifteen years ago, when she declared "Praise the Lord they fired me!" She has been living like a queen.

George is leaving in the morning on a 5:45 flight and I'm glad he came. Mom has paraded him around to every friend. It's official with her diamond solitaire; she's marring the man next month. It was the fastest world wind courtship on record. I witnessed it from day one and know 'LOVE' is Grand!

What about Me?

Chapter 53
Love Lasts

I have the biggest life altering decision to make. Decide to forget my ego, suck up ...really suck up to Rob... forgive myself for being so stupid, and go back to Chicago. Or make it on my own; still, whichever, forgive Rob ... start over, alone at fifty, in Muskegon Heights, Michigan. Self gets in the way all the time. ME!

***

Mom and I tearfully prepare for our good-byes. I lie across her bed and tell her my plans, but there isn't much to be proud of. Looking at her, I want to go back to my early childhood days, in a way. I used to listen to her read me bedtime stories; outside watch the sky, and wish on every star I saw. Then run in and tell her all my secrets.

I tearfully tell her, "I wanted you to love me and take care of my hurts, kiss my wounds and then somehow, send me off to play. But, Mom you are always looking for a man to love you. I couldn't compete with that."

The room is silent. She's looking down at the design on the comforter making circles with her finger around the appliqué. I didn't expect an answer. I know that her marriage to George is the best thing to happen in a long time. I know I'm going back to Rob. I'm hoping and praying that my dreams will come true.

I just witnessed a phenomenon! My seventy-four year old mom marries a rich man. And, like a Knight on a White Horse, he carried her away to live in his Castle in a distant land that she's always dreamed of. Miracles still happen!

The Store

But Rob, had not come for me.

***

I crept home at 55 miles an hour down highway I-94, praying. I feel like I am crawling back on my knees, but I won't show it. Not yet.

I park the Lincoln outside near the curb. Everything around The Store looks the same; the area is clean, swept, windows washed and customers are going in and out. I'm mad at myself because I can't make it on my own: I have no job, money, education, credit, or insurance.

Then I think; why shouldn't I take advantage of Rob and The Store? I deserve: food, shelter, pretty clothes and my family around me again. **"This is My Store, and I'll never be homeless again."**

I exit the car, walk into the crowded store and greet Rob with a smile. I walk straight as I pass him and ascend the stairs at the back, up to my apartment. I am going to be fifty on the 25th of November and today's the 22nd.

Chapter 54
Absolute Surrender

I am an 'Over-the-Hill,' woman, and I announced to my friends and family, my independence and cement it with a change of my name from "Cathy" which sounds childish now. Going back to "Kathleen:" more polish, mature, adult. In my mind it is a start.

This is a big launch into a new decade and it will be different. Will power isn't enough. It's up to Me to make a choice, and I know I need God's help, letting 'self' die. I know that by battling cigarettes.

Next: forgive Rob for hurting me and me hurting him. It's my mind that 'screws' me up and gets me in trouble. I think it, and then act out a crazy irrational thought, without restraint.

I don't like the fact that I'm over The Store again. Reality set in fast.

I will obey the Lord. He commands me to do something difficult and I will do that difficult assignment. He tells me to love him 'More' not less.

I'm in love with me and my needs; instead, I must do what God wants. I can't understand it and I'm not going to understand Rob but I must "Lean not to my own understanding."

***

My first night home is awkward. I start to clean the place. The laundry is all over the floor and the kitchen hasn't been cared for since I left. I look for my favorite apron and get my rubber gloves and go to the window and sit. I'm all

The Store

ready tired looking at the job before me. "I must be crazy to do this, come back to this mess and think I can fix the apartment up to where it's decent again... charming."

After Rob closes he comes straight upstairs. He stops at the archway to the kitchen and smiles, and then leans against the molding, as if to rest. I'm sitting at the window. He must think I'm sad the way I look holding my gloved hands in my lap.

"Are you hungry?" he asked softly, politely after several seconds go by.

"I'm more tired than hungry but I'll have something. What's on your mind?"

"I feel like a Rib-eye, how 'bout you?"

I smile and agree to go with him and get dressed in jeans and a jacket. My hair is a mess. I slap on a Bulls baseball cap, dab some lipstick on my lips. Looking in the bathroom mirror, my skin is rosy from pure excitement of being close to him. He waits at the top of the stairs. I'm all grins as I step behind him going down to get in the Lincoln.

This is his first time he sees the car since early August. He wants to go outside the city to Chili's restaurant in River Oaks. I am quiet as I lean back and gaze out the window. A smooth talking announcer shares his thoughts on the next musical selection. Rob breaks our silence.

"You smell nice."

"Thank you."

"I missed you. You're beautiful, you look beautiful!"

He'll never call me "Kathleen" so I smile and keep quiet. *I like the name "Honey" "Baby" and "Sugar."*...

Rob doesn't talk and I know he has shared his feelings over the phone several times while I was away. I'm the talker and try my best to stay silent for just once. I know his mind is racing and he doesn't know what to say. There are no cigarettes in my purse. Rob stopped smoking years ago with The Great American Smoke Out, and I know one way to hurt him, is if I light up. *I know he wants me back in his arms.* I can't think about it now. Rob adjusts the seats and the rear view mirror and gets comfortable. I smile. He's got the car back. He never let me know it bothered him. As far as he is concerned it was my car. He's always said several times everything he does is for me and the kids.

Mom has greatly affected me. The memories of how 'Warren' courting me; and made me love him. *I didn't want to do it.* A song rings in my head, that it's true. I didn't want to love him. I look at his hand on the steer shaft. A strong, powerful chocolate brown hand and I shake my head. *Darling I love you so much. You are so gentle. Who found my wonderful guy? I thought you were mine, all mine. No one would want you but me. I'd have you all to myself and Wham! Better word "Poof!" The entire neighborhood knows about you: The Store, then the customers and who knows what else or who, I must share you with?*

We arrive at Chili's and he searches for a parking spot. He drives around the lot several times and ends up where we started. Rob opens the door. I look up in the sky and blow a kiss. I'm so surprised at myself. Every tired bone in my body is healed. All exhaustion of the past 24 hours – All Gone. I feel like skipping inside or running around the car. I'm reminded by God's grace, how blessed I am. It feels so good to walk into this restaurant escorted by him. His hand brushes the back of my waist as if he's scared to touch me.

We sit across from each other at a secluded table. He doesn't look at my eyes as I'm searching his. I order whatever I want. It's always been that way. Price is no object when it comes to me. So spoiled, I admit it. Maybe that's where the "fight" in my soul comes from. I have tasted his sweetness and I won't give it up. If we were home, I'd have dinner in bed. Several times he brought me delicious delights to surprise me; handed on a tray. *God I love him! I am doing what You want Lord. I will, I will.*

The ride home –more wonderful. My tummy is full from his plate and I ate all of mine too… and I didn't light one cigarette. I'll get a pack when we get home."

"Did you quit smoking?"

"Not yet!" I grinned.

Rob and I pull up in front of the empty store's iron gate. The interior of The Store is beautiful through its double polished windows. There were a few low wattage bulbs in the ceiling illuminating the shelves. Tonight, the light falls out unto the sidewalk and The Store looks as if she's a Lighthouse standing guard over the corner. There are a few hours left before Rob opens her, starting another day of excitement serving anxious customers on their way. Rob stops the car longer to gaze inside. Does he think I've missed her presence these long months? I missed her, but not the way he thinks.

The area is deserted. Most evenings it's lively. As he turns into the garage we sit quietly waiting for it to open. I gather my purse and reach to open my door before Rob goes inside the tight space. I notice something against our apartment entrance. It's a large package obviously delivered while we were out. A note is attached, flapping in the breeze. Has Mom sent me a 'welcome' present? It must be from her. How sweet of her, when she's so wrapped up, getting ready to be a new bride. I'm surprised no one has taken it.

"Go, get your flowers." Rob tells me. I look over at him in amazement. I get closer to the package, he says is mine. With just the night sky helping me, I read the card.

The Store

Flowers: beautiful gigantic bloomy red roses inside a long box.

"Rob! These really are from you!" I scream when I get inside. Now, I don't know what to say. I have a tug at my heart stronger than ever.

"Rob! Who left these flowers here?" I question. "Someone has helped you with this. They've been outside all this time?"

"They are for you Cathy," is all he says. Always dumb flowers are his way of saying he loves me. "Maybe he called the florist when I went to the ladies room."

That's how I get flowers the night I came home from Michigan.

I'll sleep in Annette's room, are my thoughts. I can be in the apartment over The Store but I wasn't falling for the ploy of flowers or dinner out to sway me into getting in the big bed. Not so fast buddy. I have several plans to get my life on track now that I'm back, but when do I start?

I will begin tomorrow.

Chapter 55
How lovely is Your dwelling place

Psalm 84:1

Rob hires a cleaning woman and together, she and I clean everything. All the clothes get washed, the linen, and she polishes the apartment to my satisfaction. Everything looks the same. The paint on the walls, the carpet is ruined and must be replaced but the kitchen curtains are not. My old station, at the window, is the same. I'm not smoking; I quit last night. Rob isn't smoking and this is the third time I've quit 'Cold Turkey' in three years. Now, a legitimate reason for popping downstairs into The Store, *when I'm suspicious*, since I don't need cigarettes, has vanished.

I begin shopping for stuff I need at night when Rob closes.

Going downstairs after hours is difficult. The Store and I don't get along and I feel uneasy. Rob doesn't initiate a conversation when he sees me come down. The Store seems to tolerate me searching for a can of tomato sauce over on a far shelf and a bag of potatoes and carrots in the vegetable bin. She waits until I finish bagging the few items. They'll go back to what they were discussing the minute I go back upstairs.

Rob seems preoccupied with something on his mind, certainly not me. I don't want to be a pest but want to be with Rob at all cost.

Since I've come back, most of the time I develop excuse after excuse to hang around.

I walk back up slowly thinking as I ascend; *what was that about*? I lay my bag on the table and go to the window and sit down hard. The months with Mom haven't helped

The Store

resolve the 'feelings' of The Store being in cahoots with my husband.

"What are they downstairs talking about?" I lean over on the chair and have a familiar conversation with the window, then bury my head in my arms.

I feel different when Rob comes up the stairs, but worse when he doesn't. The man that I was so comfortable with, that wooed me, has become a stranger.

Later, Rob walks over to where I've been lingering for more than an hour. I look up at him and break the mood, instead of asking what I really want to know. *What* the *^%#, were you doing so long downstairs? Stumbling, I don't know where to start. My mind is still on so many things.

In astonishment, I use a simple conversational tone. I ask him for a suggestion as to where I should attend college. He knows I prefer to go back to school and we start a dialog that's friendly and informative. He begins by telling me about a customer that has gone to a school near us and she likes the college. I ask Rob to find out more about it.

Rob is not distant like I thought at first he'd be. He seems to act differently towards me, only when he's in The Store. Why haven't I noticed that before? Upstairs he's attentive, caring and loving; I can have him. Downstairs she has him.

Chapter 56
Life 102

It's Monday morning and I enroll in Kennedy-King Junior College, after taking a detailed entrance exam. That test qualifies me entrance without getting a GED and I am thrilled. Looking around at my new environment I am beginning to smile at life. I'm so energetic. I have a spring in my step and feel so much better about my future over The Store and with Rob. I've been out of touch with the world and it's my time to soar. My thoughts are to take introductory courses in the field of social work. One day I can help hurting women.

The clothes I'm wearing seem old fashioned compared to the young ladies walking the halls. I notice several styles that appeal to me and decide, Marshal Field's department store, here I come.

The school is teeming with energetic young men and women seemly interested in their educational pursuits. They are stylish and fresh and I don't see factitious activity that inner city colleges are known for. Like everyone else, looking at their syllabus, I scramble to get to my classes on time.

At my age, I look like a seasoned teacher. It's my turn to be an example. I walk in class, look around, sit down beside the young students pull out my things and pay attention. I have got to perform well and think; if I pay attention, do my assignments and get good grades, college life won't be difficult.

Cozette and Annette think I go to this awful college filled with dead beats and I am wasting my time. They shy away from telling their friends, and even this morning I heard Annette whisper over her phone, "My Mom has gone

The Store

back to school and guess where she's going? Kennedy-King!" Several times they've tried to discourage me.

I've made up my mind to follow my dreams. The first one is getting on my feet and pursuing my degree. I tell the kids they are so accustomed to me staying at home. They think I have everything I need; car, money, and a lifestyle of ease, plus time to devote to them. Now I am bent over several text books into the wee hours of the morning doing homework on the kitchen table. How can they know my gut fear; that their daddy will find a younger woman and leave me.

My fears were real in Michigan and slammed me in the face daily. I was convinced my husband had found another woman to live upstairs instead of me.

God was showing me daily where He wanted me to be.

I fell so short in my Christian life. I wanted to serve Him. "Absolute Total Surrender" but the more I wanted to prove Jesus was Real, the more horrible I felt falling short of the mark. God had to break me. The Potter was at work. He was patient. Asking daily, I wanted everything to miraculously transform in an instant.

I was learning to have compassion on the people that beset my husband. I realized they contributed to our livelihood coming in buying groceries. The weaker I became and knew it, the Stronger the Lord made Himself evident my life. Funny the way He works. One day at a time, but it's His time.

The Co-Dependent support group that I grew to enjoy encouraged me to locate a similar meeting as soon as I got back to Chicago. I found one immediately and go every Monday evening and wish I could attend every night, it feels that great. I stumble so many times and they are designed to help me vent. I feel safe in the group talking about my interactions with Rob and this marriage I vowed to keep.

Living over The Store is still shaky for me. I dance the wrong steps; say inappropriate things, pout, slam pots and still expect different results. I cook, clean, say sweet things but nothing works. I make the music stop; then ask Rob to change the record from a cha-cha-cha, as he holds me, over to a waltz. Then an hour later, I run back over to introduce a rumba step. No wonder I can't get a grip on my life involved with his like I do. I can't share openly my fears to anyone in my family. I'm still so suspicious. It's Me that has an entirely new prescription for my future. I am in school, go to therapy, but now Lord Jesus, it is Rob that must change. (See, I will learn one day keep my eyes on Kathleen. She's the only one I have power over. Not anyone else. Me.)

My mind goes through twist and turns on my long therapeutic ride home from my Co-Dependent meetings. I think about what I described during the round table setting. I told the group tonight that I was spread out on the floor with my ear listening through the boards trying to find out whose downstairs with Rob. This sickness is beyond measure. I can't know who comes in; whether it's a friend, customer buying cigarettes or a lover of his ... how can I know? Should I have said what I said? What does Rob mean when he tells me he loves me? The small group listens, most seem sympathetic, but, they are not designed to give direction on what to say and not to say. So, I torture myself in the car on the commute about some of my erratic behavior all week. Lord when will I be healed?

Normally, I arrive back home before The Store closes. Tonight, I hesitate a bit along the curb to view some exciting activity through the windows. The lights are so bright; The Store reminds me of an intimate stage production and Rob is the star. He's enjoying several animated players all hovering around him while others are moving around; mingling as they visit, chat and laugh while shopping. I wish I could be a part of Rob's abundant life interacting with his customers. Oh, but I am still not invited. It's his domain. I'm wondering what his day was like? Mesmerized I stay until one of the players interrupts my rambling thoughts by tapping on my window.

"Hello, Mrs. Rob. How are you?" Smiling, I lower the glass. "Thank you, I'm fine. How's your family?" I don't remember him, but, graciously act as if I do. Danny Moore stays a long time talking with me. Rob sees the guy when he walks outside to close the iron gates. Rob deliberately gets my attention, and then he motions me to drive over into the garage.

Rob tells me later upstairs, as we're eating dinner, that this guy I was talking with held up the filling station on South Chicago Avenue two weeks ago. A mixed-up guy, his mother had abandoned him as an infant. I wasn't frightened but should have been after finding out who he was. Rob tries to help guys by letting them put up stock and clean up at night. Rob thought I should have remembered his face for some reason. There are hundreds of stories circulating in and out of The Store over the years and Rob knows most of them.

I know I need to heal completely my problem of this compulsion: I search Rob's pockets because he's a creature of habit. Also I rumble through The Store, not knowing what I'm looking for, bug the car, check mileage gauges, and seat positions, if radio stations have changed. Keeping the car spotless, I search under the seats for anything, lent, hair, bobby pins, cigarettes, anything I can find to incriminate him. This isn't normal and I'm driving myself mad. I should be addressing my own life issues and what my future will hold, instead, I am trapped still fixating on Rob and he can't be fixed. This madness has to stop.

The minute I think I'm "cured" something triggers the sensation to 'look' and my mind starts sniffing all over again. When, I am actually doing what I don't want to do. I know the desire to stop is deeper than will power Lord.

My self-centered prayers aren't helping. They hit the ceiling and stay there.

Chapter 57
Absolutely Helpless

I attend my new church, Apostolic Church of God, with added gusto and so many times plead with God to remedy my situation. The church is massive and each brick has been blessed. Thousands of people find answers to life issues attending while serving the Lord. Today Bishop's sermon is wonderful, full of insight and wisdom.

Last Wednesday afternoon I went especially to be alone in the sanctuary. I walked down the aisle to pray. Down at the altar; lowering my body to the floor, I spread my arms on the hard floor. There's no outward music accept the cherished performance in my head as The Spirit engulfs me in glorious raptures of harps and organs soothing my lovesick soul. I hum along and rock, shake my head for several minutes sharing inspirational melodies with myself. My eyes never open. I plead with my Jesus to help me.

"Dear Heavenly Father." I start crying. "You know how much I am hurting. You see my pain Lord. I have come to the end of my marriage with Rob and I can't function."

I stop and blow my nose.

"Lord, Jesus, please help me! Let me know You are here ... with me today. So I can go on. Lord, I am helpless without You.

In Jesus' name amen."

I repeat this prayer so many times, begging my Lord for relief. I get up from the floor, I have to smooth my clothes... My body is trembling; to settle down; I grope for a seat in a pew against the wall. While bent over crying I finally open my eyes to experience something glorious. Warm rays of light shine down on my hands folded in prayer. I look

The Store

upward. This light trickles from high in the rafters and its colors are marvelous; like delicate specks of ice, one by one they fade to nothingness. I understand it's a sign. I can go on for another day. I can do whatever God says; just one more day and the next and the one after that. He is with me. Tomorrow will be better. I have a promise.

While at the church I make an appointment with the Bishop. He is dedicated to the Lord Jesus Christ and this church is the largest on the south side of Chicago. I know he's going to be on my side.

It's Tuesday, the sun is shining and the hour arrives that I am to see Bishop at 3:30. I've been praying all night and I don't tell Rob where I am going after school today. I park the Lincoln in the church's lot. A gust of wind catches my dress and the spring time air smells fresh. I slip into a side doorway. My eyes adjust to the interior's atmosphere and I see over in the distance is the office. I walk straight ahead and open the door. The secretary, with her pretty gray hair, knows me and announces to Bishop that Kathleen Robinson is here. I only wait a few minutes and he calls me in.

His quarters are decorated beautifully and he seats me in a big arm chair across from his desk. Silently, I am in awe as my heart pounds inside my chest and I feel I need a tissue for my eyes. The ambiance is majestic and gazing around the room the furniture is warm and inviting, I feel the Lord is here. I like Bishop and feel he knows why I have come.

I lower my head, squint my eyes tight and whisper a prayer of thanks. I'm safe. Bishop Brazier will tell me what God says from the Bible; passages that uplift and give me hope and I am anxious for that to happen. He smiles and begins to speak.

"Tell me, Mrs. Robinson, what brings you here today?"

For fifteen minutes I give my tearful detailed account; except for sneaking through Rob's pockets, the tape recorder episode and running away to Michigan. I am so nervous, my palms are wet. "Rob keeps saying he loves me," I whine.

I'm surprised Bishop has few questions for me, but he points to several passages of scripture in his Bible for me to ponder. He starts with Jeremiah 29:11. *For I know the thoughts that I think toward you, (Kathleen) saith the Lord, thoughts of peace, and not of evil, to give you an expected end.* Also, he reads, Proverbs 3:5, *Trust in the Lord (Kathleen) with all thine heart; and lean not unto thine own understanding* and finally, Judge not according to the appearance (Kathleen) ... John 7:24.

The Bishop gets up, walks around his massive desk, looks me in the eye and holds my arm firmly, "Give your husband the benefit of the doubt, Mrs. Robinson."

I leave his office holding back tears. The bright sunshine hits my face as I walk out to the parking lot. My eyes hurt, as I get into my car and drive slowly away. His last sentence reverberates in my head: *Give Rob the benefit of the doubt... give Rob the benefit of the doubt?* ...another verdict I'm unable to accept.

I scream out, "I know what I know and there is no doubt Lord!" I am hurt. God's decree rings in my ears, "Love Rob more?" The Bishop's words confirm it again. That's not what I wanted the man of God to tell me. It wasn't what I wanted to hear from Mom either when she gave me the same advice as soon as I got to Michigan. *Love Rob more and do what God says. It's against all logic. Love can't conquer all. God's Love can't fix this!* "God, what do you expect me to do? This pain is killing me. How long do you expect me to try?" Nothing will make him stay if he wants another woman, younger, prettier ... I am not a woman of steel, but of flesh.

"I can't do this Lord. I won't, I won't, and I won't."

Chapter 58
Don't question it ...let's do this again

Jeremiah 29:11

Rob and I love summers in Chicago, always have. I want to share with him my true feelings and ask him for a date. When Rob closes we go out driving. Our favorite times are near Jackson Park beach. It's a popular spot there called, Bongo Beach, where young guys bring their drums with nimble fingers and try to out drum each other. It always draws a lively crowd and tonight we stop, linger inside the open Jeep to listen. Simple pleasures are not foreign to us. Later, walking near the water our toes divide the wet sand. Rob smiles at me when I slip my fingers through his. He shares that he missed me after school today. I act surprised. "Oh, you want to know where I go?" We laugh and the joke's on him.

Rob never mentioned The Store. He is attentive and wants to get into my world. I mention the various classes I attend and he starts to yawn. We laugh again and the subject changes when a few people notice him from the neighborhood. They greet him like he's a celebrity. He smiles and gives back some courtesy with a hand shake and some other mumbo jumbo. We all comment on what the weather is like; the moon is low over the lake and the breeze is Hawaiian. They leave us and we continue walking back toward the parking lot.

Then, there is this big question looming over me. It's the main reason I led him out tonight. *Where is our marriage going?* He's so nice and the mood is perfect. The meeting with the Bishop has lent some fruit. I dare not spoil this moment with unproductive questions neither one of us know the answers to.

The Store

    The kids are our favorite subject and they keep us with plenty to talk about. I try to listen as he shares his concerns about each one. They give him a list that he loves to fill. I notice he has a favorite. Annette, can do no wrong. Together we decide what's best and I let him think he ultimately, gets his way. Finally, I tell him I'm concerned with Cozette smoking and he agrees to speak with her during her afternoon shift tomorrow.

    We both have clocks to watch and although he can stay up late, I must get some sleep. I want to be sharp in class by 8:40.

    Driving home in the open Jeep blows my hair and the night air has us both starving. White Castle hamburgers are what we crave, and we get several to gobble on the way home. I stay in a pleasant zone the entire evening. I don't notice, God in the slightest way, is answering my prayers.

***

    Plugging along, I get more involved with school and keep my grade point average above a normal 3.5. I'm friendly and mingle with a few students in my classes and also with some teachers. I'm talking with adults now on a regular basis. They couldn't care less if I'm Rob's wife or - Cozette, -Annette, -Paulette or Robbie's mom. I'm a fellow student; my conversations have nothing to do with my status over The Store. I enjoy somewhere to go each day. My routine is simple. Rob goes to work downstairs and I go to school.

    My hair style changes every day. I have it cut shorter. I'm wearing tighter jeans with easy blouse tops as the weather changes from breezy spring afternoons to smoldering humid days. The next thing on my list is a comfortable shoe style. My size elevens are hard to find and attractive ones are impossible. I want to be fashionable again.

Rob buys me my first computer for over 500.00 dollars and later, a lap top. I get started with e-mails and feel terrific spending hours sending correspondence to my social network.

I knew right away, that there were many advantages to living above a grocery store but it became acute when I started school and had to be away from the house. I had "<u>Store-itis</u>" before I knew what to call it." A condition of getting whatever you want 24/7, all less than a few feet away. Now, I experience it every day, just as the kids had to have done moving away from The Store.

There are little 'Mom & Pop' stores all around and I learn to 'wait' forgo the crave, until I get home, remembering Rob has each thing I need. Holding my weight down has been a major problem over the years. Rob never once deprived his family of getting anything on his shelves. If it was there, it was for us to enjoy.

I felt "<u>store-itis</u>" acutely in Michigan with Mom. I wanted expensive cigarettes, or cupcakes, potato chips, milk, eggs, or bread and got a painful attack a right away. Reluctantly, I had to open my purse and prayed I had enough money.

***

A couple of months go buy and I get further out of control with nasty fruitless thoughts. I can't help myself. I don't trust him and I wonder, but I have conquered the urge to 'look' through his pockets like a junkie, I've stopped smoking for good.

The Store

I count the days, then the weeks, and now ... Bam! It grips me. It starts all over again. A crazy thought. It is so powerful! It's hard not to run down those stairs to get cigarettes. But, I start searching, not knowing for what, as soon as Rob leaves at night. Deliberately, I open drawers, search shelves in The Store, feel inside his apron pockets. He doesn't know I have the key location to his safe downstairs and count the money inside. If I find a mysterious phone number, I'll investigate. Several times I have called a number, keeping my hand over the mouthpiece, listening.

I wait at the top of the stairs leading to The Store… thinking. I've given up the nasty smoking habit since coming back from Michigan; I have put it down for good. I sit for maybe an hour, looking out the window and then I find myself going down the stairs, walking inside The Store. It's dark. Only the meat case light illuminates the polished floors. Why am I here? Oh, yes, I see the cigarettes and reach up over the ledge behind the counter. I grab a pack from its rack. I ascend the stairs, but I'm not thinking clearly. I unlace the cellophane wrapper, place a cigarette stick between my lips and light it and my pitiful face. I suck its heated smoke into my lungs. Within seconds the nicotine torpedoes my brain causing thunderous jolts and delirious shocks. Weak, I stumble to my seat at the window as each cigarette draw overwhelms me. I'm so dizzy, I spin. I sit for minutes overpowered; the habit is reignited. I'll want another smoke after this one burns out. I go down in defeat. All the months working at my fears, trusting the Lord; I feel worthless. As soon as Rob comes home, he'll see my blue ash tray filled with evidence. We're still playing this game. When he arrives, I'll tell him, "Nothing has changed."

Oh, but I must not have wanted change. I'm fooling myself that The Store and Rob are taking care of me while I get my education, get on my feet and able to support myself, so I can run away as far as I can and never come back. I

The Store

stepped right up, got on the Ferris wheel and welcomed this torturous ride by coming back to the very place that hurt me.

I am sick, but I don't know how sick and I don't want to find out since I'm convinced that Rob has the problem, not me. He tells me he loves me almost every day by his actions. He fixes me breakfast, has my coffee ready before I wake up and he's already downstairs in The Store. He's been this way for years. I know this and wonder who has found him? He is mine! He's gentle and patient. He soothes me with tenderness, as his eyes look sad because I am smoking again. That hurts him. I mean it to. I feel justified in coming back here, but where else can I go?

Unconsciously, I am beset with feelings of being displaced. I must fight for my station upstairs where I think I belong. I cling to this place I live, no matter how painful. It is mine and a marriage license from the state of Arkansas proves Rob is mine.

Tonight, leaving Annette's room, the bed I retreated to, I get back in the big bed and slip under my rose printed sheets. Rob enters my space and folds me up in his arms.

Resistance isn't available. The Store has him right where she wants him for now; in my arms. She isn't going to disturb what's happening. She is holding us quietly underneath; just beneath us, so often we depend on; what she is. The Store.

After Rob drifts off to sleep, in gentle wonderment I lay awake beside him, it's so quiet. My eyes get accustomed to the dark. I can perceive images in the room, the high boy, my dresser, the chair Rob loves to retire to and the bedroom I've spent over a decade or two with an entire mirrored wall in front of me, reflecting a mere shadow of a couple in bed together. Down below The Store's refrigeration motors are humming a hum and her scent reaches my nostrils. I dose off and on trying to turn off my head. Every so often a car passes the corner outside. Its head lights pierce my room.

***Trust Me. I'm doing the work in you for My Glory

The sunshine is brighter today, or it's my heart that is filled with anticipation of something happening that's hopeful? I adjust the blinds to reduce the light inside the kitchen. The floors, sink and counter top need cleaning. My broom is exactly where I left it last Tuesday. I don't need to know how much work awaits me with the light showing up the dirt.

Mother is on the phone. I have the long cord wrapped around my fingers and my back is arched in my favorite chair in front of the window. It's finally occupied with me sitting in merriment because I choose to forget what I use my seat for.

I don't hear from my Mom daily since she has become a married lady. She chatters endlessly this morning and I am elated for her happiness but a bit wishful ... still. My thoughts run back to Michigan and her romance I was forced to preview. I don't get the slightest chance to remark within an inch of the interior of her ears about Rob and me. I know she can't conceive where I am, with thoughts about her bliss.

She wants me to visit her new home. She thinks it's big and spacious without a second level and the weather is glorious. She teases me it never rains in Southern California. We stay on the phone hours reminiscing about her new world and how happy life is with her actual wedding ceremony coming up. It's at George's church, in Parris, where she met him that wonderful Sunday afternoon and, can I come? "Oh, sure," I tell her, "I won't miss it. Mom, it will be my first trip to California!"

Neither The Store nor its customers tolerate long periods of abandonment. The only times Rob has closed The Store, it was: our pretend post honeymoon to Niagara Falls the first

The Store

time, then we drove to Houston each year in February to visit my sister Claudette, for her birthday; next it was the family's vacation to the Dells in Wisconsin or better, when we flew to the Marti Gras in New Orleans.

We are in bed and I find out that Rob seems more than happy for me to enjoy myself with Mom. He'd love to go too, but laments The Store needs him, especially on weekends. He continues to amuse himself quietly saying, it's my mother, not his. That's when my pillow, lands and hits him upside his head. We tussle back and forth and he releases it when he finds out I am not giving in. Thank God, no feathers flew from the down stuffing. I lay in his arms out of breath, and we take a moment to reflect. The room takes on a silence I enjoy and he comments on it too. He leans over closer and assures me he adores my Mom, by kissing me several places I will not mention.

***

Booking my flight this morning and making the arrangements, brings back yucky memories of my first trip on a plane. I was flying to Houston to witness Claudette's wedding to McCoy, the man of her dreams. Although it was a sun drenched afternoon, I was so anxious in anticipation of my virgin flight, my eyes stayed in a bucked position.

The airline provided everything for 'first-timers.' An air pouch for emergencies, in case I needed one. It was awkward boarding, for each attendant looked straight at me. I sat down and fastened my strap when the captain said "buckle up" and of course I read all the information they had in case we fell from the sky with engine failure. I searched the stewardess' demeanor to see if she looked scared. But she smiled as she spoke her instructions directly at me over the intercom. I couldn't help but stare out my side window clinching my

The Store

fists tearing the arm rest as the feeling of lift off had me frozen.

I felt unnatural viewing tiny images down below, that looked like toys moving in slow motion and yes they were on highways and groups of houses and entire neighborhoods were visible until they faded out of sight.

I was taking several deep breaths, trying to get accustomed to souring among the clouds, so mesmerized by the sights below but decided to turn my head to smile at the passenger seated beside me. Surely thinking they must think me weird. Strangely, she was looking straight at me. A million things darted through my mind. Was I screaming and didn't know it or were my fingers piercing her and me thinking it was the arm handle I held on for dear life? Her mascara drenched eyes searched mine. She knew I dared not ask her what she wanted from me. It was more than a glance, she knew something I didn't.

Was she someone that knew my husband? At the time he and his exploits hadn't affected me but everything from my past puzzles me now. Startled, trying to act coy I longed to ask the woman, *why are you staring at me?* I turned towards the window, seeing nothing below; I kept in a non-responsive attitude remembering not to hold my breath. I mentioned absolutely nothing to this woman until after the beverage trolley came down the aisle.

The food was plastic or my stomach was still on the ground. The woman beside me cleared her throat, brushed crumbs from her suit, and then hesitated by reaching for a hankie in her handbag. Before she spoke to me, she noticed my empty plate by pointing to the soiled napkin around my chin. I failed to settle down and she more than anything, disturbed me and now my flight status was secondary. Raising enough gumption I leaned closer, planning several openings to start a conversation, but nothing intelligent came

The Store

to mind. What the heck, I finally said "Excuse me." Trying to fake a smile by showing all my teeth, "Do we know each other?" I continued with my eyebrows raised to invade her space by hunching over closer. I wanted to hear her response despite the roaring from the engine. She finally glanced over at me again twisting her head in an awkward position, looking like the Jokester, and then started to mutter as she shyly mentions The Store. For over several minutes she hemmed and stammered about what it felt like to shop there. I could relate to that but she must have me mixed up with someone else and The Store that I know wasn't what she was talking about. Surely.

"My store?" She must be kidding, and *how did she know our grocery store and how in the world did she know who I was?* She had to notice my bucked eyes as they widened with each remembrance she uttered. Then she went further and mentioned knowing Warren. This was beginning to be ridiculous. If I could stand up I would have. Why she remembered my husband engulfed my thoughts that were racing wildly around my brain and I actually forgot I was, x number of feet up in space. My eyes never left her overweight personage and her cheap blouse never concealed her breast that was covered with more than six strands of fake oversized pearls. I noticed her brown hair matted around her fat face that enclosed beady eyes as they peeped over silver rimmed glasses even my mom wouldn't wear. Instantly, I felt awkward seated beside her, but she had my full attention and we conversed for over an hour.

Betty Mae Jones could have been her name: what she wore, the words she used, muddled my mind during the intended festive occasion for the entire time I attended my sister's ceremony. I had asked the stranger's name and where she was headed but she evaded me saying, she'd rather not say. Oh well, that was years ago but it haunts me still when I attempt to fly. What's so strange that that store, my husband

The Store

was a part of and its influence seems to pursue me. I'm glad the stranger was talking about Mrs. Fain's store in the pocket, and not The Store that I live over now.

Rob flies with me most times since that strange experience, and I never see anyone we know. I will never be anxious flying again but always check suspiciously any passenger seated near me.

Since its firm that Rob doesn't care to visit my mom, I asked a close friend, Randee, to go with me. I booked a flight the next week and when Randee and I finished dreaming about the fun we'd have, it was solid; we'd make going to California a holiday. She had several friends out west near Los Angeles, and she decided to use a family resort she had passes for and eventually we even planned a Disney adventure.

Along with making sure Mom was happy with our presence; posing endlessly, taking lots of pictures to parade in Mom's future album, eating wedding cake, finger sandwiches, punch and squeezing into a dress two sizes smaller, that I got on sale at the last minute: The entire California extravaganza was a deal we couldn't pass up. It was hot, the dress made me miserable; I couldn't wait to discard the darn thing and the flight was too long. There was not enough green grass near and around her place and there wasn't one tree lined street to boast about, but her wedding was wonderful –I wouldn't want to live anywhere near Mom and George.

As soon as Randee and I tore away from Mom's festive celebration, we really ended up enjoying ourselves. We tore up the southern California highway 215, and the 60, and beyond leaving the area called Sun City where Mom was undeniably located. We spent a full week on vacation out west, and me out of my over loaded college courses. And it was worth it.

The Store

Randee and I exchanged vows on the plane back that it's going to happen again and soon. There was too much we missed and the time got away from us. We know how to enjoy spontaneous laughter and she found every Lexus over the highway saying she's going to own one of those beautiful cars as soon as she got back to Chicago. She did get her wish, because she was Favored! We never got back to see California together. Later my friend died of cancer and I'm still crying for her.

Chapter 59
How lovely is Your dwelling place

Psalm 84:1

I know I was expecting too much signing up for all the courses but I attend my in-depth Co-Dependent meetings every Monday. But nothing makes sense when it comes down to an unfulfilled mundane life over The Store.

The rest of evening's arduous hours are spent studding for three tests: Biology, United States History and Business Law with a review in Bookkeeping. I have started getting back aches and need glasses to read even the screen on my computer. This is ridiculous, I've let everything pile up like this. I like using a computer. It's so much better than the word processor Paulette had a couple of years ago. I have a seven make-up assignments in College Algebra alone, left over from my trip to California and last but not least I spend at least an hour and a half arranging an adorable outfit I'm going to wear that has everything to do with my future success.

I have to surrender completely. Through a series of challenges over The Store, mishaps and trials in Michigan, finding out that I was hopeless, even my mother left me again when I thought we'd live together. When all of a sudden, my mother, bless her soul, gets a prince to rescue her, just to satisfy God's Plan for my life. He worked it out that I had to crawl back to Rob. I had to give up my quest for control. Obviously, the events in my childhood had built up a wall. Nothing was going to surprise me again. I have to know what's going to happen next.

My biggest scare; I don't know if it's a dream or my vivid imagination.

The Store

The vision keeps me awake at night as I stare wide eyed lying next to Rob. He's peaceful in a sweet sleep purring and me? Not wanting to count each crack in the ceiling, I rehearse the same thing ever again.

Let's say, I have really loss my 'cotton-picking' mind. I'm hiding out and don't talk to Rob for days. Mad at him for not coming home before the sun came up.

Off in the distance, as if in The Store, I hear Rob dialing the authorities and he whispers, "She's upstairs, come get her." Then, minutes later, I hear noise, as if thundering hooves. They are authorized soldiers, like the ones in white coats, rushing up the stairs, busting through my bolted door. Searching, for my hiding place; like I would do with Rob's things; in every nook and cranny.

"Oh, this isn't happening! Oh yes!" Determined, they find me! The grip is powerful. They throw me against the wall, then tie me in a straight jacket, drag me, as I holler uncontrollably down the stairs.

"Don't take me, Oh, gosh, Pleeeze don't take me." I ferociously shout and cry.

I'm pulled into the street outside helpless, where a mob of The Store's customers, with Mrs. Fain, Rob and so many others stand gawking at me, while I'm screaming and then, they are cheering as they take me off in a padded patty wagon, never to be seen of again.

The Store

It's too high a price to pay. Leave my home and still go stark mad? I resolved last week, for that idea didn't hold water.

Placing my empty coffee cup down in the dirty sink, filled with yesterday's dishes, I leave the kitchen undone, like I do most mornings. I'll be late again if I dawdle any longer and this record plays in my head, incessant tunes of; *I'm lost without you.*

Opening my closet, drawers and over the chair, I can't find a thing to wear. The mirror shows me still shedding pounds and I love that.

Nothing looks just right. I have to look especially nice when I pass through The Store on my way to school today. Rob will see me 'sane' this morning; as pretty as can be and he's going to wonder by my head held up and my breast, oh, my chest out, Where is she going? He'll ask. I know he will. He's been after me for a week now and this morning was the best love ever.

"Where are you headed, so charming? Can I join you?" Rob conveys and says exactly what I envisioned and more. The customer leaves when I approached from the rear. Rob glanced over at me, then up at the clock on the wall. He knew it was my time to get an anticipated welcome at 8:46 a.m.

His voice is sincere and warm as he leans on the enclosed glass around the register as his manly chin rest on folded hands. His eyes searching me up and down; everything I did was worth it.

The clothes: the blouse he bought at Neiman's with blue sparkles trailing down the side, my tan slacks with heels to match. I decided to wear my hair flipped over my eye a bit, that I've teased and sprayed to perfection. The Lord Jesus tells me "Our mistakes are like footsteps in the sea."

The Store

Tapping his counter with manicured nails, he reaches for my hand; I lift it out of reach to search my purse; feigning misplaced keys. I'm equipped for all the flattery I can hold. My mind is satisfied, this man that I love, loves me and most of all longs for me.

"You know I am on my way to class Rob." An exhilarated half snigger and then look deeply into his eyes. "Can I have one chilled mamba juice?" He visibly chuckles to himself, and then leaves the register to scramble toward the back of The Store to fetch the cold bottle.

I survey the area, where past hurts originated and nightmares were born. The Store is bright today with rays of sunshine beaming through her front windows. It lights up the entire atmosphere and Rob, the magician he is, has caught its glow. There's not a speck of dust floating in the hue's luminosity. The golden rays bounce off his shelves of can goods stocked to perfection.

The sound of motors humming soothes my beating heart. This moment, no one's in The Store. Alone, a thought bounces through my brain: rush, double lock the door and grab him as he rounds the aisle. My dancing eyes convey my 'naughty' thoughts as I lick my lip: *boy, I'll sneak you back up the stairs, throw you on the big bed to continue our morning wish.*

Some days it bites me, how The Store treats me but not today! I am wishful, hopeful, but most of all forgiving; I get another dose of sweet attention waiting for Rob to hand me the beverage while he takes his time. Blindly he reaches for a brown paper bag from its rack under the counter. His eyes never leave mine to ask; do I want anything else? *Oh, sweetheart, if you only knew.*

"You smell brand new Cathy." He whispers softly for me to hear, as if a herd of customers were around him, and that murmur is just to tickle my private ear.

The Store

As Rob opens his door, I have to duck to pass under his arm; my hair, along with my clothes blows freely from a brisk breeze and the pavement leaves my feet. I don't remember reaching the warm air outside. The trees all clap their leaves down Woodlawn Avenue circling the corner of Rob's little grocery store.

He longs to escort me all the way but some unfamiliar guys are loitering on the corner. My smile is contagious as he hesitates there in his archway. Anyone can tell we're in love and Rob assures me he's my man and he says it's true with more than his glance then pats me on my hip, "See you when you get back."

I feel young, ladylike, treasured and loved. Like the girls walking the halls of Kennedy-King or down windy Michigan Avenue or the sandy beaches of Hawaii. No one could feel like I do this morning; but knowing something was brewing all week. I prayed for this sensation when love songs linger in my head and God is in everything. With each step; I sense his scrutiny, watching me, while he's still in the doorway.

Everything is happening as a long awaited dream has come true. I'll never have to awake and it goes away, as if this day didn't happen to me.

Passing through The Store, he was treating me like I am treasured, responding, tit for tat, like we're courting. The entire morning overwhelmed me.

I skip a step to sit down cradled inside my leather seats, then lowering the windows I stall starting the sweltering car. Where did that blessed momentous encounter with Rob come from? Was it as he awoke, and he held me sweetly in his arms, snuggling his nose in my neck, with me ever grateful *"Lord, thank You. Please, by the mercies of God, can I stay here forever this morning?"*

A brief glance up toward my cloudless sky to whisper out loud. "Thank You Jesus!" … wish I could hang around

The Store

The Store, like a school girl at play, peering through the monkey bars at the 'sweetness' I hunger for.

***

During class, I can't concentrate on the lecture analyzing 'bout my husband.

Tap – tap Professor Barclay wants my attention. "Mrs. Robinson, are you here today?" I straighten up and look up in his direction.

"Yes, Sir." Everyone laughs and I smile and I keep on smiling… continuing my conclusions: this is a major breakthrough for me: *he's still in love and I realize he loves the spunk in me, kicking, out raged and torn up over him.* I smile and keep on grinning. Oh, is that the excitement he craves? And why my *naughty actions* never bothered him; *wild, moody, unpredictable in daily life*, and keeping the secret in bed; *as his kitten* or is it *vise versa*? But he can't tell me what he wants. Its me that has to guess.

He also wants me spared from gawking men: *that what he has, to love upstairs, is private.* He wants me to enjoy my "somewhat baffling" lifestyle he's afforded me.

Lovingly he gives to me and the kids what he can, no reservations. It may be true. My husband has saved me *the daily drudgery* and *countless hours* of working and cleaning and fixing The Store for *immeasurable* reasons.

I have to search my mirror differently.

Chapter 60
What's eating you hurts

The doctors at the VA medical clinic on Jefferson told Rob about a serious condition in his heart. The 4 x 4 foot room was cold and Rob sat on the paper laden slab waiting for the results of a stress test he'd been given.

"Eating the wrong foods" Dr. Winter told him, closing the door behind him. He took a towel from over the sink and finished wiping his hands, then sat down on a stool facing Rob.

"I think this grocery business you told me about is your main problem." It was something Rob had to reckon with ten years ago. Although The Store was a testimony of supplying everyone else with staples, she was killing him. The indictment the doctor gave him was astronomical. Rob wanted to live.

The doctor's words broke through Rob's heart like a pick during an ice storm. Rob and I had been sitting for over two hours in the waiting room before he was called. The nurse surveyed his chart. By the look on her face, he told me later, he knew it wasn't going to be good news.

I was there in the waiting room area an hour longer, reading a home decorating magazine. The pictures were bright and cheerful, like my first apartment in Hyde Park and I still had memories of that place as I turned the pages slowly trying to forget I was in this awful place. The men at this clinic, seated around me, looked twice as old as my husband. They looked dazed in the mustard colored leatherette chairs, placed around the room. I felt relieved that at Rob's age he wouldn't get a death sentence like they obviously have. Rob was having a simple test to prove he's fine. Minutes later, I was called to sit next to the man I'd see muster up a grin as he looked up at me peep inside the room.

The Store

"I got a stiff sentence, Cathy, my doctor will explain." I came in with that remark fresh on his lips and sat down looking straight at the doctor's white coat. They try to look professional but they know how it feels to get bad news, whether it's from a minister attending your last rights or a coach at your football game. The doctor leaned over from his stool and whispered to my husband, "Listen young man, by giving up all the rich foods on the danger list you'll live another twenty years," He stopped with that statement as Rob's face showed promise. He grinned. "You'll live well beyond sixty."

Was he going to do it? Give up the treats? He even had me snacking on souse meat and crackers that had a taste of its own. Rob proved his strength when he quit smoking but his main problem; was eating that junk in The Store.

I interrupted the doctor. "Excuse me. My husband won't eat right and I'm not going to be like his 'mother' and force him to." I asked for a tissue. Rob knew this exchange wasn't easy for me.

"Anyway, I don't see him when he's downstairs for hours. I don't have a clue what he's snacking on." Rob didn't say a word. His eyes glazed, fixed on the floor searching each crack in the marble.

For several minutes he listened to me quiz the doctor about his heart, eating right, and an exercise course of therapy. I wanted to find out what ever I could to understand what was on our plate. This news affected our entire family but Rob had to implement it. We were already reeling from the untimely death of Charolette. She was going in the hospital for a simple procedure and never recovered. We didn't like operations, or hospitals, because of his sister's mishap... and Mrs. Fain's cancer, and Mr. Baker, his uncle-friend. Warren had had enough tragic untimely deaths in his family.

The Store

"Work with him Mrs. Robinson." Dr. Winter got up, reached over and patted Rob on his shoulder, bent over if as to kiss him but offered an endearing embrace as Rob rose up to give a hand of mutual concern when their arms wrapped around each other. It was two men knowing the seriousness of a situation and something between them clicked.

As the doctor left the room I sat there numb searching my husband's face.

"The Store that you love so much is killing you." I said it out loud.

Rob began buttoning up his jacket and positioned his cap securely on his head and we were out the cubical down the hallway leading to the double doors. Several men standing around leading up to the entrance of the hospital gave both of us a sullen look as the bright crisp sunshine caught us unapologetically walking to the car. Those three blocks seemed miles away. I braced myself against the wind, clutching his arm tighter than ever. I tried to keep in step with his gait, and my long coat was bristling in all sorts of directions against the Chicago wind.

A notion to stop for lunch crossed my mind but I dared not mention it. Rob had at each visit to the VA, taken me to a familiar joint over on the next street. He has a nose for finding the choices places. The entire fare: poppy seed buns, his favorite oversized polish sausages sizzling on the grill, onions sweltering in juice, towering potato fries in metal buckets, all you can drink cherry colas or ample strawberry shakes; gets him every time.   I wanted to see if he would make the same decision today; pig out on everything or keep walking. What was going through his head?

The doctor's words were still in my thoughts about changing his eating habits, as we continued walking briskly. We reached the sidewalk's end, waiting for the green light. I viewed our car in the distance and welcomed it, for its warmth, if nothing else.

Rob looked down at me, his gloved hand secure in mine. I bucked my eyes back at him as if to say "What now, Brown Cow?" We ran across the street a bit hurried than usual and shivering still, settled inside the car, but out of breath. He started the Lincoln and drove to that restaurant he loved, as before.

Chapter 61
It's a fun filled package

I am going through a major healing. I have to learn to "trust." This is a major hurdle I must master. I am learning to trust myself too. I put my faith in me as the Lord directs and I stay focused on His Perfect Will.

I will walk out of this pain for good. The test will come when Rob leaves at night or comes up missing during the afternoon on Sunday or anytime I can't explain where or why he's not with me. Then wham! My mind thinks of something stupid and I am helpless to obey it. I am convinced "The hardest thing in life to do is sit in a stupor, totally out of it."

I graduated from Kennedy-King College kicking proud of myself. Rob and Mom go with me all excited for an interview for Governors State University. I entered and enrolled in classes following Paulette's dream of becoming a Speech Language Pathologist. If she can do it, then maybe I can too.

Paulette, coming out of Hampton, is talked into buying an adorable house we find instead of her renting a high-rise place downtown. She's convinced I was right. But the house needs serious fixing up and I find pleasure in making sure it looks like a place she'd find assessable in the Loop somewhere. Rob sends me crafters, plumbers, electricians and anyone handy with a hammer and screw driver to make it her Doll House.

When I got into renovating Paulette's place and left all interest in Rob's business: where he's going, what he's doing and who he's talking to was the biggest REVEAL ever. Even The Store wasn't an issue for me. I noticed a shift with Rob, and his devotion to The Store. It was slow but measurable.

The Store

Looking back he wanted the attention I was giving him, although negative, he enjoyed the sweet/evil/crazy probing into his world and in subtle ways, he wanted it back. He missed me. He calls and asks for dates, taking me out to lunch on my breaks. It's a Wow! Knock, Knock, Anyone listening? Leave the man alone and he ends up wondering Why? Don't you "love" me anymore? Ha aha h hahah.

When he fell in love with me it was real. What took us so long and why did going into business get us side tracked? What's meant to be, is meant to be. Maybe writing this book you had to understand my crazy story. A rocky marriage environment but I had no choice but to stick it out. I guess he felt he was stuck with me or wanted to be. Who's the winner? God gets the Glory.

God worked in my children. All of them.

Cozette was the first to break out on her own and why I have my PhD in child rearing today. Look me up in the Yellow Pages.

Her brief story goes like this:

There is a wall separating two apartments upstairs in our building. Our budding family needed more space. When the wall came down it gave Cozette her first taste of separating from her sisters, with a room of her own. This added space also gives her mom added decorating delights. Cozette never helped. Whatever I place in her room: decorate the walls, placed on the floor, colors of bed linen, whatever, is no mind to her.

Is she my kid?

She works for The Store along with my friends restaurant, Catfish Digby's, and while there meets a young man that she ends up, leaving us for and living with him. Another friend of mine, Corla Wilson, helps me rescue my daughter out of that horrible situation.

The Store

Then Cozette finds a guy in the neighborhood and fakes a marriage arrangement just so her parents will leave her alone. That didn't pan out. She finds an apartment near 70th and Harper desperately trying to make it on her own. Sadly she comes back to stay with us again.

I am notorious about hoarding money and had hidden several hundred dollars in a jar among my spices. One of Cozette's visitors finds the stash searching for something to season two pork chops she was frying. The visitor steals the cash. When I noticed the money missing, I didn't confess to Rob about my secret. But, I was forced to give Cozette her private quarters in the rear. A wall separating the two upper units had to go back up. Now, I hired a guy to put the separating wall in its original position, and it was done overnight.

Months later –Cozette's maverick arrangement of 'Three's Company' became the 'new' thing. They all crowd together when; Cozette moves her old boyfriend, Dennis, and her best girlfriend, Jennifer, into her private rear, one bedroom apartment. Are you shaking your head? I did for the longest. They knew that was a horrible situation and tempers might have flared.

But take heart. Years later, Cozette is the wisest daughter, empathic and a marvelous Christian. I wouldn't trade her for anything.

***

Rob frequently follows me on different excursions just doing the things we used to do. He has someone babysit The Store. Now we window shop on Michigan Avenue and love to investigate the interiors of Neiman Marcus, Saks Fifth Avenue, and Bloomingdales, to name a few. On Saturdays, if the weather's permits have lunch at Ann Sather's restaurant,

The Store

brose quaint boutiques, and resale shops, picking up stuff we think we'll treasure one day. We've toured Chicago as tourist many times trying out the double deck buses, boat rides over to Navy Pier and biking along the lake front.

I start working for Paulette. We'd started her PYR Services company on my kitchen table with a fax machine and will power. Her business is booming. She's hired Cozette as office manager, by taking her away from a lucrative position she had at Motorola Corporation. They were both bent on releasing their father from The Store as soon as possible. They knew he worked too hard and Paulette never fails to leave the house telling me I'm 'sitting pretty.' She thinks I do 'nothing' and have 'nothing' to do with her daddy spoiling me like he does.

Warren and I get extra travelling time when Robbie takes over The Store for his father when Dwight gets a position with an Airline. Our first trip together is to Nigeria. I've met a guy on the Internet chasing a singing group I'd been listening to on WCLR. The group, The Lighthouse Family, sings wonderful songs that I can't get out of my head. Rob doesn't mind me playing their CD's constantly.

While in Lagos, Nigeria we meet Shaggy Kings. He's a sweet young man that worked at the hotel we checked into and he ends up calling me Mama. Shaggy sets up this trick on Robbie to get him into coming to Nigeria to meet Donutz. She's a young woman I had met while there, thinking she'd be perfect for my son. Robbie goes to Nigeria, meets Shaggy and Donutz. Believe me you can't choose a wife for your sons. He ran from my choice. It was an experience for Robbie to see Africa. Can't say he hasn't been.

One of the strangest things that happen: September 8, 2001

On Rob's sixtieth birthday celebration just before we leave for Amsterdam was on a Saturday. Paulette gives her

The Store

father a Big Birthday Bash. She orders a clown that paints faces and the kids' line up under a decorated canopy outside the store waiting to get their faces painted. A "Grand" festive time for all: men, women and children in attendance. Music is playing, balloons flying and birthday cake and food for the entire neighborhood "Rob style."

Then we board the plane the next day Sunday. His birthday, September 9th. We are assured The Store is well taken care of by Robbie. Then we meet Dwight in New York to board the second flight to Amsterdam, nonstop, first class. Dwight brings Rob a birthday cake down the aisle with a single candle and Rob blows it out x number of feet in the air. On wings of Glory jetting to a place we'd never been.

I loved Amsterdam, so did Rob, we're touring the city September 10th. So many bicycles, hooked up everywhere; too many to count and the river running thru the town, Fantastic. Rob got to see the ladies in cubicles waiting for Johns to bid their services too. Prostitution is legal there.

We check in a hotel that evening full of food and merriment. Dwight had everything ready for us. The next day, early in the morning, we decide to leave to head on back to Chicago. Nothing was wrong with The Store, but we're not fond of going nonstop into New York again. We choose an earlier flight nonstop into Atlanta. We tell Dwight we're leaving and he understands. Holland is known for flowers and Rob buys me an arm full. Several bunches, so many I can hardly carry them, while we wait to board the bus to the airport...

On the flight back we notice a difference in the direction of the plane. It's been diverted to Nova Scotia, Canada. The German woman I am seated next to tells me it's not supposed to be. "Something is seriously wrong." She says. Rob and I aren't seated together and on this first class arrangement we couldn't get twin seats. Well, I meet this

The Store

German lady and we become "close" friends. We don't know the Twin Towers in New York has been hit and the horror of 911 is in full force. In fact no one on the plane is told what happened. We're in the air and nowhere to land our plane but in Canada.

Landing we stay in a holding pattern on the landing strip for hundreds of planes are stranded. We're searched like criminals and dogs are going through our luggage. We get to a bingo hall and a lady walks up to Rob and asked if she could house him at her home. He says sure. But first let me ask my wife. The lady I'm with can't be left alone I tell my husband. Go ask the head social worker if she can house three of us?

This lady is an angel because not only does she house us, she takes complete care of us for three days until the sky opens up and the USA officials lets us fly again. Her name? Veronica Murphy. She has a wonderful husband Eric, who moved heaven and earth for us and two beautiful daughters, Jasmine and Nadine, that adjusted their lives totally. They are a Christian family and take my German friend, Sabine in like she's family too. The next year we go to Disney World to celebrate our new blended family and Rob loves the theme park. Nothing like it.

Chapter 62
24 Hours

Rob agreed to move to Paulette's house and I am still reeling from the thought. Paulette for weeks had begged her father to try it, take over her house and let her move downtown into a high rise somewhere on Michigan Avenue. We started packing and moving some smaller things and it's going to be a hushed transition. Even The Store might not know Rob's plan. We kissed and had a toast over the prospects of living together far away from anything we're accustomed to. We made love and it was surely the last night we'll be here over The Store.

I love it when a day starts out full and promising. Something sparked the air along with the sunshine this Saturday morning.

I just happened to look out, while adjusting my blinds, at my bedroom window overlooking 72nd street and Rob is talking to a woman on the corner. The lady was pointing over in the direction of Horde Park, one block west of our place. I later found out that Ms. Becky, a neighborhood organizer, was heading up her first Christian Outreach Rally. She commandeered a huge stage, sound equipment, an hundred white chairs and a large covering, making area look so North Side; all donated from the city of Chicago. She wanted The Store to join in on the excitement and to get free publicity. First, Rob offered a bike to raffle off for his Audi 4 marching group, which started in 1988 with Veronica coming in to ask if Rob would sponsor her marchers. That started them marching in the parade and Rob's love affair with the group. Everyone was excited about that, then he gave her food and beverages and whatever else she needed, to make her affair successful. He favored religious gatherings for JESUS and this was destined to become the largest Christian event our little neighborhood had ever seen. Customers were motivated to buy more than ever before as if everyone needed to get in on the revelry.

Rob has the great idea of cooking Bar-B-Q ribs. Exhausted he comes upstairs and falls asleep in the bedroom after asking Cozette's boyfriend Darron to finish grilling for him. What makes it significant, Rob never gives anyone permission to do steaks, chops and sausages, on his personal Weber grill anchored on our upstairs deck. Darron gets the prestige of using our grill for the first time and he does a great job.

Rob wakes up startled when he hears a man's voice and rushed from the bedroom to investigate. While at the rally had I invited Donald Raickett's son, Stephen, a Christian comic, scheduled to be on the program, up to our place. We were talking and looking at my computer when Rob heard him. It was a man's voice and that alarmed him right away!

After Stephen left Rob seemed concerned about something. Maybe he still wasn't feeling well, a little drowsy I thought. But I became really surprised when he mentioned he'd like to see Robbie take over The Store for a year. "Cathy he's so pig headed, I'd like to see what he would do." I had learned to listen when Rob discussed his kids. He thought they shouldn't get paid as much since he supported them. All of them had to work downstairs at one time. They ate free and had a roof over their heads plus use of the car. He rambled on some more about what young people now days thought and what happened when he was growing up. "But that's why they're all gone. We charged them rent Rob." We laughed, then he hurried back downstairs, someone had called him. I walked back over to the park and found a chair in the shade. I had felt so awkward earlier trying, unsuccessfully to sell tickets for the Audi 4 raffle.

The Store

The Rally's sound system generated Heavenly music throughout the day. It could be heard over the entire area for blocks. The merriment was contagious. The delightful line up of various pastors, speakers, singers, and bands of every size and description were used on the program Ms. Becky provided. All primed and designed to introduce the love of Jesus to the crowd. The people continued to bring over their private picnic baskets, blankets to spread over the grass, with tables, chairs, and big sun umbrellas. And the food was plentiful: tuna fish sandwiches, fried chicken, potato salads, and corn on the cob. Ice cream trucks paraded up and down the streets ringing their special chimes.

As evening came the crowd became overwhelming. I phoned The Store. Rob answered with a jovial, "Yo." I told him the raffle was ready and everyone was eager for him to announce the winner. He said he'd close early and come by 7:00PM. I told him he'd find us gathered under the largest tree.

I could see Rob from a half block away. Lord knows, I was so spittin' proud of him. I sat back beaming at his demeanor: the way he walked, so self-assured with his body language that I never grew tired of. The pride in each step, for he owned this entire arena he helped to create.

He stopped his proceedings, every now and then, with a smile and requests the purchase of his tickets. The way he does it was purely Rob, with the charm we all knew. "You look like a 5 dollar ticket." He told one woman, as she grinned up at him, probing an apron pocket for her dollars. "You've got 2 dollars don't you, for this winning ticket?" to another sweet soul smiling back at him, quickly giving Rob the money, just because he said her bike was almost won. It's considered a proud pleasing privilege to give Rob whatever he asked for.

The Store

Rob enjoyed all exchanges with his customers and total strangers; it made no difference to him. They were sucked into his enchanted web; he didn't realize he had over them. I sat there smiling, watching him weave among the crowd. His mind was on his Audi 4 dance group performing in the Bud Billiken Parade the second week in August. Their new outfits would represent The Store.

The atmosphere of cheers and laughter all over the grounds never stopped. Seems everyone was there, it was the place to be. A day like no other with drums, tambourines and entertainers that kept on performing. It was a true spiritual awakening. A few tears on tissues could be found too as ministers gave their speeches, sermons and testimonies about the Lord and His Grace.

Now the time came for the stage to introduce the man they all knew and loved. The announcer gave the preliminary introduction: Rob, humbly with his famous grin that he tried so badly to hide; carefully stepped up on the platform to speak to the audience of admirers.

There was a hush of silence over the crowd. Every eye was on him. He nervously took the microphone to his lips and cleared his throat, then waited for the whistles to subside…

That speech was a tribute to the customers of Rob's Spotlite Foods on the corner since 1969. He tried not to stumble with thoughts impromptu; to recall all he had to say; to each one and their meaning to him and his family over the years. His gratitude was evident, as he told of his sacrifice, struggles and victories. The rays of a perfect sunset caught his moist brow. The glow engulfed his head, as a halo, as he spoke. He made mentioned of his Audi 4 group that danced in the parade and his focus on their raffle was only to raise funds for each participant. Rob had given from his heart and those beats inside was sure to continue each year. I love the

The Store

Lord and I find it fitting that this occasion is without a doubt, what our neighborhood needs more of. He stammered to find more words to share. Then he smiled again his chuckle, and bid a fond farewell with a towering broad wave of his brown hand, so wide for all to see. It had to reach to the back areas and also to his closest fans, standing underneath the stage, looking up at his sincere tear stained face. Then he turned respectfully to his son, "He's going to take over." Rob said with pride, that he had a son, that "He can do the same job or even better at doing the raffle; Warren I. Robinson III." Then Rob did another chuckle twice. "Here is my son!" and passed over the microphone.

Robbie moved closer, next to his dad. With a hearty "Thanks Dad" with an embrace of warmth, he grabbed the mic and smiling, thanked his dad again.

"Did you all get your tickets? And then waved the mic in the air, "Let this little one pull the ticket." pointing the mic to a cute youngster in the front row. "On behalf of The Store, she will give, …a lucky member of this audience, …the Bike!!" And with new found confidence with his father still on stage, Robbie announced the winning ticket from the little girl's hand. "And the winner is: Mrs. Kinnard, you know her; she's the pillar of our neighborhood. Hey, Mrs. Kinnard gets a beautiful Mountain Terrain Bike!" All applauded wildly and Mrs. Kinnard was more surprised than anyone with her $2.00 raffle ticket she waved high in the air.

Some people in the crowd still lingered around Rob. They had to mention what a great time they were having and his speech made them grateful he belonged to their neighborhood. "We love you Rob." A customer hovers close and says. "Rob you've had a colorful life, and know everything. You should write a book." Rob says: I'm looking forward to my 60th decade –what God has for me – I'm married to Cathy, now that's a book, I'll let her write it."

The Store

"You married? Then yoYou've got all it takes to make a best seller."

My cousin Margie Hale and her brother Dicky had come for the festivities. I was going to take them with me to show them our new place over Paulette's house. We got packed and ready to leave.

In the car ride, Rob drove with our cousins in the back seat enjoying the ride in my new black Jeep. Everyone wanted to reflect on the marvelous time our whole day turned out to be. But Rob stayed extremely quiet, focused on the road.

We filed into Paulette's kitchen still laughing, reminiscing about our family and the rich history we shared. Each of us pulled out a chair and sat around Paulette's big round table. You could hear me louder than everyone, mostly glad Audi 4's raffle was over. I couldn't sell a single ticket. As usual, Rob excused himself to rest and walked towards the fireplace room in the rear of the house. I continued to talk to my cousins and share their lives as we went back and forth, until they left an hour later.

I closed the front door. Now, more than ever, I'm missing my sweet husband. And I wanted to know where he had gone, yep, still stretched on the sofa where he said he'd go, looking so peaceful, with his eyes closed. He had his hands crossed over his chest, his clothes unperturbed and perfect. I leaned over next to his ear, letting the scent of his cologne fill my nostrils. *I love him so much dear Lord, Thank You.*

I gently whispered, "It's time for us to go up to bed." I hated to disturb his rest. Rob opened his eyes, looked around and then spread his lips wide. I'm close to him with my face in his. With raised eyebrows, we're still welcoming the idea of being together in our new home.

The Store

He raided the refrigerator and fixed a sandwich and some chips with a tall glass of red punch and a slice of cake. He gobbled the cake and placed the rest of the food on a saucer. I watched him do all this patiently standing next to the pantry. He slowly finished cleaning the crumbs.

I understood what The Store wanted for the first time. Since he opened, she had him tucked upstairs and at any moments notice, she could at her whim, summon him, and down the stairs he'd come. Whatever she needed, Rob was there… Well its over!

The Store, somehow knew she had lost him. It was a crazy "revelation" but I had won. I had his heart, the one that beats exclusively for me now, and that boyhood devotion I remembered too well.

Everything remained the same from our beginnings. Only I'm fresh, our love so vibrant and real, and the years have cemented us. I am supposed to enjoy him, love him and be his Mrs. Robinson. I wasn't going to lose him again. Ever! I had him staying with me at Paulette house 27 blocks away. Oh, he could drive over and open her doors but never live with her; no, never again!

Who would do that but Rob? Leave a perfectly grand arrangement by not having to drive to work; if he wasn't totally committed to our marriage, and me. I know it's going to last a lifetime.

I followed, behind him up the stairs clutching his belt. Our bedroom in the rear of the house had large patio doors, as windows, overlooking an expansive wooden deck. I closed its drapes. On the bed soft duvet covers bid us to come inside. I sank in towards the middle waiting for Rob to enter. He finished his sandwich and placed the plate on the side table. His pants were folded and placed on the chair, now undressed he could come over towards me.

The Store

I held the African pouch with the money he'd generated from the raffle next to me. I counted all of it, 739.84 cents. Rob was at peace. Looking over at him I thought this was such a sweet picture, his black skin glistens, he was my man, that did it all today; made the entire community affair spectacular! That was his reward. Mine was to have him finally away from The Store, asleep, our first night in our new place. I snuggled up to him in my favorite position and he instantly, instinctively wrapped his arms around me, now, my opportunity to say thankful prayers.

Chapter 63
Brighter than Sunshine

Opening my eyes, Yes, I am here, not there. I was aware that the sunshine greeted us brighter somehow our first morning apart from The Store. Ahhhh.

I ran his bath water; clicked on Elton John's favorite hits on the CD player that's on the bathroom shelf. The melodic sounds of those particular songs were heavenly, "I can feel the love tonight" a lyric pierces my ear. He'll finish listening to the end while bathing looking upward at the rays leaking through the skylight window over the tub.

I came downstairs to start his breakfast. I couldn't stop smiling as I fixed everything, so domestic like. I was totally engulfed in paradise, envisioning the way we'll be "forever" in this place. I am anxiously waiting for him to finish so he could eat my food. It's something to be a lover. The years ahead wonderful in my mind already, in this home, fixing it up like a dollhouse, soon to be all mine. My head was still in love with Rob, my actions proved it.

Paulette's kitchen had an old fashioned charm to it; with a cast iron sink and circa '40's gas stove. I had to hurry and put something decent on because I wanted to drive Rob to The Store. I'll celebrate and gawk at her when I drive up.

A few strawberries were in the strainer. Bacon frying and the table set for one. Over The Store Rob got up, dressed and made his way down the stairs to The Store in one forth the time. Today was different. I could taste the favor of it. I had just cut the strawberries and placed them in a bowl when he appeared behind me dressed in a crisp shirt, olive slacks and very ready to eat. He reached for the shaker and sprinkled salt on the berries. I looked crossed at him; that he would not obey doctor's orders. His sheepish grin told it all.

The Store

I took it for what it was. He ate what he wanted to eat in The Store.

The plate arranged to serve a King; he waited for me to join him. I didn't have time to sit and enjoy his morning. I vowed to change Monday. "Wait and see Rob, it should be so different tomorrow with you helping me!" Kissing him on his forehead, I ran upstairs and quickly changed from my nightgown and robe.

We said good bye to Paulette. She was sitting over in her favorite soft chair in her living room adjacent to the door. She smiled at us leaving, seeing her daddy use his familiar charm that she had grown to love and which worked on everyone. Wow! you're finally taking over my house! She beamed, looking more like her father daily with that special grin.

Rob is very comfortable sitting high in the passenger seat of my black Jeep. I am glowing, thinking how sweet our new commute will be; me, from now on driving my husband to The Store. I placed my right hand softly over to rub his tummy, as I kept my eyes on him longer than I should. We smiled. This was going to be our new norm: I was his chauffer, and he was my precious cargo. You'd think I was a teenager, acting this way, so young and fresh. Rob was normal I think.

The ride took longer than anticipated. Since this was our first morning, he must have been preoccupied timing us. How much time should it take to get from Paulette's house to The Store and open her by 7 or 8 each day?

We drove up to the building on 72nd and Woodlawn at 7:48. The sunshine beaming off her windows and all seemed well. I sure didn't miss staying there last night. I am so happy. Rob doesn't mention the difference one way or the other. It's just another Sunday morning to him and The Store wants to open for business. She waits…

The Store

I kiss him with only a peck. He has to work all day and it never bothers him. I am going to church, but first, I have a few necessities to gather together, put in a box, from this soon to be, old apartment; like my coffee cup. The move that would take us away from The Store to Paulette's was a bit-by-bit test. I can move things as the Jeep's insides permits and plus there's no hurry. We haven't thought about who would live in the old place when it's empty. That is down the road and it might be a couple of months at least before winter. I wasn't hurried and neither was Rob. Easy going was what I call real living.

The stairs are the same for these 33 years. They were quite used to my cadence, the leap from one over the other. I walked all the way through to the computer cabinet next to my bed and checked a few emails; my chair was so comfortable leaning forward and reversing it twirling around; the time flew. I only wanted to stay a short while.

Rob gets something out of the freezer. Another customer needs something we had and Rob, more than willing, gives it to them. I holler back over my shoulder, to make small sport and kid with him a little. "Now! Who needs it!?" He didn't hear me and I go back to typing an email to little Leslie Corley, a twelve year old second cousin that emails me often. I gather some more favored items, bounced down the stairs with some small boxes and clothes and I dump them inside the back seat and close up the Jeep.

Making a U-turn I stop at the curb across from The Store in front of the yellow building. Rob sees me and crosses over to stand next to the driver's side of the Jeep. I lovingly listen for all his excuses for not helping me load up. "Where were YOU?" I said.

Apologetically, Rob goes into a short dissertation of his private moment in the John that kept him from me. "Baby, I was stuck and couldn't help you. But you know I was here.

The Store

Why didn't you wait?" We give each other that Look: I know, you know, ... I know 'we' know! I knew he wasn't teasing me. He wished to be upstairs, for me.

The Store wanted all of his time from the beginning. Today, he opened at 8 and he was due to leave her at 4:00. Then I'll be ready. "You know sweetheart, you're not going upstairs, but with me." I said that, and loved every word. Nope! Rob was not going upstairs today! Smiling, in my thoughts, *he had another place he was headed to; and that's a fact!*

I went on to explain to Rob my misuse of time upstairs and that my friend Shirley was going to the beach after church. I was going to go with her. I winked at him, with my left eye, and smiled.

"Go, have a good time." While he's using those brown eyes, looking twice as sincere, he meant each word spoken, as I have heard them countless times. The same sentiment I couldn't say to him and mean it. I could have whispered ("YOU have a great time too!")

He said it again, "Just have a good time, I'll see you when you get back." Then he leaned through the Jeep's window and gave me a soft peck on my pursed lips. That twinkle in my eye was all he needed. My thoughts were so kid-dish, and silly. (In just a few months I will turn 60.) I saw him walk across the street in my mirror. But I kept his voice in my head all the way home and couldn't erase the silly grin on my face.

Go have a good time ... He keeps saying it. *Go have a good time ... Go have a good time!* It rang in my ears. His gracious attitude towards me with only my joy in mind; then he sends me off to play, as he works to secure my happiness. He was consistent; for years with the same bequest. Go! Have a good time.

The Store

It was coming back into focus, my feelings more matured now, solid, and I knew they were lasting. The trust, the "love" I had known before The Store came between us; Rob and me; me and Rob, skipping through life again. Don't need petals from a daisy: "He loves me, he loves me not." I was enjoying a feeling that I knew my man loved me and he loves no one else!

I positioned the rear view mirror and beamed at myself. I had that school girl glow about me, how many women were in love with their husbands and knew it? I smiled at my image and shook my head back and forth as if singing a happy tune. I was so happy to have Rob back in my arms, together in our new love nest. Our first morning 'tryout' transferring Rob from our 'new' house to The Store was so warm, so wonderful. He was mine. Rob was mine. Forever!

I drove down the street turned the corner and my friend, Gloria Jean, calls on my cell. The plan: meet her at Apostolic Church 2nd service, with Shirley, in our favorite spot, fifth row, right side, along the aisle... "and, try to be there on time!"

"Forget about me coming," I told her, "I stayed too long fussing around upstairs; Girl, doing who knows what!" She didn't take that well. "Come on, you know God wants you there."

"Okay, I'll try." And, I meant it.

I got to Paulette's and drove up in her drive-way beside the house. I had to unload three boxes some needed toiletries and clothes. Paulette was still home talking on the phone. I placed my treasured coffee cup down on the kitchen counter. In the morning it would be there waiting.

I ran up the stairs and started to undress, kicked my shoes off and started my bath. Pulling my T-shirt over my head, covering my ears, I heard the strangest sound barely audible. The sound was as if, Paulette was screaming. I moved out of the bedroom to the top of the stairs, so I could listen. I looked down; leaned over the banister to see if I could have helped her in some way.

Yes, Paulette, was shouting! Deep and guttural! She sounded horrible!
"Uggggggggh, uggggggggg, He's dead? uggggggggggg,"

"What do you mean he's dead?" I said. Seconds went by; I still didn't know who she was talking about.

I heard the most dreadful words! Ever!

"Uggg, uggg, Daddy … is… dead!!"

I can't comprehend it, because it can't be true!

No! Not in a million years. "I had just left him minutes ago and no way! No way!" I don't know why I don't drop to my knees, but I don't.

I am suspended as flashes of light, milliseconds apart, shoot through my brain. I am frozen! Numb, for seconds. It takes the longest for what Paulette shouts to sink in. I revive and I move with nothing but pure will power. Flash backs of times together moments before- dance through my mind; and then my voice screams out of my gut with such force, it would have frighten Geronimo himself.

"What are you talking about?" My world stop turning it seems, oh, but I died… no one knows it.

I can't believe she is talking about her daddy.

_(There are words that heal and words that will change your life forever.)

I find the bedroom, nervously I slip my T-shirt back over my head and run down the stairs. Paulette is down on the floor; she is in a daze, her mouth is open, with the phone in her hand holding it to her breast. She stares, wide eyed, up at me with eyes full of tears –blinding tears. I feel as if I am moving in slow motion, but I am racing faster than lighting. I

The Store

don't have time to question anything. I grab the keys off the counter, rush out, bang the side door behind me and step in the Jeep. Paulette runs out chasing me and jumps in the other side to hold on as I reverse out her driveway. Mopping tears from my eyes with my bare palm, I drive as fast as I legally dare, down Crandon Street. "No! No! No! No!" Over and over I keep pounding the steering wheel with my clinched fist. Cozette had told Paulette something I can't accept.

I just left Rob and he was fine. "What in the world happened?"

Outside The Store is eerie; no one is out front when I pull up to see for myself, what is this? The Store is closed! What happened? The Jeep screeches to a halt. I open my door and slam it behind me and race over to the entrance of my place. "The Store?"

She is shut down and an iron gate covers her door. The strange thing is; she is NEVER closed during operation hours! Never would The Store close if Rob was around! Where are the workers? The cashier is gone and the stock person, the butcher. "Where is Rob?"...

"Mom, daddy was in The Store!" Paulette keeps saying. "You left him right there with The Store!" I don't have time now, to think it out, but this I remember: (or is The Store telling me)

"I did it!" I can hear it faintly in my left ear, but she stands there, closed, saying nothing. "**The Store has killed my husband!**"

I see Darron pull up. He had seen me racing down the street, like a maniac, turned his truck around and followed me from Paulette's house. He'd heard from Cozette what had happened. From Cozette's phone call. He came as fast as he could for me. Franticly, he runs over to console me, knowing he has the strength to hold me up, right there in my doorway.

The Store

My eyes are wide and searching, looking up at the sky, and then I look back suspiciously over towards The Store. Seconds pass. What to do, what to say, where to go? I am silently screaming inside, "What happened to my husband?"

I know what happened! I can feel Darron's strong hands grasp my trembling ones, holding me back from running. He has an ashen look, as his eyes find mine; they prove later to be right. I wouldn't, couldn't believe them. I audibly call out, **"Satan, you are a liar!" The Store is a liar! I know all this is a horrible mistake! Paulette, please say this isn't happening!"**

I had just left the area minutes ago, there were teems of people milling around, shopping, joking, and having their morning routine, with The Store and Rob. Seemed like seconds ago when Rob wished me a "Great Day!" I have to drive away from The Store and this area that can't tell me anything. It never does.

Paulette can't drive any more than I can. We are both a nervous wreck. I attempt to get behind the wheel again. Reluctantly I try to drive to the hospital where Darron told me a Fire Department ambulance had taken Rob.

Dashing through streets I wonder why the grass is still green on Stony Island and the sun over my head still shines? My Jeep races in and out of the traffic as if the traffic is stationary. I whizz by cars screaming "Get out of my way!" I didn't notice a blue siren light to help me get to my destination. Why doesn't the universe know I am begging for "Truth." I pray, "Dear Lord PLEEEEEZE!!! Give me another chance, Please Lord, give us another chance!"

Rob and I had started out this morning wishing everything to be behind us, and then eternally sharing our lives. I scream so loud everybody can hear me,

The Store

"Lord!

Let my husband be fine!

Lord Jesus Pleeeze!

I am trying to breathe, and I am screaming!

"Oh, Lord if I get to this place, Lord, Pleeeze, Darron said he would be there at that stinky dirty place!"

I yanked the Jeep up the ramp, and parked in an emergency area at the Jackson Park Hospital. I left Paulette behind and tore out of the vehicle and broke immediately through two wide double doors, then up a short polished hallway, out of breath but determined to find Rob.

Paulette rushes in beside me to give me my purse, car keys and glasses. "I'll hold them Mother," she softly said dabbing her tears.

We are standing in a large place with stark white walls and an odor of Pine Sol is in the air. I look around and it's strangely empty. Then over at the far counter a woman obviously crying is standing. Then another person is coming over to console her. Maybe they are waiting for news or just got it.

Then, out of the blue a man, stops us. "Where are YOU going?" he said curtly.

"They said my husband, Warren Robinson, was rushed here by ambulance."

"Wait here." Seconds later, maybe longer, shorter, I can't remember? I look around for someone I know or recognize to assure me this is a damn dream and I would wake up drenching wet, but relieved that dreams sometimes don't come true. "What is the hold up? Why don't they let me inside to see my husband; and see, if he is all right? He's got to be!"

The Store

"What are you here for lady?" Another man appeared. I close my eyes, untie my hands and put them up to my face, then smooth my hair. I try to act like a sane woman, really I do. This isn't normal.

Nothing I have ever been through prepared me for this. Nothing has been said, or done, or given me or shown me how to act, or even how to feel, at a time like this! How can I give some measure of sanity before I fall under this uncertainty?

Where is my husband? I hate hospitals and the secret places they hide loved ones -like we deserve to live with undue pain, all alone, and they can relieve it. If only.

Chapter 64
Oh, Lord let not this cup

I am on the ceiling looking at myself and the entire arena. My eyes open, I see the man's lips moving. I am not there. I am up here looking down and I see it all from someplace else. It is playing out like a III act play, or like a script in a block buster movie and I am the star of it.

All eyes are on my performance. "An Oscar goes to: Kathleen Robinson, in the heroic performance of, '_____ " it is blank.! My life blanked out and my life 'act' isn't a dream. It isn't a dream after all!"

Aaah, I don't find out what I get the award for.

"Lady –lady! Are you alright?" I open my eyes and take a deep breath. Oh, I am here in this place, talking to a stranger. Okay, "No, I am not all right… take me to my husband. His name is Warren Robinson."

The hospital staff worker did not take me to Rob. He ended up asking physical questions about my husband: marks on his body, heart condition, allergies, stress level and blood pressure? All those inquiries did not point me to Rob's condition! I hate this stupid question and answer session. "They are asking weird things to throw me off my quest to see Rob!"

The man finally asks me if I will wait in a Special Room. Reluctantly, Paulette and I enter the room down the hall and sit down. I'm near the door and Paulette is next to me. Cozette and Darron come in 10 minutes later. We are silent. We look at each other, then away, then back and forth. Every eye red. I grab some tissues. Rob's relatives; Aunt Peggy's daughters, Marsha, and Tarish arrive. They have been escorted into this special room along with some others.

The Store

I don't care who's here with me. The arduous seconds pour into countless minutes. We sit there, not a word spoken. Praying, I am spell bound. I gaze around the depressing room that has several phones lined along the wooden shelf and (sure enough) boxes of tissue, all being used. The wallpaper looks dull. The sun light doesn't penetrate the drab windows. The carpet is horrible. All the chairs are occupied with friends and family. I feel all eyes are on me. I don't feel a hand, a touch or comfort of any kind. I sit all alone... Why?

Why doesn't the staff open the door and talk with me; assure me that all is well?

What is wrong? I pray that this is all some stupid mistake. *"It isn't happening to us, not today. This wonderful day; Rob and I were together, on our first commute. We were so happy; so in love and in anticipation of a future living far away...*

Finally, a sigh of relief and with a grin on my face I think: *"They are still working with Rob, trying to save his life. That's what's taking so long.*

Otherwise, where will I go? Where will I stay? Who will take 'care' of me?

The scene starts. I see it! It's familiar! The entire dramatic production begins:

"Shoot! Roll the cameras!"

Rob's paperwork is signed and his position secured; Warren Isaac (Rob) Robinson is thrust into his New Place.

It is early Sunday morning, July 14, 2002, at 10:32 and breathing in a sigh of relief; it is done!

The Store

As with the anticipation of a 1st date, Rob takes out The Key to unlock his long awaited Dream.

There are Three Glorious Lights shining brighter than Day over The Store as Rob stands inside alone.

Through un-shaded eyes Rob envisions splendid shelves filled with stock: the meat counter lit, with rows of fresh meats, poultry and sausage lined neatly with fresh greens. He can hear the register sing as many familiar customers, all line up jovially, to purchase their groceries.

It is like his Birthday! All at once! He gets everything he has been longing for.

~~~

There is an unusual aroma in the air that is quite pleasant; ~sweet like Cotton Candy.

Rob instantaneously moves to the back of The Store, and then to the front, for everywhere The ~Scent captures all of him, filling his big heart with Peace beyond measure, on Wings of Glory!

It stopped! Right there it stopped!

Rob pulls out and unfolds a chair that is leaning against the back wall and gradually sits down, to soak it in. He can feel the gentle Rays of Dazzling Wonder encircle his mental impressions, ~of what he is soon to become.

Suddenly! With Marvelous Thunder, Those Brilliant Lights enters The Store: Violet and Golden vapors of Smoke envelope him from head to toe. He feels as tranquil, as if in a Magnificent Dream.

"This is not a dream." He quickly stands up! A grin of Grand Assurance that only 'faith' in God can give, envelopes him. With proud demeanor, chest stuck out and his

The Store

I don't care who's here with me. The arduous seconds pour into countless minutes. We sit there, not a word spoken. Praying, I am spell bound. I gaze around the depressing room that has several phones lined along the wooden shelf and (sure enough) boxes of tissue, all being used. The wallpaper looks dull. The sun light doesn't penetrate the drab windows. The carpet is horrible. All the chairs are occupied with friends and family. I feel all eyes are on me. I don't feel a hand, a touch or comfort of any kind. I sit all alone... Why?

Why doesn't the staff open the door and talk with me; assure me that all is well?

What is wrong? I pray that this is all some stupid mistake. *"It isn't happening to us, not today. This wonderful day; Rob and I were together, on our first commute. We were so happy; so in love and in anticipation of a future living far away...*

Finally, a sigh of relief and with a grin on my face I think: *"They are still working with Rob, trying to save his life. That's what's taking so long.*

Otherwise, where will I go? Where will I stay? Who will take 'care' of me?

The scene starts. I see it! It's familiar! The entire dramatic production begins:

"Shoot! Roll the cameras!"

Rob's paperwork is signed and his position secured; Warren Isaac (Rob) Robinson is thrust into his New Place.

It is early Sunday morning, July 14, 2002, at 10:32 and breathing in a sigh of relief; it is done!

The Store

As with the anticipation of a 1st date, Rob takes out The Key to unlock his long awaited Dream.

There are Three Glorious Lights shining brighter than Day over The Store as Rob stands inside alone.

Through un-shaded eyes Rob envisions splendid shelves filled with stock: the meat counter lit, with rows of fresh meats, poultry and sausage lined neatly with fresh greens. He can hear the register sing as many familiar customers, all line up jovially, to purchase their groceries.

It is like his Birthday! All at once! He gets everything he has been longing for.

~~~

There is an unusual aroma in the air that is quite pleasant; ~sweet like Cotton Candy.

Rob instantaneously moves to the back of The Store, and then to the front, for everywhere The ~Scent captures all of him, filling his big heart with Peace beyond measure, on Wings of Glory!

It stopped! Right there it stopped!

Rob pulls out and unfolds a chair that is leaning against the back wall and gradually sits down, to soak it in. He can feel the gentle Rays of Dazzling Wonder encircle his mental impressions, ~of what he is soon to become.

Suddenly! With Marvelous Thunder, Those Brilliant Lights enters The Store: Violet and Golden vapors of Smoke envelope him from head to toe. He feels as tranquil, as if in a Magnificent Dream.

"This is not a dream." He quickly stands up! A grin of Grand Assurance that only 'faith' in God can give, envelopes him. With proud demeanor, chest stuck out and his

The Store

strong arms stretched out wide, his palms lifted high and upward, in welcomed thankfulness Rob cries!

"This is mine! He yells it out over and over again in a loud grateful voice dancing, twirling all around The Store!

"This is mine! ~ This is mine! ~This is mine!"

Over again Rob affirms to himself what was done!

"God has given me everything, if only to Ask!" From that instant, he is lovingly captured, taken up to his Reward!

The Store was his and he grinned and looked over where the Sky Never Ends: where throngs of onlookers were cheering and applauding, welcoming Rob with Grand Accord!

He recognizes someone:

"Yo! Mom! Oh, Mrs. Fain! The Lord Jesus was with her and both walking towards him across The Way, smiling, with nothing left to do.

"Son, this IS your Birthday!"

Epilog:

The Store stands with humility on the corner waiting and she'll keep her promise to Rob and his wife, Kathleen. To be a bountiful blessing to anyone that just might tap on her window, every now and then.

It's all in God's Plan.

***

Kathleen's memories that used to hurt her deeply are all forgiven. Rob never knew how soon she would deeply learn to Love what he loved: The Store and the apartment over it, his customers and the entire neighborhood.

God walks through her heart and she wouldn't live any other place than near The Store where her husband's spirit still hovers over the corner, but she doesn't search the window or smoke anymore. She knows where Rob is; saying, "I'll be in your dreams,... wait for me."

Truly Rob left a legacy of **LOVE**

My ears were dulled by traffic; my thoughts preoccupied.

Yet I have not been happy, while leaving You outside.

Then come Lord Jesus enter, my house of life and be

A gracious Savior blessing the days allotted me.

Author Unknown

About the Author

Oil painting by Silvia Gray of Temecula California.

Kathleen Yvonne Robinson is a Mixed Media Artist, Bible Teacher, Photographer, and Author.

A Chicago native: she earned her AA degree at Kennedy-King College.

Her four children; Cozette, Annette, Paulette and Warren III plus her three grandchildren; Mia, Logan and Liam, all live near Chicago and affectionately call her Big Momma.

Kathleen resides in Sun City, California and spends her summers in Chicago.

THREE REASONS WHY YOU NEED JESUS

Jesus loves you! He desires to have a relationship with you, and to give you a life full of joy and purpose. Why do you need Him in your life?

1. BECAUSE YOU HAVE A PAST.

You can't go back, but He can. The Bible says, "Jesus Christ the same yesterday, and today, and for ever" (Hebrews 13:8). He can walk into those places of sin and failure, wipe the slate clean, and give you a new beginning.

2. BECAUSE YOU NEED A FRIEND.

Jesus knows the worst about you, yet He believes the best. Why? Because He sees you not as you are but as you will be when He gets through with you. What a friend!

3. BECAUSE HE HOLDS THE FUTURE.

Who else are you going to trust? In His hands you are safe and secure – today, tomorrow, and for all eternity. His Word says, "For I know the plans I have for you …plans for good and not for evil, to give you a future and a hope. In those days when you pray, I will listen" (Jeremiah 29:11-12 TLB).

If you'd like to begin a personal relationship with Jesus today, please pray this prayer

Lord Jesus, I invite You into my life.

I believe You died for me and that Your blood pays for my sins and provides me with the gift of eternal life.

By faith I receive that gift, and I acknowledge You as my Lord and Savior. Amen

Bob Gass

Used by permission

The Word For You Today

www.bobgass.com
1-800-964-9846